MULTICULTURAL EDUCATION SERIES
James A. Banks, Series Editor

CULTURALLY RESPONSIVE TEACHING

Theory, Research, and Practice

GENEVA GAY

FOREWORD BY JAMES A. BANKS

Teachers College, Columbia University
New York and London

—To Vida, a shining star who illuminated what many others considered impenetrable darkness. Though you're no longer with us, the gifts you gave to the youth you taught, their children, and their children's children are continually cherished. The model you set for other teachers to follow remains undaunted.

and

—To students everywhere. May you be likewise blessed as those who were fortunate to be taught by Vida. Like them, you deserve the very best of our teaching genius and ingenuity.

Published by Teachers College Press, 1234 Amsterdam Avenue, New York, NY 10027

Copyright © 2000 by Teachers College, Columbia University

Library of Congress Cataloging-in-Publication Data

Gay, Geneva.
  Culturally responsive teaching : theory, research, and practice / Geneva Gay.
    p. cm. — (Multicultural education series)
  Includes bibliographical references (p.   ) and index.
  ISBN 0-8077-3955-3 — ISBN 0-8077-3954-5 (pbk.)
  1. Multicultural education—United States.   2. Educational equalization—United States.
  3. Teaching—Social aspects—United States.   I. Title.   II. Multicultural education series
  (New York, N.Y.)
  LC1099.3 .G393   2000
  370.117—dc21   99-088478

ISBN 0-8077-3954-5 (paper)
ISBN 0-8077-3955-3 (cloth)

Printed on acid-free paper
Manufactured in the United States of America

07   8   7   6

Contents

Series Foreword

The nation's deepening ethnic texture, interracial tension and conflict, and the increasing percentage of students who speak a first language other than English make multicultural education imperative as the twenty-first century begins. The U.S. Bureau of the Census estimated that people of color made up 28% of the nation's population in 2000 (U.S. Bureau of the Census, 1998). The Census predicted that they would make up 38% of the nation's population in 2025 and 47% in 2050.

American classrooms are experiencing the largest influx of immigrant students since the beginning of the twentieth century. About a million immigrants are making the United States their home each year (Martin & Midgley, 1999). More than 6 million legal immigrants settled in the United States between 1991 and 1996 (U.S. Bureau of the Census, 1998). A large but undetermined number of undocumented immigrants also enter the United States each year. The influence of an increasingly diverse population on the nation's schools, colleges, and universities is and will continue to be enormous.

In 1995, 35% of the students enrolled in public schools were students of color; this percentage is increasing each year, primarily because of the growth in the percentage of Latino students (Pratt & Rittenhouse, 1998). In some of the nation's largest cities and metropolitan areas, such as Chicago, Los Angeles, Washington, DC, New York, Seattle, and San Francisco, half or more of the public school students are students of color. In California, the population of students of color in the public schools has exceeded the percentage of White students since the 1988–1989 school year.

Language diversity is also increasing among the nation's student population. Fourteen percent of school-age youth lived in homes in which English was not the first language in 1990 (U.S. Bureau of the Census, 1998). Most teachers now in the classroom and in teacher education programs are likely to have students from diverse ethnic, racial, and language groups in their classrooms during their careers. This is true for both inner-city and suburban teachers.

An important goal of multicultural education is to improve race relations and to help all students acquire the knowledge, attitudes, and skills needed to participate in cross-cultural interactions and in personal, social, and civic action that will help make our nation more democratic and just. Multicultural education is consequently as important for middle-class White suburban students as it is for students of color who live in the inner city. Multicultural education fosters the public good and the over-arching goals of the country.

The major purpose of the *Multicultural Education Series* is to provide preservice educators, practicing educators, graduate students, and schol-ars with an interrelated and comprehensive set of books that summarize and analyze important research, theory, and practice related to the educa-tion of ethnic, racial, cultural, and language groups in the United States and the education of mainstream students about diversity. The books in the series provide research, theoretical, and practical knowledge about the behaviors and learning characteristics of students of color, language-minority students, and low-income students. They also provide knowl-edge about ways to improve academic achievement and race relations in educational settings.

The definition of multicultural education in the *Handbook of Research on Multicultural Education* (Banks & Banks, 1995) is used in the series: "Multicultural education is a field of study designed to increase educa-tional equity for all students that incorporates, for this purpose, content, concepts, principles, theories, and paradigms from history, the social and behavioral sciences, and particularly from ethnic studies and women studies" (p. xii). In the series, as in the *Handbook*, multicultural education is considered a "metadiscipline."

The dimensions of multicultural education, developed by Banks (1995) and described in the *Handbook of Research on Multicultural Education*, provide the conceptual framework for the development of the books in the series. They are: *content integration, the knowledge construction process, prejudice reduction, an equity pedagogy,* and *an empowering school culture and social structure.* To implement multicultural education effectively, teachers and administrators must attend to each of the five dimensions of multicul-tural education. They should use content from diverse groups when teach-ing concepts and skills, help students to understand how knowledge in the various disciplines is constructed, help students to develop positive intergroup attitudes and behaviors, and modify their teaching strategies so that students from different racial, cultural, language, and social-class groups will experience equal educational opportunities. The total environ-ment and culture of the school must also be transformed so that students from diverse groups will experience equal status in the culture and life of the school.

Although the five dimensions of multicultural education are highly interrelated, each requires deliberate attention and focus. Each book in the series focuses on one or more of the dimensions, although each book deals with all of them to some extent because of the highly interrelated characteristics of the dimensions.

Latinos are the fastest-growing ethnic group in the U.S. population and in the nation's schools. There are wide gaps between the academic achievement of Latinos and non-Hispanic Whites and Latinos and some groups of Asian Americans, such as Chinese Americans, Japanese Americans, and Korean Americans. The academic status of Latinos exemplifies a serious problem within the nation: as the knowledge and skill requirements for jobs in this Internet age escalate, the fastest-growing population of future citizens is experiencing serious academic problems in the schools and in society. African Americans and Native Americans, as groups, are also not achieving on parity with Whites and some Asian groups. We should recognize, of course, that there are high achievers within all racial and ethnic groups, including Latinos.

Within the last three decades, a group of insightful and committed scholars and researchers—including Kathryn Au, Roland G. Tharp, A. Wade Boykin, Sonia Nieto, Lisa Delpit, Jacqueline Irvine, and Gloria Ladson-Billings—have been concerned about the serious academic achievement problems among low-income students and students of color. They have constructed a theory of culturally responsive pedagogy (also called culturally sensitive pedagogy) that gives hope and guidance to educators who are trying to improve the academic achievement of these students. This theory postulates that discontinuities between the school and low-income students and students of color is an important factor in their low academic achievement. The theory also postulates that the academic achievement of these students will increase if schools and teaching are changed so that they reflect and draw on their cultural and language strengths.

Geneva Gay is one of the progenitors of this theory. She has contributed scholarship, staff development, and teaching to it for a quarter of a century. Gay has listened to the failures and victories of thousands of teachers in inservice settings, written a score of articles about diversity and teaching, and mentored a cadre of doctoral students in multicultural education. She brings a lifetime of scholarship, teaching, and reflection to this informative book. Gay synthesizes the research on culturally responsive pedagogy, provides new insights and nuances on her work and the work of others, shares stories of successful teachers, and describes how teachers can make a difference in their students' lives. Like Gay's previous scholarship and her powerful teaching, this book will make a difference in the lives of teachers who read it and listen.

James A. Banks
Series Editor

REFERENCES

Banks, J. A. (1995). Multicultural education: Historical development, dimensions, and practice. In J. A. Banks & C. A. M. Banks (Eds.), *Handbook of research on multicultural education* (pp. 3–24). New York: Macmillan.

Banks, J. A., & Banks, C. A. M. (Eds.). (1995). *Handbook of research on multicultural education*. New York: Macmillan.

Martin, P., & Midgley, E. (1999). Immigration to the United States. *Population Bulletin, 54*(2), 1–44. Washington, DC: Population Reference Bureau.

Pratt, R., & Rittenhouse, G. (Eds.). (1998). *The condition of education: 1998*. Washington, DC: U.S. Government Printing Office.

United States Bureau of the Census. (1998). *Statistical abstract of the United States* (118th edition). Washington, DC: U.S. Government Printing Office.

Acknowledgments

I am deeply indebted to all of the professional colleagues, graduate students, personal friends, and family members who shared their observations, experiences, and memories about teaching and learning. These personal stories were incredibly enriching to the information gleaned from published accounts about the educational needs of underachieving, ethnically diverse students. They enliven, personalize, energize, and crystallize what might otherwise have been a purely academic and dispassionate analysis.

A special note of gratitude is due my friend and colleague, James A. Banks, who extended the invitation and encouragement to write, and then provided expectations and assistance for me to write better. Even when it seemed most unlikely, I was, and continue to be, very appreciative of his scholarly mentoring.

Many thanks also to "Peppers," who helped most by listening to my expressed concerns and implied doubts about being capable of completing the task. You probably have no idea how much it meant to know that you were there, and how talking to you helped me to refocus, persevere, and reaffirm belief in my capabilities.

The school struggles of all my "fictive children" and their right to receive a better education are the motivation behind the ideas, explanations, and recommendations presented herein. I take their academic situations as my personal cause and professional responsibility, and act accordingly.

Preface

Significant changes are needed in how African, Asian, Latino, and Native American students are taught in U.S. schools. Two characteristics of their current achievement patterns highlight this imperative. One is the *consistency of performance patterns* among ethnic groups across different indicators and measures of school achievement. The other is the *variability of achievement* of subsets of individuals within ethnic groups. These characteristics suggest the need for systematic, holistic, comprehensive, and particularistic reform interventions, simultaneously.

Systemic reforms must be undertaken that deal with multiple aspects of achievement (academic, social, psychological, emotional, etc.) within different subject areas (math, science, reading, writing, social studies) across school levels (prekindergarten, elementary, middle, and high schools) and through different aspects of the educational enterprise (curriculum, instruction, administration, assessment, financing, etc.). These reforms also need to be diversified according to the social variance of students, attending deliberately and conscientiously to such factors as ethnicity, culture, gender, social class, historical experiences, and linguistic capabilities. Dealing adequately with all these influences on student achievement and their implications for reform is far beyond the capabilities of a single book. Some choice is needed to ensure quality of analysis. The choice for this book is using their cultural orientations to teach ethnically diverse students who are not performing well, especially in reading, writing, math, and science.

Merely belaboring the disproportionately poor academic performance of certain students of color, or blaming their families and social-class backgrounds, is not very helpful in implementing reforms to reverse achievement trends. Just as in health care treating symptoms does not cure diseases, simply pointing out achievement problems does not lead to their resolution. If this were the case, there would be no need for a book like this. The underachievement of some ethnic groups has been spotlighted again and again over several generations, and the situation has not gotten any better. It may even have worsened in recent years. It is also true that some of the disparity in academic achievement across ethnic groups is attributable to racism and cultural hegemony in the educational enterprise. But to declare this is not enough to direct a functional and effective change agenda. More constructive reform strategies must be employed. Culturally responsive pedagogy as characterized in this book meets these needs.

OVERVIEW OF CHAPTERS

In Chapter 1, "Challenges and Perspectives," a particular perspective on the challenges of teaching underachieving students of color more effectively is presented. It sets the tone and establishes the conceptual parameters for the remaining chapters. A storytelling motif is used to frame the critical issues underlying the need to incorporate the cultural orientations and experiences of students from different ethnic and racial backgrounds into teaching strategies. The achievement patterns among ethnic groups in the United States are too persistent to be attributed only to individual limitations. The fault lies as well within the institutional structures, procedures, assumptions, and operational styles of schools, classrooms, and the society at large.

A conceptual proposal for correcting these achievement problems is presented in Chapter 2, "Power Pedagogy Through Cultural Responsiveness." The theoretical parameters of this proposal—achieving power pedagogy through culturally responsive teaching—are constructed from ideas suggested by different scholars, researchers, and practitioners about teaching modes that work best with ethnically diverse students. This characterization of culturally responsive teaching includes explanations of its salient components as well as its potential power for reversing the achievement trends of students of color. Its key anchors are the simultaneous cultivation of the academic success and cultural identity of ethnically diverse students. These general features serve as benchmarks for organizing and assessing the quality of specific teaching ideas, programs, and actions discussed later in other chapters. Consequently, Chapter 2 acts as a *conceptual bridge* between the need for and the doing of culturally responsive teaching, between theory and practice, between achievement problems and solutions.

Chapters 3–6 develop in greater detail four critical aspects of culturally responsive teaching introduced in Chapter 2. These are caring, communication, curriculum, and instruction. No priority ranking is intended, nor should any be attached, to the order in which these chapters are presented. Just because a teaching disposition of caring is discussed first does not mean that it is more important than the other aspects of culturally responsive teaching. The sequence in which these components and the related chapters appear is merely a reflection of one "logical patterning" for thinking about and classifying these issues. Other organizing schemas are possible. Nor should the boundaries drawn for the various components of culturally responsive teaching be perceived as mutually exclusive. The divisions are artificial and arbitrary, and they are used to focus attention, facilitate discussion, and make the presentation of information more managerial. In reality, the components of culturally responsive teaching are dynamic, dialectical, and interwoven.

Interactions between students and teachers as well as among students in the classroom are frequently identified as the "actual sites" where learning success or failure is determined. They are prominent among the major attributes of culturally responsive teaching. Conventional wisdom and research studies suggest that teachers play a pivotal role in these interactions. In fact, the tone, structure, and quality of instruction are determined largely by teachers' attitudes and expectations as well as their pedagogical skills. Therefore, some careful attention to how teachers relate to students is central to realizing the purposes of this book. What these relational patterns are and how they affect the achievement of students from various ethnic groups are presented in Chapter 3, "The Power of Caring." Since issues other than intellectual ability have profound effects on assumptions about what students can or cannot achieve, explorations of teachers' expectations are not limited to the academic. Personal, social, and ethical dimensions are included as well.

Effective communication is simultaneously a goal, a method, and the essence of quality classroom instruction. Yet communicating with ethnically diverse students is often problematic for many teachers. Numerous misconceptions and confusions surround interactions among communication, culture, and education. A graphic example of these is the recurring controversy over the place of Ebonics (a style of communication used by many African Americans that is sometimes referred to as Black, African American, or nonstandard English) in the educational process. It, more than any other communication issue related to students of color, symbolizes the complexity, challenge, and academic potential of incorporating elements of different cultural communication styles into classroom instruction. Chapter 4, "Culture and Communication in the Classroom," explains the close interaction among culture, communication, teaching, and learning. It builds upon Saville-Troike's (1989) conviction that "there is a correlation between the form and content of a language and the beliefs, values, and needs present in the culture of its speakers" (p. 32). Since how one thinks, writes, and speaks reflects culture and affects performance, aligning instruction to the cultural communication styles of different ethnic groups can improve school achievement. To this end, features of communication styles, how they are manifested in instructional situations, and programs and practices that actually demonstrate the positive effects of using cultural communication as a tool for effective teaching are discussed in Chapter 4. These analyses concentrate on discourse features instead of linguistic structures. An explanation, supported with research evidence, is provided for this choice.

Chapter 5 is devoted to culturally diverse curriculum content. It develops the idea that effective teaching and learning for culturally and ethnically different students makes high-quality, high-status knowledge accessible to them. A major part of this accessibility is recognizing the worth of the information and contributions ethnic groups have made to the fund of knowledge students should learn and making it available to them. The current status of cultural diversity in curriculum designs and instructional materials is explored, along with research about practices that produce positive outcomes for students of color. Formal (e.g., textbooks) and informal (e.g., literary and trade books, mass media) curricular materials are examined. The analyses are limited to teaching reading, writing, math, and science. These subjects are selected because of their function as "academic cores" in the educational process, the high status typically attached to them, and the prominent role they play in the determination of student achievement. Squire's (1995) explanation about the importance of "literacy skills" to all educational quality supports this choice. He says, "Reading, writing, and language are the bedrock subjects of the curriculum, for they develop the competencies on which virtually all subsequent instruction and learning depend" (p. 71). The analyses of curricular programs and research presented in Chapter 5 are complemented with suggestions for how to further improve the quality of multicultural curriculum content and its effects on student achievement.

Chapter 6 continues to develop the proposition that deliberately incorporating *specific* aspects of the cultural systems of different ethnic groups into instructional processes has positive impacts on student achievement. It emerges from arguments presented by some educational analysts that interferences to the achievement of ethnically diverse students are often more procedural than substantive. Compelling research demonstrates that school achievement improves when protocols and procedures of teaching are synchronized with the mental schemata, participation styles, work habits, thinking styles, and experiential frames of reference of diverse ethnic groups.

The discussions in Chapter 6, "Cultural Congruity in Teaching and

Learning," go beyond the frequent tendency to merely catalogue descriptive traits of bipolar learning styles. They probe the interior of these descriptors to determine their qualitative attributes and implications for instruction. The argument is made that a learning style is actually a *construct* that has multiple elements embedded within it, such as motivational, environmental, relational, and sensory stimulation preferences. All of these may impact the learning process differently. Knowing what these are is necessary to making teaching culturally responsive. Thus, the key message of Chapter 6 is that modifying teaching and learning processes at the level of their component parts generates greater academic success than "generalized global pedagogical reforms."

Four major features are common to the discussions across Chapters 3–6. First, a combination of information from theory, research, and practice is brought to bear on the issues examined. Thus, *simultaneous and integrated multiperspective* analyses are emphasized. While much, if not most, educational scholarship includes these three aspects, the usual convention is to explore theory, research, and practice separately from one another. The juxtaposition of them in this book seems more reasonable and useful for filling existing conceptual voids and expanding effective instruction for improving the achievement of ethnically diverse students.

Second, *multiethnic* examples and points of references are woven throughout the discussion of topics, issues, themes, and strategies. Concerted efforts are made to achieve some ethnic balance in these, but the results are not always ideal, or even desirable. The units of analysis in research, theory, and practice are often skewed more toward some ethnic groups than others. For example, more data are available on the need for and experience with culturally responsive teaching as it relates to African Americans than to other groups of color. Consequently, African Americans appear more often as referents or case examples of practices and proposals throughout the book. This disproportionality is countered somewhat by targeting other ethnic groups in suggestions for extending, refining, and enriching current culturally responsive instructional practices.

Third, whenever possible other factors, such as gender, age, and social class, that influence the validity and effect of research, theory, and practice on teaching ethnically diverse students are openly discussed. As with ethnicity, many imbalances exist among these variables. For instance, much of the research available about the effects of gender on communication, interactional styles, and classroom performance deals with middle-class, European American females. Most of the information on teaching students of color is derived from studies of individuals from low socioeconomic and urban backgrounds. Asian Americans are underrepresented in all aspects of research, theory, and practice about culturally responsive teaching.

Fourth, individual scenarios and personal stories are interspersed throughout the presentation of theoretical ideas and research findings. These are included in order to recognize autobiography as a legitimate source of knowledge and research, to create a more comprehensive portrait of and compelling case for the power and potential of culturally responsive teaching, and to demonstrate how it is made manifest in actual behaviors.

A case of "Culturally Responsive Pedagogical Praxis" is presented in Chapter 7. It emerges from the premise that the most powerful evidence of teaching effectiveness is the personal story. Operating on this premise, I provide some brief descriptions of my own beliefs about and styles of teaching. These are presented not as prototypes that everyone should emulate, but as a living example of how one individual exemplifies some of the principles and practices of culturally responsive pedagogy. They also show how this approach to teaching can be used with college and university students enrolled in teacher education programs.

Stories often end with epilogues. They provide glimpses into future developments of the characters that occur after the culmination of the present situation. An epilogue signifies an ending, but without the total cessation of all action related to the story. Thus, it is simultaneously a closure and a continuation. Such is the case with the epilogue to the story of culturally responsive teaching constructed here. This function is served by Chapter 8. Its content looks backward to earlier analyses and forward to other possibilities for teaching ethnically diverse students. The information presented is both reflective and projective. It summarizes major messages and principles for future practice in culturally responsive teaching extrapolated from discussions presented in the previous chapters. This is why it is entitled "Moving Forth." *Culturally Responsive Teaching* ends as it begins, continuing the search (1) to make education more successful for students like Aaron and Amy throughout the United States and (2) to stop the vicious cycle of academic failure so that Amy's and Aaron's children will have a very different story to tell about their school experiences.

READING THE TEXT

Improving the school achievement of students of color who are currently not performing well requires comprehensive knowledge, unshakable convictions, and high-level pedagogical skills. The information presented in the chapters of this book is intended to facilitate the development of these and to resist the temptations of some educators to provide superficial analyses, simplistic interpretations, and quick-fix responses to these complex issues.

This book incorporates research, theory, and practice about culturally contextualized or mediated teaching for marginalized African, Asian, Latino, and Native American students. It is based largely on national data sources and local projects that have gained national recognition. Herein lies a major but unavoidable limitation. Local programs and practices that have not gained national visibility are not included. Many of these probably exist and are worthy of inclusion. No doubt their presence would have further enriched the analyses and recommendations made, but they were not accessible to me.

Culturally Responsive Teaching is about *teaching*, and the teaching of concern is that which *centers* classroom instruction in *multiethnic cultural frames of reference*. Consequently, pedagogical paradigms and techniques that may be effective but are not culturally situated for marginalized, underachieving ethnic groups—such as Latinos, Native Americans, and African Americans—are not included in the discussions. Other dimensions of the educational enterprise that affect student achievement, such as funding, institutional-based school reform, the recruitment and assignment of teachers, and administrative leadership, also are not discussed. Their importance in the scheme of total educational improvement is unquestionable. They simply do not fit within the conceptual parameters of this project. Making all aspects of schooling culturally diverse at the same time would be ideal. But this project was not geared to such a massive task.

Furthermore, schools cannot solve society's problems. This is accepted as a given and is not discussed here. In fact, schools could effect much more rapid reforms if society changed first. For instance, if society really stopped being racist, it would insist (and enforce the expectation) that all its institutions, including schools, do likewise. Then the problems of concern to, and even the need for, books like this one would cease. The education of too many students of color is too imperiled for us to wait for these grand hopes to happen. We must act now, and incremental changes are better than none at all. *Culturally Responsive Teaching* recognizes the power of teaching while fully realizing that, without accompanying changes in all other aspects of schooling and society, the very best of teaching will not be able to accomplish the systemic reforms needed for ethnically diverse students to receive genuine educational equity and achieve excellence.

The story of culturally responsive teaching that unfolds in the chapters of this book, like any other story, has setting, plot, characters, and action.

The separate chapters serve all these functions for their specific topics of analysis, while contributing significantly to the construction of the more comprehensive "character profile and narrative development" of culturally responsive teaching. These characterizations reflect the beliefs that (1) test scores, grade point averages, course enrollments, and other indicators of the school achievement of many students of color are the *symptoms*, *not causes* of the problems; (2) academic achievement is not the only significant indicator of school success and/or failure; and (3) while school failure is an *experience* of too many ethnically diverse students, it is not the *identity* of any. These ideas represent both an invitation and a mandate to teachers. The discussions presented in this book are designed to help equip more teachers to meet them and to accomplish higher levels of success for underachieving students of color.

A CREDO FOR PEDAGOGICAL ACTION

Several years ago Marva Collins (1992), the founder of the Westside Preparatory School in Chicago, created a metaphorical image of educational excellence that captures its spirit and meaning as intended in this book. Using poetic form, Collins gives excellence a personal voice and allows it to speak for itself. Part of this characterization is quoted here because of its inspirational and invigorating quality. Speaking in the first person, "Excellence" says:

> I bear the flame that enlightens the world. I fire the imagination. I give might to dreams and wings to the aspirations of men.
> I create all that is good, stalwart, and long-lasting. I build for the future by making my every effort superior today . . .
> I am the parent of progress, the creator of creativity, the designer of opportunity, and molder of human destiny . . .
> I wear the wisdom and contributions of all ages. I dispel yesterday's myths and find today's facts. I am ageless and timeless . . .
> I banish mediocrity and discourage being average . . .
> I stir ambition, forge ideals, and create keys that open the door to worlds never dreamed. . . .
> I am the source of creation, the outlet of inspiration, the dream of aspiration (pp. 218–219)

This credo should inspire all teachers committed to improving the school performance of underachieving students of color. It can serve as the anchor and torchlight for their pedagogial practices. The values, expectations, commitments, and actions it conveys are certainly congruent with the intentions of *Culturally Responsive Teaching*.

CHAPTER I

Challenges and Perspectives

Too many students of color have not been achieving in school as well as they should (and can) for far too long. The consequences of these disproportionally high levels of low achievement are long-term and wide-reaching, personal and civic, individual and collective. They are too devastating to be tolerable. We must insist that this disempowerment stop now and set into motion change strategies to ensure that it does. To realize this transformation, classroom teachers and other educators need to understand that achievement, or lack thereof, is an experience or an accomplishment. It is not the totality of a student's personal identity or the essence of his or her human worth. Virtually every student can do something well. Even if their capabilities are not directly translatable to classroom learning, they still can be used by teachers as points of reference and motivational devices to evoke student interest and involvement in academic affairs. Teachers must learn to how to recognize, honor, and incorporate the personal abilities of students into their teaching strategies. If this is done, then school achievement will improve.

INTRODUCTION

The book offers some suggestions for reversing the underachievement of students of color. They are embodied in the proposal for implementing *culturally responsive teaching*. Research, theory, and practice attest to their potential effectiveness. However, culturally responsive teaching alone cannot solve all the problems of improving the education of marginalized students of color. Other aspects of the educational enterprise (such as funding, administration, and policy making) must also be reformed, and major changes must be made to eliminate the social, political, and economic inequities rampant in society at large (Anyon, 1997; Kozol, 1991; Nieto, 1999). While the need for comprehensive educational and societal changes is readily recognized, analysis of them is beyond the parameters of this project. It focuses, instead, on teaching in K–12 classrooms.

This chapter sets the tone for the remainder of the book, which builds on the notion of creating a story of culturally responsive teaching. The reason for using a storymaking motif is to suggest that culturally responsive teaching has many different shapes, forms, and effects. A "story" perspective allows the integration of more types of information and styles of presentation than are customary in more conventional styles of scholarly writing and research. This demonstrates how research, theory, and practice are woven together to develop major ideas; establishes the fact that school achievement involves more than academics; attempts to convey a feeling for the personhood of the students of concern in the analyses; and explains why culturally responsive teaching is a dynamic process. To accomplish these goals, the chapter is divided into four parts. The first part explains the importance of storymaking as a technique of educational analysis, research, and reform. The second section includes a "symbolic story" of the achievement problems encountered by many students of color. It is followed in the third part by a discussion of some national achievement trends among students of color. The four part of the chapter introduces some assertions made about how student achievement can be improved. These are developed in greater detail in subsequent chapters.

THE NEED FOR AND NATURE OF STORY

Dyson and Genishi (1994) believe that "we all have a basic need for story." They define *story* as a process of "organizing our experiences into tales of important happenings" (p. 2). Stories, according to Denman (1991), are "lenses through which we view and review all of human experience. . . . They have a power to reach deep inside us and command our ardent attention. Through stories we see ourselves. . . . Our personal experience . . . takes on a cloak of significance . . . we see what it is to be alive, to be human" (p. 4). Bruner (1996) adds that narratives, or stories, are the means through which people make sense of their encounters, their experiences, their *human affairs*. He explains further:

> We frame the accounts of our cultural origins and our most cherished beliefs in story form, and it is not just the "content" of these stories that grip us, but their narrative artifice. Our immediate experience, what happened yesterday or the day before, is framed in the same storied way. Even more striking, we represent our lives (to ourselves as well as to others) in the form of narrative. (p. 40)

Narratives encompass both the modes of thought and texts of discourse that give shape to the realities they convey. Their style and content give form to each other, "just as thought become inextricable from the language that expresses it and eventually shapes it" (Bruner, 1996, p. 132). Furthermore, the whats and whys of narratives are never chance occurrences or mere happenstance. They have deliberate intentionality, "voice," positionality, and contestability. Bruner (1996) believes that stories are motivated by certain values, beliefs, desires, and theories; that they seek to reveal intentional states behind actions, or reasons, not causes; that they are rarely taken as "unsponsored texts"; and that "those worth telling and worth construing are typically born in trouble" (p. 142).

Stories also "shape, rather than simply reflect, human conduct . . . because they embody compelling motives, strong feelings, vague aspirations, clear intentions, or well-defined goals" (Rosaldo, 1989, p. 129). They serve many different functions. They can entertain, educate, inform, evoke memories, showcase ethnic and cultural characteristics, and illuminate abstractions. Stories are means for individuals to project and present themselves, declare what is important and valuable, give structure to perceptions, make general facts more meaningful to specific personal lives, connect the self with others, proclaim the self as a cultural being, develop a healthy sense of self, and forge new meanings and relationships, or build community. Stories give life to characters, concepts, and ideas through word pictures and verbal rhythms, which, in turn, convey new experiences and possibilities (Bruner, 1996; Denman, 1991; N. King, 1993).

In reflecting on incorporating storymaking and storytelling in her own teaching experience, N. King (1993) declares that these techniques "help make the abstract more concrete, diverse facts more understandable, and arouse interest in learning as students become engrossed, not only in the story itself, but in the cultural or social context in which it is told" (p. 2). The telling of one story is the genesis of yet other stories. The images, rhythms, and experiences it evokes "reverberate in the memories of audience members, who reconstruct the story with the stuff of their own thoughts and feelings. In such ways, individual lives are woven together through the stuff of stories" (Dyson & Genishi, 1994, p. 5). These attributes certainly fit the character and functions of the "story" of culturally responsive pedagogy presented in this book.

Even though "story" is usually associated with people telling about themselves and/or events in which they have been involved, the explanations of educational ideas, paradigms, and proposals constitute "story" as well. Educators need to organize their conceptions and experiences in working with students of color into meaningful "tales of important happenings," as much as individuals need to do so with their personal encounters. Without being so ordered, successful efforts cannot be easily shared or replicated. And educating some students of color is in dire need of much more success than currently exists. This is why I want to create a "story" of power pedagogy in the form of culturally responsive teaching.

In constructing this story, the images, ideas, meanings, and experiences produced by other researchers, scholars, and practitioners are woven together with my own interpretations to create even richer meanings and broader possibilities. The results are intended to be more effective ways of improving the educational achievement of students of color. Thus, *Culturally Responsive Teaching: Theory, Research, and Practice* is presented as a *story for academic success*. In some instances it is already happening, but in most it is still an envisioned possibility yet to be realized.

A PERSONAL STORY AND SYMBOL OF A TREND

Any good story has a setting and context, and develops around some topic, issue, event, theme, or situation of *felt* importance to the storyteller. Sometimes this is accomplished by using smaller events or experiences to launch larger ones. This is how the creation of the story of culturally responsive teaching begins—that is, with a ministory as an entrée into the bigger story. This ministory acts as a preview, a prelude to what is developed in greater detail later on. It is simultaneously metaphorical and literal, symbolic and representative, personal and collective, real and imagined, factual and fictional. It gives name to the motivation for and message of this book, and it places them within somewhat of a personal context. It acts as a point of reference and identifies the constituent issues and individuals for whom culturally responsive pedagogy is advocacy and agency.

This beginning story might be entitled "Simultaneously Winning and Losing." While its situations are about real-life individuals and events, the characters' names are pseudonyms. The story begins:

> As learners, siblings Aaron and Amy are a study in contradiction. Outside of school they exhibit some of the attributes typically associated with giftedness, but in school they are, at best, average students. They are caring, conscientious, and courteous teens who are sought out by peers as friends. They are insatiably curious about people, events, and experiences that they encounter in their social lives. They interact easily, confidently, and effectively with a wide range of people, diversified by age, position, gender, ethnicity, race, and education. They are as comfortable with deans of colleges of education as they are with agemates and their little toddler nephew.
>
> Amy and Aaron know how to ask engaging, thoughtful, probing questions so that they can gain information about things they do not understand and simultaneously be actively, engaged participants in conversations. Not knowing something is not perceived by them as a negative reflection on

their egos, intelligence, or self-worth. They consider inquiry and questioning as natural means of knowing, and they use them prolifically in their social settings. They are very adept at making contributions to interactions with others that are appropriate to the context and purpose. Amy and Aaron love to learn and are interested in exploring a wide variety of topics and issues. They are not reluctant to try out new experiences and think about different things, but this is done with thoughtful care, not impulsiveness or irresponsibility. They probe diligently with others to extend their knowledge, but with respect and honor. They "process" their experiences and knowledge, are good listeners, and know how to help others build conversations. They routinely reflect on, analyze, evaluate, and classify knowledge and experiences into arrangements other than those in which they were initially received. Amy and Aaron love to tell stories about their encounters and to share their experiences and knowledge with others. Consequently, they are verbally articulate and very skilled in their interpersonal and social relations.

Aaron and Amy also are good problem solvers and critical thinkers. They know well how to assess their strength and weaknesses and to determine what needs to be done to deal effectively with problematic situations. They are honest and above-board about their responsibilities and the fallacies of their behaviors; they do not shirk obligations or make disavowing excuses for irresponsibilities. They are resourceful and self-initiating in finding answers and solutions to problems. A case in point happened when they were several years younger. A frightening experience with a severe thunderstorm left them very much afraid of thunder and lightening. After some time living with this fear, they decided to find a way to manage it. So they began to watch the weather channel on TV and taught themselves how to read weathermaps in newspapers. This way they could determine in advance what the weather was going to be like, and emotionally and mentally prepare themselves for it. Thus, instead of letting this fear overwhelm them, they took control of it and taught themselves to grow beyond it.

With all of these attributes and skills, one would expect Amy and Aaron to be high achievers in school. Unfortunately, this is not the case. They have struggled academically from the time they began school as kindergartners. They complain about their subjects being dull and boring; about not being able to understand what the teachers are talking about; about teachers who are impatient with students asking them questions; about teachers who don't seem to care or be genuinely concerned about students; about all the tests they have to take, with no one explaining *why* the answers they gave to the questions weren't correct; and about not having time to get everything done that school and classes require. These are agonizing and disconcerting concerns for them. Yet Aaron and Amy are able to separate their achievement problems from their personal quality. While they talk candidly about failing a test or not performing adequately on a class task, they are never heard saying, "I am a failure." They also continue to view school as a place where they go to learn. This is evident in their conversations about happenings in school. More often than not, events they recount have something to do in some way with learning. Although they have a wide and diverse circle of friends at school, socializing and connecting with them is not their primary point of reference in talking about going to school and the events that occur in the course of the school day.

Amy and Aaron are high school seniors now. Despite their academic struggles, they have never expressed a disdain for education or schooling. They have never complained about or considered not going to school. On occasion they have even found a teacher, lesson, task, or reading exciting and intellectually stimulating. One of their teachers who wove lots of information about African Americans into U. S. history, and had the students do critical analyses and alternative interpretations of historical events, is remembered fondly and held in high esteem. His teaching style is considered by them to be "the way all teachers should teach." Reading The Cay (T. Taylor, 1969), Let the Circle Be Unbroken (M. Taylor, 1981), Roll of Thunder, Hear My Cry (M. Taylor, 1984), and The Autobiography of Malcolm X (Malcolm X & Haley, 1966) and viewing Roots (Haley, 1976) were particularly memorable and intellectually successfully events for them that generated much excitement and exuberant sharing of insights and reactions with family and friends at home. Reports written and tests taken on these learning tasks received high grades and positive accolades from their teachers.

As they approach the end of their senior year, Aaron and Amy wait, with trepidation yet cautious hopefulness, for the results of their latest attempts on their school district's proficiency tests. Math and writing have been the particular nemeses for one, and math and science for the other. They have taken these tests several times before, unsuccessfully. If they do not pass them, what will they do? Will they try yet again to pass? How many more times will they go through this agony before becoming so discouraged and demoralized that they refuse to persist any longer in trying to pass these tests? Most certainly, if they do not pass the proficiency tests, they will not be allowed to graduate, even though they have completed all the required courses with passing grades. If they do not graduate, the chances of their pursuing any postsecondary educational opportunities are virtually nil.

What's happening to Amy and Aaron inside school? Why are these youths intelligently curious and capable out of school, but not in? Is this seemingly contradiction in their academic capabilities because they are African American and poor urban residents? What is repeatedly not passing a set of tests doing to their internal sense of self, although outwardly they still seem to be very confident and positive about who they are? If teachers knew how, or cared, to *consistently* incorporate African American content and styles of learning into their classroom instruction and preparation for testing, would Aaron's and Amy's academic story be different?

THE ACHIEVEMENT DILEMMA

Amy and Aaron began their testing saga in eighth grade. They passed some of the required tests in the subsequent years, but not math, science, or writing. Thus, they have been taking some form of proficiency tests for the last five years. Their school district now tests in grades 4, 6, 8, 9, and 12, and will soon add all the other grades to this schedule.

Unfortunately, Aaron's and Amy's situation is not an idiosyncratic or isolated one. There are hundreds of thousands of students like them in schools throughout the United States. As of the 1994–1995 school year, school districts in 17 states were requiring students to pass minimum-competency tests in order to graduate from high school. Another 28 states use standardized testing for other reasons, such as diagnosis of student needs and placement, improvement of instruction, program evaluation, and school performance reporting (*Digest of Education Statistics*, 1999). Thus, only 5 of the 50 states have not instituted standardized testing for any reason. Added to these figures are local school districts that are instituting various forms of required standardized tests of essential learnings, performance proficiencies, and graduation requirements. The numbers are growing by leaps and bounds annually.

But rarely are these policy declarations accompanied by detailed provisions for how they are to be accomplished instructionally. Nor do they specify accountability consequences for school personnel when students fail to meet the performance expectations. A case in point is Seattle, Washington. The public schools in that city began their 1997–1998 academic year with new graduation standards for the incoming ninth-graders. They require students to (1) have a cumulative 2.0 (C) or better grade point average in all required courses in English, language arts, math, science, and social studies; (2) read, understand, and evaluate at least 20 books over 4 years; (3) write a comprehensive research paper to be presented orally and defended during the senior year; (4) demonstrate their ability to write a variety of other types of work effectively; (5) master five basic areas of mathematics at the tenth-grade level of proficiency; and (6) complete 20 hours of service learning (Lilly, 1997).

Mandatory proficiency, or "exit," testing in grades 2, 5, and 8 will be added in 1998. These are all part of the superintendent's master plan to make the educational experience more rigorous and to raise levels of academic performance throughout the district. No operational definitions, explanations, or guidance were provided for how these policy regulations are to be implemented, such as what books will be acceptable to read, who will make these decisions, how the evaluations will be presented, and who will determine whether they are acceptable. Without these kind of provisions students who are already at risk for academic failure will be further jeopardized.

Students struggling to pass proficiency tests and other presumed "high standards of academic excellence" throughout the United States are not only African American, but Native American, Latino, Asian American, and European American; male and female; poor and middle class; urban and rural dwellers; English-dominant speakers and others who have limited proficiency in English. Many are in worse shape than Aaron and Amy. At least, Aaron and Amy continue to go to school, find some moments of value and intellectual stimulation in their classes, and have not internalized their academic difficulties as negative statements about their value as human beings. They know well the meaning of an inspirational motto advertised recently by a small-business enterprise that says, "Failure is an experience, not any individual." Unfortunately, this is not true for many students who are unsuccessful in school. They and their teachers connect their academic difficulties to their personal worth, and the individuals are deemed failures.

ASSERTIONS ABOUT IMPROVING STUDENT ACHIEVEMENT

Five major premises or assertions undergird the discussions in this book. They give shape to the text and tone of the analyses presented and the strategies proposed for improving the performance of underachieving students of color. Since echoes of them reverberate throughout the development of the narrative text of all the chapters, it seems best to make them explicit up front.

Culture Counts

The first premise is that culture is at the heart of all we do in the name of education, whether that is curriculum, instruction, administration, or performance assessment. As used here, *culture* refers to a dynamic system of social values, cognitive codes, behavioral standards, worldviews, and beliefs used to give order and meaning to our own lives as well as the lives of others (Delgado-Gaitan & Trueba, 1991). Even without our being consciously aware of it, culture determines how we think, believe, and behave, and these, in turn, affect how we teach and learn. As Young Pai (1990) explains, "There is no escaping the fact that education is a sociocultural process. Hence, a critical examination of the role of culture in human life is indispensable to the understanding and control of educative processes" (p. 3). George and Louise Spindler (1994) extend and further clarify these arguments. In so doing they make a compelling case for teachers to understand how their own and their students' cultures affect the educational process. They explain:

> Teachers carry into the classroom their personal cultural background. They perceive students, all of whom are cultural agents, with inevitable prejudice and preconception. Students likewise come to school with personal cultural backgrounds that influence their perceptions of teachers, other students, and the school itself. Together students and teachers construct, mostly without being conscious of doing it, an environment of meanings enacted in individual and group behaviors, of conflict and accommodation, rejection and acceptance, alienation and withdrawal. (p. xii)

Wade Boykin (1994) provides another perspective on the interaction between culture and education that helps to frame the analyses presented in the various chapters of this book. He, too, believes that "there has always been a profound and inescapable cultural fabric of the schooling process in America" (p. 244). This "cultural fabric," primarily of European and middle-class origins, is so deeply ingrained in the structures, ethos, programs, and etiquette of schools that it is considered simply the "normal" and "right" thing to do. Because of these, formal education

> is about learning how to read, write, and think . . . in certain prescribed ways consistent with certain beliefs, prescribed vantage points, value-laden conditions and value-laden formats. These prescribed ways of educating, these certain vantage points, conditions, proper practices and inherent values are the materials and texture of a profound cultural socialization process that forms the very fabric of the medium through which schooling is done (pp. 245–246).

The connection between culture and education suggested by Pai, Boykin, and the Spindlers is made even more explicit by Flippo and associates (1997). They declare that "the relationship between literacy and culture is bidirectional. Not only will cultural diversity mediate the acquisition and expression of literacy, but literacy education will also influence and mold an individual's cultural identity" (p. 645). These observations underscore the importance of placing culture at the center of the analysis of techniques for improving the performance of underachieving students of color.

Culture, like any other social or biological organism, is multidimensional and continually changing. It must be so to remain vital and functional for those who create it and for those it serves. As manifested in expressive behaviors, culture is influenced by a wide variety of factors, including time, setting, age, economics, and social circumstances. This expressive variability does not nullify the existence of some core cultural features and focal values in different ethnic groups. Instead, members of ethnic groups, whether consciously or not, share some core cultural characteristics. Shade, Kelly, and Oberg (1997) refer to these as the *modal personality*, which means cultural characteristics most likely to be found in a sample of an ethnic population. Designating core or modal characteristics does not imply that they will be identically manifested by all group members. Nor will these characteristics be negated if some group members do not exhibit any of them as described. How individual members of ethnic groups express their shared features varies widely for many different reasons. Some of the causes of this variance, and the relationships among them as conceived and applied throughout this book, are depicted visually in Figure 1.1.

The information in this figure suggests that *culture is dynamic, complex, interactive, and changing, yet a stabilizing force in human life.* "Ethnicity and culture," at the bottom of the figure, are the *foundational anchors* of all other behaviors. They operate on a continuum of intensity, ranging from high to low, as symbolized by the double-headed arrow. How core characteristics of ethnic groups' cultures are manifested in *expressive behaviors* (e.g., thinking, talking, writing, etc.) is influenced by different *mitigating variables* such as gender, education, social class, and degrees of affiliation. The variables identified in the model are representative of *types* of influences rather than being all-inclusive. The two-directional arrows between ethnicity and culture, the mitigating variables, and the expressive behaviors suggest that the relationships among all of these are dialectic and dynamic.

The mitigating variables also interact with and influence each other, as do the various kinds of expressive behaviors. These relationships are indicated by the bidirectional arrows in each block. However, the influences are not always in the same directions or of equal degrees of intensity. For instance, high levels of education do not necessarily correlate positively with high degrees of ethnic affiliation and learning-style characteristics. High degrees of ethnic affiliation do correlate with high cultural identity and ownership. Chronological maturity does not guarantee heightened ethnic affiliation or cultural identity. Although males and

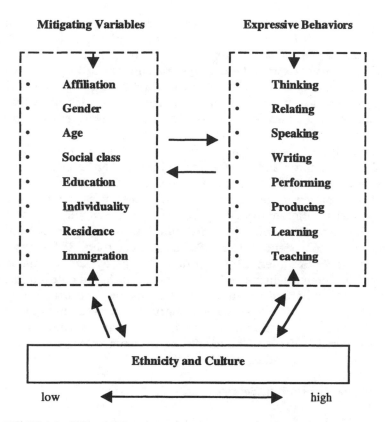

FIGURE 1.1. Cultural Dynamics

females express their cultural heritage in somewhat different ways, this is due more to their engendered socialization than to their being more or less culturally affiliated because of their gender.

The discussion of cultural influences on teaching and learning presented in this book focus on core characteristics, as manifested on a range of clarity, specificity, purity, and authenticity that is closer to the "high" end of the continuum. The imagined individuals exhibiting these cultural characteristics are *highly ethnically affiliated with a strong cultural identity*. The descriptions are not intended to capture every conceivable manifestation of culture for every single individual and circumstance for all individuals within different ethnic groups. Furthermore, cultural features are *composite constructions* of group behaviors that occur over time and in many different situations. They are not pure descriptors of specific individuals within groups or behaviors at a particular point in time. Instead, *descriptions of culture are approximations of reality—templates, if you will—through which actual behaviors of individuals can be filtered in search of alternative explanations and deeper meanings.* In this sense the cultural descriptions included in this book are intended to serve similar purposes as any other educational phenomena, such as characterizations of good teaching, being at-risk, giftedness, and gender-related behaviors. Few, if any, individuals will manifest the characteristics, as described, in every place and at all times.

The cultures of schools and different ethnic groups are not always completely synchronized. These discontinuities can interfere with students' academic achievement, in part because how students are accustomed to engaging in intellectual processing, self-presentation, and task performance is different from the processes used in school. Demonstrating knowledge and skills may be constrained as much by structural and procedural inconsistencies (Au, 1980a; Cazden, John, & Hymes, 1985; Holliday, 1985; Spindler, 1987; Spring, 1995) as by lack of intellectual ability. Therefore, teachers need to understand different cultural intersections and incompatibilities, minimize the tensions, and bridge the gaps between different cultural systems. Congruency between how the educational process is ordered and delivered, and the cultural frames of reference of diverse students will improve school achievement for students of color (Spindler & Spindler, 1994).

Conventional Reform Is Inadequate

The second guiding assumption of this book is that *conventional* paradigms and proposals for improving the achievement of students of color are doomed to failure. This is due largely to their being deeply enmeshed in a deficit orientation—that is, concentrating on what ethnically, racially, and linguistically different students don't have and can't do—and their claims of cultural neutrality. These positions are evident in current thinking about "at-risk" students and instructional programs that emphasize only the technical and academic dimensions of learning. There are some high-profile innovations of this kind that appear to be having some significant positive impacts on the achievement of students of color, such as Reading Recovery, DISTAR, and Accelerated Schools. But their effects may not stand the test of time or be as comprehensive as they claim. They may inadvertently cause students to compromise their ethnic and cultural identity to attain academic achievement.

These programs attempt to deal with academic performance by divorcing it from other factors that affect achievement, such as culture, ethnicity, and personal experience. The Advancement Via Individual Determination

(AVID) project, which began in 1980 in the San Diego public schools, has proven the fallacy of this for Latino and African American students from urban areas. The directors and teachers of AVID found that achievement was much higher when academic interventions are reinforced by an infrastructure of social supports. These included personal caring, mutual aid and assistance, use of cultural anchors and mediators in instruction, and creating a sense of community among students and teachers (Mehan, Hubbard, Villanueva, & Lintz, 1996; Swanson, Mehan, & Hubbard, 1995).

Intention Without Action Is Insufficient

A third assumption is that many educators have good intentions about not being academically unjust and discriminatory toward ethnically and racially different students. Others understand and even endorse the importance of being *aware* of cultural differences in classroom interactions. However important they are, good intentions and awareness are not enough to bring about the changes needed in educational programs and procedures to prevent academic inequities among diverse students. Goodwill must be accompanied by pedagogical knowledge and skills as well as the courage to dismantle the status quo. Many years ago Carter G. Woodson (1933/1969) made some provocative observations about the limitations of good intentions without skill proficiency evident in attempts to educate African Americans shortly after the end of the Civil War. The missionary workers who went south to enlighten the freedmen were earnest and admirable in their endeavors but were largely ineffective because they

> had more enthusiasm than knowledge. They did not understand the task before them. This undertaking, too, was more of an effort toward social uplift than actual education. Their aim was to transform the Negroes, not to develop them. The freedmen who were to be enlightened were given little thought, for the best friends of the race, ill-taught themselves, followed the traditional curricula of the times which did not take the Negro into consideration except to condemn or pity him. (p. 17)

Even though these observations were prompted by situations a century and a half ago and Woodson's comments were first made more than 65 years ago, they are not mere historical events and memories. Nor is it reasonable, unfortunately, to dismiss them as obsolete. The fact that they are still applicable today indicates that the issue of providing appropriate education for African Americans and other ethnic groups of color is a longstanding and persistent one.

The worst kinds of condemnation of groups of color no longer exist in very overt ways, but residuals of the missionary zeal in dealing with social issues affecting them continue. They take the form of benign oversight, in which students of color often are ignored and left alone as long as they are not challenging teachers or disrupting classroom procedures. Another frequent contemporary manifestation of the "enlightenment intentions" described by Woodson are declarations that awareness of and appreciation for cultural differences are sufficient for dealing with the challenges of providing effective education for ethnic groups of color. Defenders of these positions seem to be unaware of the complexity of the issues; awareness or appreciation without action will not change the educational enterprise. Mastery of knowledge and skills related to working with culturally diverse students in pedagogical situations is imperative for this task.

Another "good intentions" position often taken is that "race, culture, and ethnicity are not important. The educational issue of utmost concern is the individual and his or her academic outcomes." The race, culture, ethnicity, individuality, and intellectuality of students are not discrete attributes that can be neatly assigned to separate categories, some to be ignored while others are tended to. Instead, they are inseparably interrelated; all must be carefully understood, and the insights gleaned from this understanding should be the driving force for the redesign of education for cultural diversity. In the spirit of Woodson's message, this comprehensive understanding is a more appropriate basis for developing the intellectual capabilities of students of color than is the attempt to get them to transcend their ethnic identities and cultural foundations.

Strength and Vitality of Cultural Diversity

A fourth major assertion of this book is that cultural diversity is a strength—a persistent, vitalizing force in our personal and civic lives—although this may not be realized. It is, then, a useful resource for improving educational effectiveness for all students. Just as the evocation of their European American, middle-class heritage contributes to the achievement of White students, using the cultures and experiences of Native Americans, Asian and Pacific Islander Americans, Latino Americans, and African Americans facilitates their school success.

Several researchers and practitioners have provided evidence to support the verity of these claims. For example, McCarty, Wallace, Lynch, and Benally (1991) found that the image of Navajo children as silent and passive students was totally destroyed by teaching that connected school learning with cultural backgrounds and lived experiences. When their social experiences were incorporated into curriculum and instruction, and their cultural and linguistic resources were used to solve academic problems, the Navajo students became physically energized, intellectually engaged, and verbally fluent in the classroom. Boggs, Watson-Gegeo, and McMillen (1985), Tharp and Gallimore (1988), and Au (1993) report similar results from using culturally familiar content and styles of teaching on the academic achievement of Native Hawaiian students. Krater, Zeni, and Cason (1994), as well as Lee (1993) have done likewise for African Americans; Escalante and Dirmann (1990) as well as Sheets (1995a) with Latinos; and Philips (1983) with students on the Warm Springs Reservation and Greenbaum (1985) with Cherokee elementary school students. Practices such as these, and the effects they have on student achievement, give name, substance, and validity to the title and intentions of this book. They support the transformative effects of sociocultural contextual factors on the academic achievement of students of color. In other words, "matching the contextual conditions for learning to the cultural experiences of the learner increases task engagement and hence increases task performance" (B. Allen & Butler, 1996, p. 317).

Learning experiences and achievement outcomes for ethnically diverse students should include more than cognitive performances in academic subjects and standardized test scores. Moral, social, cultural, personal, and political developments are also important. All of these are essential to the healthy and complete functioning of human beings and societies. If education is, as it should be, devoted to teaching the whole child, then this comprehensive focus should be evident throughout curriculum, instruction, and assessment. John Gardner (1984) makes this point powerfully and persuasively. He tells us that excellence in education is a process of

> perpetual self-discovery, perpetual reshaping to realize one's best self, to be the person one could be. It includes not only the intellect but the emotions, character, and personality . . . not only surface but deeper layers of thought and action . . . adaptability, creativeness, and vitality . . . [and] ethical and spiritual growth. (p. 124)

Fostering this comprehensive scale of development for culturally diverse students in U. S. schools should take place within a framework of ethical values and multiple cultural perspectives because "every age, in every significant situation, in every conceivable way" (J. Gardner, 1984, p. 125) has to recreate itself. These important nonacademic learnings typically are not included on standardized test scores. If tests are the only measures used to determine student performance, some critical areas of achievement will be systematically and repeatedly overlooked. Therefore, just as achievement should be seen as multidimensional, many different types of techniques should be routinely used to assess student performance in schools.

Jeffrey Kane, the executive editor of *Holistic Education Review*, offers another perspective of quality education that resonates with the assumptions and intentions of this book. It is about "knowing and being" (1994), and it speaks to the moral dimensions of education. It is presented here because education in general and specific reform actions to eliminate the educational injustices perpetuated toward students of color are most certainly moral as well as being pedagogical. Kane (1994) explains:

> Knowing and being are intimately entwined. Knowledge is embedded in and created by a constellation of human intelligences, and such intelligences exist within a universe of inner experience, of the experience of being. Every fact, every skill a child acquires, however small and seemingly discreet, addresses our sense of meaning, purpose, and identity. . . . Whether we develop the capacity to wonder, to explore the depth of our own being, to rise to the challenge to speak the words "I am" or whether we resign ourselves to questions of technique and method to problems . . . may well depend upon the equality of the experiences we provide for children in the course of their education. (p. 4)

Test Scores and Grades Are Symptoms, Not Causes, of Achievement Problems

The final key premise underlying the discussions in the forthcoming chapters is that scores on standardized tests and grades students receive on classroom learning tasks do not explain why they are not performing at acceptable levels. These are the symptoms, not the causes, of the problems. Unless teachers understand what is interfering with students' performance, they cannot intervene appropriately to remove the obstacles to high achievement. Simply blaming students, their socioeconomic background, a lack of interest in and lack of motivation for learning, and poor parental participation in the educational process is not very helpful. The question of "why" continues to be unanswered. Some other reasons may explain why disproportionally high percentages of African Americans, Latinos, Native Americans, and some Asian American groups are not doing well in school. Among these are intragroup variability, differential skills and abilities, stress and anxiety provoked by racial prejudices and stereotypes, and discontinuities between the cultures of the school and the homes of ethnically diverse students. They offer insights that can generate more hopeful possibilities for reversing current achievement patterns.

The search for reasons that different students are performing as they are should begin with a much more careful disaggregation of achievement data. Describing performance in "averages" across ethnic groups and for "composite skills" can disguise more than illuminate. For example, reports that African American students have the lowest reading scores of any ethnic group on National Assessment of Educational Progress measures leave out a lot of critical information. They do not specify how performance is distributed by gender, social class, immigrant status, and linguistic background of the students, nor do they specify the various skills (e.g., vocabulary, comprehension, inference, decoding, etc.) that comprise reading. These reports blatantly ignore the *within-group variability* that exists among African Americans. Yet this variance must be understood, and the insights gained should influence the design and implementation of instructional reforms to facilitate better school achievement for these students.

No ethnic group is ethnically or intellectually monolithic. For instance, African Americans include people who are descendants of Africans enslaved in the United States, others whose origins are in the Caribbean, and recent immigrants from various African nations. Some are native speakers of English, some are dialect speakers, and others speak English as a second language. Some African Americans are academically gifted, some are average students, and some are failing in school. This kind of variability exists in all ethnic groups, and it affects the achievement of students in different ways. What these differences are must be more clearly defined if teachers are to further encourage those students who are already performing well and remediate those who are not. Thus, effective teaching and learning for diverse students are contingent upon the thorough disaggregation of achievement data by student demographics and types of academic skills.

Research on the education of recent Asian immigrants to the United States provides a graphic illustration of why immigration should be understood as one of the reasons for the achievement patterns of some ethnic groups. Vernez and Abrahamese (1996) found that immigrants were less likely to attend high school (87 percent) than U. S.-born students (93 percent). Latino immigrants, especially those from Mexico, accounted for almost all of this difference. In 1990 only one in four Mexican immigrant youths between the ages of 15 and 17 were enrolled in school; Latino immigrants performed lower than other immigrant groups, but higher than their U. S.-born counterparts. McDonnell and Hill (1993) and Fass (1989) reported that the highest-performing Asian immigrant students are Japanese, Chinese, Filipinos, Koreans, and Asian Indians. Southeast Asians, such as Vietnamese, Cambodians, and Thais, do not perform as well.

Some researchers (First & Carrera, 1988; Igoa, 1995; Olneck, 1995) suggest that many immigrant families and their children are caught in a paradox. They come to the United States to escape poverty and persecution, and to improve the general quality of their lives. In doing so, they often suffer deep affective losses of supportive networks and familial connections. The formal schooling of many of these children prior to immigration was sporadic and fragmented. After arriving in the United States, some immigrant families experience frequent changes in residence, which interferes with the children's educational continuity. They have to adjust to a new culture, language, style of living, and educational system. This geographic, cultural, and psychoemotional uprootedness can cause stress, anxiety, feelings of vulnerability, loneliness, isolation, and insecurity. All these conditions can have negative effects on school achievement.

Both immigrant and native-born students of color may also encounter prejudices, stereotyping, and racism that have negative impacts on their self-esteem, mental health, and academic achievement. The work of several researchers attests to these effects on African, Asian, and Native American students. Plummer and Slane (1996) found racism to be highly stress-provoking for African Americans, requiring them to engage in coping behaviors quite different from those of European Americans. They concluded that individuals do not have to experience racist attitudes and actions directed at them personally to be victimized because "race, in and of itself, is a potential source of stress" (p. 314).

Steele (1997) and Steele and Aronson (1995) have examined how societal stereotypes about ethnic and gender groups can affect the intellectual functioning and identity development of individual members. They call this effect a "stereotype threat." It is defined as "the event of a negative stereotype about a group to which one belongs becoming self-relevant, usually as a plausible interpretation for something one is doing, for an experience one is having, or for a situation one is in, that has relevance to one's self-definition" (Steele, 1997, p. 616). Steele and Aronson (1995) propose that stereotype threat is most salient for those students who care most about performing well. Allegations about their ethnic group's intellectual inability create additional self-threat, which interferes with achievement by reducing the range of intellectual cues students are able to use, diverting attention onto task-irrelevant worries, creating self-consciousness and undue caution, and causing them to disengage from academic efforts. Similar results also have been reported by Landrine and Klonoff (1996) and Gougis (1986).

The racial discrimination against Navajo students recorded by Deyhle (1995) was a serious threat to their achievement. It took many different forms, ranging from explicit acts of racism to more subtle paternalism, to distortion of cultural values, to belittling the students' intellectual capability. The youth who attended school off the Navajo Reservation talked about the psychoemotional pressure, embarrassment, and anger caused by repeatedly being picked on, ridiculed, and subjected to overt declarations of dislike for and demeaning assumptions about Navajos; teachers' being uncomfortable with or afraid of them; and being offered low-level, nonacademic instruction, presumably because Navajo students "do better in basic classes and with hands-on instruction." Their cultural beliefs and practices are often mocked or dismissed as insignificant. Some Navajo students retaliate by stereotyping European American students and teachers in kind, while others try harder to dispel the stereotype and avoid the limelight. Still others overtly resisted classroom rules or removed themselves from the situation entirely—by dropping out of school or, more accurately, being "pushed out."

Kiang and Kaplan (1994) reported similar examples and effects of racial stress and anxiety on Vietnamese students at a Boston high school. The students told about encountering racial conflicts daily that included being rendered irrelevant and invisible; being ridiculed for speaking Vietnamese; being called derogatory names and subjected to racist slurs; witnessing and experiencing harassment on a regular basis; feeling threatened and angry; and being teased and insulted (Kiang & Kaplan 1994). These experiences may be carryovers from what is happening in society at large. Min (1995) provides some evidence that anti-Asian prejudices and "bias crimes" are on the rise, due to the increase of Asian Americans in the U. S. population being considered an economic threat by some other groups. It is not difficult to imagine the profound negative consequences these kinds of experiences have for academic, social, and personal achievement, or the emotional and intellectual benefits that could result from the removal of prejudicial conditions from schools and society.

Other factors that help to explain the achievement patterns of ethnically different students and locate opportunities for reform are offered by Fordham (1993, 1996) and Goto (1997). They posit that some students with high academic potential deliberately sabotage or camouflage their intellectual abilities to avoid being alienated from their ethnic friends who are not as adept in school. Fordham explains that the intellectually capable African American females in her study sometimes engage in "intentional silence," wherein they rarely spoke in class, answered questions but only tersely and without elaboration, and generally avoided bringing attention to themselves. Goto found that Chinese Americans students did the same kinds of things. To escape being ridiculed by peers or spotlighted by teachers, the students worked hard to give the impression that they were just "normal." They sought a classroom identity that would grant them "comfortable anonymity."

"Double dealing," or being at once highly ethnically affiliated and academically achieving, can take a terrible toll on students when the two agendas are not complementary, as is frequently the case in conventional schools. Negotiating both ways of being can be stress-provoking and emotionally exhausting; it can even cause some students to drop out of the academic loop entirely. Others may sacrifice their friendship networks and ethnic connections for school success. Neither of these choices is desirable for the students involved, nor does either offer the best conditions for maximum achievement of any kind. Students should be able to achieve academically, ethnically, culturally, and socially simultaneously without any of these abilities interfering with the others.

CONCLUSION

Much intellectual ability and many other kinds of intelligences are lying untapped in ethnically diverse students. If these are recognized and used in the instructional process, school achievement will improve radically. Culturally responsive teaching is a means for unleashing the higher learning potentials of ethnically diverse students by simultaneously cultivating their academic and psychosocial abilities.

The best-quality educational programs and practices can never be accomplished if some ethnic groups and their contributions to the development of U. S. history, life, and culture are ignored or demeaned. All schools and teachers, regardless of the ethnic and racial makeup of their local student populations, must be actively involved in promoting equity and excellence, and all students must be benefactors of these efforts. Education that is minimally adequate has to teach students the knowledge, values, and skills they need to function effectively as citizens of the pluralistic U.S. society. These are requirements, not voluntary choices, for all students.

Despite an increasingly diverse population, most people in the United States live in communities with others more alike than different from themselves. Students from these communities arrive at school knowing little of significance about people who are different. Yet their lives are intertwined with these "unknown others" and will become even more so in the future. If we are to avoid intergroup strife and individuals are to live the best-quality lives possible, we simply must teach students how to relate better with people from different ethnic, racial, cultural, language, and gender backgrounds. These *relational competencies* must encompass knowing, valuing, doing, caring, and sharing power, resources, and responsibilities. Hence, developing sociocivic skills for effective membership in multicultural communities is as important a goal of culturally responsive pedagogy as improving the academic achievement and personal development of students of color.

CHAPTER 2

Power Pedagogy Through Cultural Responsiveness

Teaching is a contextual and situational process. As such, it is most effective when ecological factors, such as prior experiences, community settings, cultural backgrounds, and ethnic identities of teachers and students, are included in its implementation. This basic fact is often ignored in teaching some Native, Latino, African, and Asian American students, especially if they are poor. Instead, they are taught from the middle class, Eurocentric frameworks that shape school practices. This attitude of "cultural blindness" stems from several sources.

One of these is the notion that education has nothing to do with cultures and heritages. It is about teaching intellectual, vocational, and civic skills. Students, especially underachieving ones, need to learn knowledge and skills that they can apply in life, and how to meet high standards of academic excellence, rather than wasting time on fanciful notions about cultural diversity. Second, too few teachers have adequate knowledge about how teaching practices reflect European American cultural values. Nor are they sufficiently informed about the cultures of different ethnic groups. Third, most teachers want to do the best for all their students, and they mistakenly believe that to treat students differently because of their cultural orientations is racial discrimination. Fourth, there is a belief that good teaching is transcendent; it is identical for all students and under all circumstances. Fifth, there is the claim that education is an effective doorway of assimilation into mainstream society for people from diverse cultural heritages, ethnic groups, social classes, and points of origin. These students need to forget about being different and learn to adapt to U. S. society. The best way to facilitate this process is for all students to have the same experiences in schools.

INTRODUCTION

This chapter calls these assumptions into question. It begins by exposing the fallacy of cultural neutrality and the homogeneity syndrome in teaching and learning for Native, African, Latino, and Asian American students who are not performing very well on traditional measures of school achievement. It also debunks the notion that school success for students of color can be generated from negative perceptions of their life experiences, cultural backgrounds, and intellectual capabilities. Instead, instructional reforms are needed that are grounded in positive beliefs about the cultural heritages and academic potentialities of these students. A pedagogical paradigm that has these characteristics is presented. The conceptual explication of this paradigm includes a brief historical background, descriptive characteristics, two case examples of its theoretical principles exemplified in practice, and some suggestions for how teachers can begin their transformation toward greater cultural responsiveness in working with students of color.

FROM CAN'T TO CAN

Many educators still believe that good teaching transcends place, people, time, and context. They contend it has nothing to do with the class, race, gender, ethnicity, or culture of students and teachers. This attitude is manifested in the expression "Good teachers anywhere are good teachers everywhere." Individuals who subscribe to this belief fail to realize that their standards of "goodness" in teaching and learning are culturally determined and are not the same for all ethnic groups. The structures, assumptions, substance, and operations of conventional educational enterprises are European American cultural icons (Pai, 1990). A case in point is the protocols of attentiveness and the emphasis placed on them in classrooms. Students are expected to pay close attention to teachers for prolonged, largely uninterrupted periods of time. Specific signs and signals have evolved that are associated with appropriate attending behaviors. These include nonverbal communication cues, such as gaze, eye contact, and body posture. When they are not exhibited by learners at times, at intervals, and for durations designated by teachers, the students are judged to be uninvolved, distracted, having short attention spans, and/or engaging in off-task behaviors. All these are "read" as obstructive to effective teaching and learning.

Many students are admonished by teachers to "Look at me when I'm talking to you." Direct eye contact as a signal of attentiveness may be perceived as staring, a cultural taboo that causes resentment among some Apache students (Spring, 1995). Other discontinuities in behavioral norms and expectations are not isolated incidents or rare occurrences in culturally pluralistic classrooms. They happen often and on many different fronts, simply because teachers fail to recognize, understand, or appreciate the pervasive influence of culture on their own and their students' attitudes, values, and behaviors.

Decontextualizing teaching and learning from the ethnicities and cultures of students minimizes the chances that their achievement potential will ever be fully realized. Pai (1990) agrees with this assertion and makes the point even more emphatically, explaining:

> Our goals, how we teach, what we teach, how we relate to children and each other are rooted in the norms of our culture. Our society's predominant worldview and cultural norms are so deeply ingrained in how we educate children that we seldom think about the possibility that there may be other different but equally legitimate and effective approaches to teaching and learning. In a society with as much sociocultural and racial diversity as the United States, the lack of this wonderment about alternative ways often results in unequal education and social injustice. (p. 229)

Another common and paradoxical manifestation of the notion that good teaching is devoid of cultural tenets is the frequent declaration that "respecting the individual differences of students is really what counts in effective teaching, not race, ethnicity, culture, or gender." Simultaneously, too many teachers plead ignorance of Latinos, African Americans, Native Americans, Laotians, Vietnamese, and other immigrant groups. It is inconceivable how educators can recognize and nurture the individuality of students if they do not know them. Ignorance of people different from ourselves often breeds negative attitudes, anxiety, fears, and the seductive temptation to turn others into images of ourselves. The individuality of students is deeply entwined with their ethnic identity and cultural socialization. Teachers need to understand very thoroughly both the relationships and the distinctions between these to avoid compromising the very thing they are most concern about—that is, students' individuality. Inability to make distinctions among ethnicity, culture, and individuality increases the risk that teachers will impose their notions on ethnically different students, insult their cultural heritages, or ignore them entirely in the instructional process. In reality, ethnicity and culture are significant filters through which one's individuality is made manifest. Yet individuality, culture, and ethnicity are not synonymous.

The second troubling feature of the conventional educational ethos and practices with respect to improving the achievement of ethnically diverse students is the "deficit syndrome." Far too many educators attribute school failure to what students of color don't have and can't do. Some of the specific reasons given for why Navajo students do poorly in school are representative of this kind of thinking. In a school district in which 48% of the students are Navajo, and one of every four Navajos leave before graduation, the causes of school failure identified by the administrators were all "deficits." Among them were lack of self-esteem; inadequate homes and prior preparation; poor parenting skills and low parental participation in the schooling process; lack of language development; poor academic interests, aspirations, and motivation; few opportunities for cultural enrichment; high truancy and absentee rates; and health problems, such as fetal alcohol syndrome (Deyhle, 1995). Except for fetal alcohol syndrome, similar "deficits" have been attributed to underachieving Latinos, African Americans, and some groups of Asian Americans.

Trying to teach from this "blaming the victim" and deficit mindset sounds more like a basis for "correcting or curing" than educating. Success does not emerge out of failure, weakness does not generate strength, and courage does not stem from cowardice. Instead, success begets success. Mastery of tasks at one level encourages individuals to accomplish tasks of even greater complexity (Ormrod, 1995). High-level learning is a very high-risk venture. To pursue it with conviction, and eventual competence, requires students to have some degree of academic mastery, as well as personal confidence and courage. In other words, learning derives from a basis of strength and capability, not weakness and failure. Ormrod (1995) refers to this as having self-efficacy, meaning that "students feel more confident that they can succeed at a task . . . when they have succeeded at that task or similar ones in the past" (p. 151). Conversely, "when students meet with *consistent* failure in performing a particular task, they will have little confidence in their ability to succeed . . . in the future," and "each new failure confirms what they already 'know' about the task—they can't do it" (p. 152, emphasis in original). This "learned helplessness" and "cumulative failure" are devastating to many different kinds of achievement possibilities—academic, school attendance, personal well-being, dropout prevention, and avoidance of discipline problems.

Therefore, a very different pedagogical paradigm is needed to improve the performance of underachieving students from various ethnic groups—one that teaches *to and through* their personal and cultural strengths, their intellectual capabilities, and their prior accomplishments. Culturally responsive teaching is this kind of paradigm. It is at once a routine and a radical proposal. It is routine because it does for Native American, Latino, Asian American, African American, and low-income students what traditional instructional ideologies and actions do for middle-class European Americans. That is, it filters curriculum content and teaching strategies through their cultural frames of reference to make the content more personally meaningful and easier to master. It is radical because it makes explicit the previously implicit role of culture in teaching and learning, and it insists that educational institutions accept the legitimacy and viability of ethnic group cultures in improving learning outcomes.

These are rather commonsensical and obvious directions to take, particularly in view of research evidence and classroom practices that demonstrate that *socioculturally centered teaching* does enhance student achievement. This is especially true when achievement measures are not restricted solely to academic indicators and standardized test scores. Most of this research and practice have focused on African Americans (for example, Chapman, 1994; Erickson, 1987; M. Foster, 1991, 1994, 1995, 1997; Hollins, 1996; Irvine, 1990; Ladson-Billings, 1992, 1994, 1995a and 1995b, 1995c; Lee, 1993; Lee & Slaughter-Defoe, 1995) and Native Hawaiians (Au, 1993; Au & Kawakami, 1994; Boggs et al., 1985; Cazden et al., 1985; Tharp & Gallimore, 1988).

The close interactions among ethnic identity, cultural background, and student achievement (that is, between culture and cognition) are becoming increasingly apparent. So is the transformative potential of teaching grounded in multicultural contributions, experiences, and orientations. It is these interactions, and related data, that give source and focus, power and direction to the proposal made here for a paradigmatic shift in the pedagogy used with non-middle-class, non–European American students in U. S. schools. This is a call for the widespread implementation of *culturally responsive teaching*.

If educators continue to be ignorant of, ignore, impugn, and silence the cultural orientations, values, and performance styles of ethnically different students, they will persist in imposing cultural hegemony, personal denigration, educational inequity, and academic underachievement upon them. Accepting the validity of these students' cultural socialization and prior experiences will help to reverse achievement trends. It is incumbent upon teachers, administrators, and evaluators to *deliberately create cultural continuity* in educating ethnically diverse students. To the extent that all this entails is done systematically and effectively, dilemmas like those described by Fordham and Ogbu (1986) and Fordham (1996) may decrease significantly. Academically capable African American students (or any other ethnic group of color) will feel less compelled to sabotage or camouflage their academic achievement to avoid compromising their cultural and ethnic integrity or relationships with peers from ethnic groups that are not as successful. Nor will children like Amy and Aaron (described in Chapter 1) continue to have such painful experiences and memories of school.

IDEOLOGICAL BEGINNINGS

The ideas on which culturally responsive teaching are based have been a major part of education for and about cultural diversity from its inception. Their persistence is not surprising, since multicultural education originated in the early 1970s out of concerns for the racial and ethnic inequities that were apparent in learning opportunities and outcomes, and that continue to prevail. Abrahams and Troike (1972) argued that if racial-minority students are to be taught effectively, teachers "must learn wherein their cultural differences lie and . . . capitalize upon them as a resource, rather than . . . disregarding the differences . . . [and] thereby denigrating . . . the students" (p. 5). Educators also need to analyze their own cultural attitudes, assumptions, mechanisms, rules, and regulations that have made it difficult for them to teach these children successfully. This is imperative because there is "no other way of educating . . . [racial-minority] students than to provide them with a sense of dignity in the selves they bring with them into school, and to build on this by demonstrating the social and linguistic and cultural alternatives around them" (Abrahams & Troike, 1972, p. 6).

Chun-Hoon (1973) suggested that teaching cultural diversity in schools offers intellectual and psychological benefits for both mainstream society and Asian Americans. It helps to circumvent dangers to open, democratic communities by not homogenizing diverse peoples, and it assists Asian Americans in transcending the psychological colonization promoted by the mass media, which make them virtually invisible and totally silenced. Without these kind of educational interventions, individuals of color and society at large are short-changed, because "intellectual freedom can exist only in the context of psychic space, while psychic space can be created only between distinct and contrasting points of view" (Chun-Hoon, 1973, p. 139). Both "intellectual freedom" and "psychic space" are necessary to facilitate maximum academic and other forms of school achievement. Teaching students of color from their own cultural perspectives is one way to make this happen.

The strong convictions expressed by Abrahams and Troike and by Chun-Hoon about the potentials of using diverse cultural referents in teaching also permeate the thinking of educators who were instrumental in shaping the multicultural education movement. Early comments from several of them illustrate the similarity of these messages. Arciniega argued in 1975 that "educational processes are needed which enable *all* students to become positive contributors to a culturally dynamic society consistent with cultural origins" (p. 165, emphasis in original), to understand each others' cultures, and to attain higher levels of academic achievement. One of the most powerful benefits to be derived from a culturally pluralistic educational paradigm is "the creative ability to approach problem-solving activities with a built-in repertoire of bicultural perspectives. This is what is involved when we talk about eliminating incongruities between the cultural lifestyles of ethnic minority students and current schools" (Arciniega, 1975, p. 167). Carlson (1976) advised educators to stop trying to avoid the realities of ethnic differences and the roles they play in U. S. education. He reasoned that "since it is a fact that ethnic differences exist in important dimensions . . . it must be acknowledged that they exist and that they affect learning and academic outcomes" (p. 28).

Forbes (1973) developed this theme further as it relates to teaching Native American students. He outlined an educational agenda centered in the focal values of Native American cultures and comprehensive components of learning. Forbes suggested that cultural values, and the socio-cultural, religiophilosophical, and political behavioral styles resulting from them, should be the foundation of all curricular and instructional decisions. Native American students should be taught knowledge and skills for the continued survival and development of their tribal groups or nations; personality characteristics valued by particular Native American societies; means of functioning harmoniously with nature and with other people; and ways to achieve the highest levels of mastery possible in different spheres of life. All these skills were to be developed within the context of reciprocal relationships, mutual sharing, showing hospitality toward others, self-realization, and spiritual and character development of individuals and groups. Forbes also expressed some ideas about the importance of community building and "success" for Native American students, which later became core elements of culturally responsive teaching in general. He advised:

> The individual should develop a profound conception of the unity of life, from the fact of his belonging to a community of related people in which he owes his existence and definition of being, to the total web of natural life, to which he and his people also owe their existence. . . . The individual should develop a realization that "success" in life stems from being able to contribute to the well-being of one's people and all life. This means that the individual seeks to perfect behavior and skills which will add "beauty" to the world. To create "beauty" in actions, words, and objects is the overall objective of human beings in the world. (Forbes, 1973, p. 205)

Banks admonished teachers of racial-minority students to stop conducting business as usual, or using traditional instructional conventions. Instead, they should "respect the cultural and linguistic characteristics of minority youths, and change the curriculum so that it will reflect their learning and cultural styles and greatly enhance their achievement." Moreover, "minority students should not be taught contempt for their cultures. Teachers should use elements of their cultures to help them attain the skills which they need to live alternative life styles" (J. Banks, 1975, pp. 165–166). Cuban (1972) warned educators to avoid looking for simple, one-dimensional solutions to complex challenges in educating students of color. The mere inclusion of ethnic content into school curricula would not resolve these dilemmas. Some radical changes were needed in the instructional process as well. While ethnic content has the potential to stimulate intellectual curiosity and make meaningful contact with ethnically diverse students, it should be combined with instructional strategies that emphasize inquiry, critique, and analysis, rather than the traditional preferences for rote memory and regurgitation of factual information.

Aragon (1973) shifted the focus of reform needs to teacher preparation. He argued that the reason ethnic minorities were not doing well in school was more a function of teacher limitations than student inabilities. Teachers, rather than students, were "culturally deprived" because they did not understand or value the cultural heritages of minority groups. Educational reform needed to begin by changing teacher attitudes about nonmainstream cultures and ethnic groups, and then developing skills for incorporating cultural diversity into classroom instruction. These changes would lead to improvement in student achievement.

As early as 1975, Gay identified some specific ways to develop multicultural curriculum content and some important dimensions of achievement other than basic skills and academic subjects. Her conceptions of achievement encompassed ethnic identity development, citizenship skills for pluralistic societies, knowledge of ethnic and cultural diversity, and cross-cultural interactional competence as well as academic success. She suggested that content about cultural diversity has both intrinsic and instrumental value for classroom instruction. The instrumental value includes improving interest in and motivation for learning for diverse students, relevance of school learning, and establishing linkages among school, home, and community. Specifically, Gay (1975) suggested:

> Ethnic materials should be used to teach such fundamental skills as reading, writing, calculating, and reasoning. Students can learn reading skills using materials written by and about Blacks, Mexican Americans, Italian Americans, and Jewish Americans as well as they can from reading "Dick and Jane." Ethnic literature . . . can be used to teach plot, climax, metaphor, grammatical structure, and symbolism as well as anything written by Anglo Americans. . . . [Teaching] ethnic literacy, reflective self-analysis, decision making, and

social activism . . . are as essential for living in a culturally and ethnically pluralistic society as are knowing how to read and having a salable skill. . . . Ethnic content serves the purpose of bringing academic tasks from the realm of the alien and the abstract into the experiential frames of reference of ethnically different youth. (pp. 179–181)

DESCRIPTIVE CHARACTERISTICS

Although called by many different names, including *culturally relevant, sensitive, centered, congruent, reflective, mediated, contextualized, synchronized,* and *responsive,* the ideas about why it is important to make classroom instruction more consistent with the cultural orientations of ethnically diverse students, and how this can be done, are virtually identical. Hereafter, they are referred to by my term of preference, *culturally responsive pedagogy.* It represents a compilation of ideas and explanations from a wide variety of scholars. Throughout this discussion, labels other than "culturally responsive" appear only when the scholars quoted directly use different terminology.

Culturally Responsive Teaching Is Validating

Culturally responsive teaching can be defined as using the cultural knowledge, prior experiences, frames of reference, and performance styles of ethnically diverse students to make learning encounters more relevant to and effective for them. It teaches *to and through* the strengths of these students. It is culturally *validating and affirming.* Furthermore, culturally responsive teaching has the following characteristics:

- It acknowledges the legitimacy of the cultural heritages of different ethnic groups, both as legacies that affect students' dispositions, attitudes, and approaches to learning and as worthy content to be taught in the formal curriculum.
- It builds bridges of meaningfulness between home and school experiences as well as between academic abstractions and lived sociocultural realities.
- It uses a wide variety of instructional strategies that are connected to different learning styles.
- It teaches students to know and praise their own and each others' cultural heritages.
- It incorporates multicultural information, resources, and materials in all the subjects and skills routinely taught in schools.

Thus, the study of different literary genres is replete with samples and examples from a wide variety of ethnic authors. The study of math concepts and operations (such as calculations, pattern, proportionality, statistics) in everyday life can engage students in explorations of the crafts, economics, architecture, employment patterns, population distributions, and consumer habits of different ethnic groups. Opportunities provided for students to practice and demonstrate mastery of information, concepts, and skills in language arts, social studies, and science can include a wide range of sensory stimuli (visual, tactile, auditory), individual and group, competitive and cooperative, active participatory and sedentary activities in order to tap into the learning styles of different ethnic students. These approaches to teaching are based on the assumption that positive self-concepts, knowledge of and pride in one's own ethnic identity, and improved academic achievement are interactional. Furthermore, the cultural affiliation and understanding, knowledge and skills needed to challenge existing social orders and power structures are desirable goals to be taught in schools.

Culturally Responsive Teaching Is Comprehensive

Ladson-Billings (1992) explains that culturally responsive teachers develop intellectual, social, emotional, and political learning by "using cultural referents to impart knowledge, skills, and attitudes" (p. 382). In other words, they teach the whole child. Hollins (1996) adds that education designed specifically for students of color incorporates "culturally mediated cognition, culturally appropriate social situations for learning, and culturally valued knowledge in curriculum content" (p. 13). Along with improving academic achievement, these approaches to teaching are committed to helping students of color maintain identity and connections with their ethnic groups and communities; develop a sense of community, camaraderie, and shared responsibility; and acquire an ethic of success. Expectations and skills are not taught as separate entities but are woven together into an integrated whole that permeates all curriculum content and the entire modus operandi of the classroom. Students are held accountable for each others' learning as well as their own. They are expected to internalize the value that learning is a communal, reciprocal, interdependent affair, and manifest it habitually in their expressive behaviors.

Ladson-Billings (1994) observed these values being exemplified in actual instruction in the elementary classrooms she studied. She saw expectations expressed, skills taught, interpersonal relations exhibited, and an overall esprit de corps operating where students were part of a collective effort designed to promote academic and cultural excellence.

They functioned like members of an extended family, assisting, supporting, and encouraging each other. The entire class was expected to rise or
fall together, and it was in the best interest of everyone to ensure that
each individual member of the group was successful. By building an
academic community of learners, the teachers responded to the sense of
belonging youths need, honored their human dignity, and promoted their
individual self-concepts. Students engaged in caring relationships, shared
resources, and worked closely together and with the teacher to attain
common learning outcomes. Educational excellence included academic
success as well as cultural competence, critical social consciousness, political activism, and responsible community membership. A strong belief in
the right of students to be part of a mutually supportive group of high
achievers permeated all these learning processes and outcomes (M. Foster,
1995, 1997; Irvine & Foster, 1996; Ladson-Billings, 1995a, 1995b; Lipman,
1995).

Culturally Responsive Teaching Is Multidimensional

Multidimensional culturally responsive teaching encompasses curriculum
content, learning context, classroom climate, student–teacher relationships, instructional techniques, and performance assessments. For example, language arts, music, art, and social studies teachers may collaborate
in teaching the concept of protest. It can be examined from the perspective
of their respective disciplines, such as how protest against discrimination
is expressed by different ethnic groups in poetry, song lyrics, paintings,
and political actions. The students and teachers may decide to simulate
time periods when social protest was very prominent, analyzing and role-
playing various ethnic individuals. Within these simulations, coalition
meetings can be held in which individuals from different ethnic groups
express their positions on the issues of contention in various genre (e.g.,
rhetoric, sit-ins, songs, political slogans). Part of the challenge is for students to understand the major points made in these different forms of
expressions and to see whether any consensus and collaborative action
can be achieved across ethnic groups. Students can also help teachers
decide how their performance will be evaluated, whether by written
tests, peer feedback, observations, ability to extrapolate information about
ethnic protest presented in one expressive form and transfer it to another,
or some combination of these.

To do this kind of teaching well requires tapping into a wide range
of cultural knowledge, experiences, contributions, and perspectives. Emotions, beliefs, values, ethos, opinions, and feelings are scrutinized along
with factual information to make curriculum and instruction more reflec-

tive of and responsive to ethnic diversity. However, every conceivable aspect of an ethnic group's culture is not replicated in the classroom. Nor are the cultures included in the curriculum used only with students from that ethnic group. Cultural responsive pedagogy focuses on those elements of cultural socialization that most directly affect learning. It helps students clarify their ethnic values while correcting factual errors about cultural heritages. In the process of accomplishing these goals, students are held accountable for knowing, thinking, questioning, analyzing, feeling, reflecting, sharing, and acting.

Culturally Responsive Teaching Is Empowering

Because culturally responsive teaching is empowering, it enables students to be better human beings and more successful learners. Empowerment translates into academic competence, personal confidence, courage, and the will to act. In other words, students have to believe they can succeed in learning tasks and be willing to pursue success relentlessly until mastery is obtained. Teachers must show students that they expect them to succeed and commit themselves to making success happen. These can be high-risk endeavors. Culturally responsive teachers are aware of the risks involved in learning and the need for students to have successes along the way to mastery. They plan accordingly and create infrastructures to support the efforts of students so that they will persevere toward high levels of academic achievement. This is done by boostering students' morale, providing resources and personal assistance, developing an ethos of achievement, and celebrating individual and collective accomplishments.

The Advancement Via Individual Determination (AVID) project is an excellent example of how this empowering process operates in practice (Swanson et al., 1995; Mehan et al., 1996). Low-achieving Latino and African American students are encouraged to enroll in advanced-placement classes. The accompanying instructional interventions are reinforced by what Mehan and associates (1996) call a system of "social scaffolding." These are social and personal supports that buffer students as they are being taught high-level academic skills and how to take ownership of their own learning. They include students'

- explaining their problem-solving techniques to each other in small groups,
- displaying insignia (e.g., emblems, signs, pins, badges, logos) that identify them as AVID participants,
- spending time together in a space specifically designated for AVID,

- learning the "cultural capital" of school success (test-taking strategies, self-presentation techniques to fit teaching styles, study skills, note-taking, time management),
- being mentored in academic and social skills by other students who have successfully completed the program.

Shor (1992) elucidates further on the nature and effect of empowering education. Although his explanations do not derive explicitly from concerns about improving the school achievement of marginalized students of color, they are nonetheless apropos. He characterizes empowering education as

> a critical-democratic pedagogy for self and social change. It is a student-centered program for multicultural democracy in school and society. It approaches individual growth as an active, cooperative, and social process, because the self and society create each other. . . . The goals of this pedagogy are to relate personal growth to public life, to develop strong skills, academic knowledge, habits of inquiry, and critical curiosity about society, power, inequality, and change. . . . The learning process is negotiated, requiring leadership by the teacher, and mutual teacher–student authority. In addition, . . . the empowering class does not teach students to seek self-centered gain while ignoring public welfare. (pp. 15–16)

Implicit in these conceptions of education for empowerment are ideological mandates as well as parameters for the substantive content to be taught, the instructional processes to be used, and the behavioral outcomes expected of students. Within them students are the primary source and center, subjects and outcomes, consumers and producers of knowledge. Classroom instruction embodies and unfolds within a context of what Shor (1992) calls "an agenda of values" that emphasize participatory, problem-posing, situated, multicultural, dialogic, desocializing, democratic, inquiring, interdisciplinary, and activist learning.

Culturally Responsive Teaching Is Transformative

Culturally responsive teaching defies conventions of traditional educational practices with respect to ethnic students of color. This is done in several ways. It is very explicit about respecting the cultures and experiences of African American, Native American, Latino, and Asian American students, and it uses these as worthwhile resources for teaching and learning. It recognizes the existing strengths and accomplishments of these students and then enhances them further in the instructional process. For instance, the verbal creativity that is apparent among some African

Americans in informal social interactions is recognized as a storytelling gift and used to teach them writing skills. This can be done by having the students verbalize their writing assignments, recording and transcribing them, and then teaching technical writing skills using the transcriptions of their own verbalized thoughts. The tendency of many Japanese, Chinese, and Filipino students to study together in small groups can be formalized in the classroom, providing more opportunities for them and other students to participate in cooperative learning.

Culturally responsive teaching makes academic success a non-negotiable mandate for all students and an accessible goal. It promotes the idea, and develops skills for practicing it, that students are obligated to be productive members of and render service to their respective ethnic communities as well as to the national society. It does not pit academic success and cultural affiliation against each other. Rather, academic success and cultural consciousness are developed simultaneously. Students are taught to be proud of their ethnic identities and cultural backgrounds instead of being apologetic or ashamed of them. Culturally responsive teaching also circumvents the tendency toward learned helplessness for some students of color in traditional public schools, where their achievement levels decrease the longer they remain in school (Holliday, 1985).

The features and functions of culturally responsive pedagogy meet the mandates of high-quality education for ethnically diverse students proposed by J. Banks (1991). He contends that if education is to empower marginalized groups, it must be transformative. Being transformative involves helping "students to develop the knowledge, skills, and values needed to become social critics who can make reflective decisions and implement their decisions in effective personal, social, political, and economic action" (p. 131). Students must learn to analyze the effects of inequities on different ethnic individuals and groups, have zero tolerance for these, and become change agents committed to promoting greater equality, justice, and power balances among ethnic groups. They practice these ethics and skills in different community contexts—classrooms, schools, playgrounds, neighborhoods, and society at large. Therefore, the transformative agenda of culturally responsive teaching is double-focused. One direction deals with confronting and transcending the cultural hegemony nested in much of the curriculum content and classroom instruction of traditional education. The other develops social consciousness, intellectual critique, and political and personal efficacy in students so that they can combat prejudices, racism, and other forms of oppression and exploitation.

Culturally Responsive Teaching Is Emancipatory

Culturally responsive pedagogy is *liberating* (Asante, 1991/1992; Au, 1993; Erickson, 1987; Gordon, 1993; Lipman, 1995; Pewewardy, 1994; Philips, 1983) in that it releases the intellect of students of color from the constraining manacles of mainstream canons of knowledge and ways of knowing. Central to this kind of teaching is making authentic knowledge about different ethnic groups accessible to students. The validation, information, and pride it generates are both psychologically and intellectually liberating. This freedom allows students to focus more closely and concentrate more thoroughly on academic learning tasks. The results are improved achievement of many kinds. Among them are more clear and insightful thinking; more caring, concerned, and humane interpersonal skills; better understanding of interconnections among individual, local, national, ethnic, global, and human identities; and acceptance of knowledge as something to be continuously shared, critiqued, revised, and renewed (Chapman, 1994; M. Foster, 1995; Hollins, 1996; Hollins, King, & Hayman, 1994; Ladson-Billings, 1992, 1994, 1995a and 1995b; Lee, 1993; Lee & Slaughter-Defoe, 1995).

Crichlow, Goodwin, Shakes, and Swartz (1990) provide another explanation for why education grounded in multiculturalism is emancipatory for teaching and learning. According to them, it

> utilizes an inclusive and representational framework of knowledge in which students and teachers have the capacity to produce ventilated narratives. . . . By collectively representing diverse cultures and groups as producers of knowledge, it facilitates a liberative student/teacher relationship that "opens up" the written text and oral discourse to analysis and reconstruction. (p. 103)

In other words, culturally responsive pedagogy lifts the veil of presumed absolute authority from conceptions of scholarly truth typically taught in schools. It helps students realize that no single version of "truth" is total and permanent. Nor should it be allowed to exist uncontested. Students are taught how to apply new knowledge generated by various ethnic scholars to their analyses of social histories, issues, problems, and experiences. These learning engagements encourage and enable students to find their own voices, to contextualize issues in multiple cultural perspectives, to engage in more ways of knowing and thinking, and to become more active participants in shaping their own learning (Crichlow et al., 1990; J. King & Wilson, 1990; Ladson-Billings & Henry, 1990). These revelations about knowledge and their attendant skills comprise the heart of the intellectual and cultural liberation facilitated by culturally responsive teaching. They are analogous to Freire's (1980) notions that critical consciousness and cultural emancipation are the gateways to each other. To them can be added that the freedom to be ethnically expressive removes the psychological stress associated with and psychic energy deployed in "covering up" or "containing" one's cultural inclinations. This reclaimed psychoemotional energy can be rechanneled into learning tasks, thereby improving intellectual attentiveness and academic achievement.

Cooperation, community, and connectedness are also central features of culturally responsive teaching. Students are expected to work together and are held accountable for one another's success. Mutual aid, interdependence, and reciprocity as criteria for guiding behavior replace the individualism and competitiveness that are so much a part of conventional classrooms. The goal is for all students to be winners, rather than some winning and others losing, and for students to assume responsibility for helping each other achieve to the best of their ability. In her studies of effective African American teachers, M. Foster (1989, 1994, 1995) found that these values and behaviors were demonstrated in their classrooms. The teachers were personally affiliated with and connected to the African American cultural community. They taught the students values, knowledge, and skills for participating in the larger society as well as their own cultural communities. They also drew on community patterns and norms to structure and operate their classrooms, and they incorporated the students' cultural and communication styles into instructional practices.

CULTURALLY RESPONSIVE TEACHING PERSONIFIED

Two stories are presented here to illustrate how the attributes of culturally responsive teaching operate in practice. Neither alone is a complete portrait. Each provides a capsule view of one or a few dimensions of this style of teaching. Together, they come closer to creating a complete picture. It is helpful to consider them both separately and together in visualizing the move of culturally responsive teaching from theory to practice. Doing so is consistent with a major feature of the paradigm itself—that is, the importance of dealing simultaneously with general issues and particular cases in teaching African American, Latino American, Asian American, and Native American underachieving students. The stories deal with critiquing and symboling.

Critiquing

The setting is a teacher education class. The students are studying the philosophical foundations of culturally responsive pedagogy. The principle under analysis is "K–12 education is a free, public, and equal access enterprise for all students in the United States." Students are expected to engage in critical, analytical, reflective, and transformative thinking about the issues, ideas, and assertions they encounter. The instructor invites them to "think about" what this principle means within the context of ethnic and cultural diversity. The students respond to this invitation as follows:

Student 1: What does "educational freedom" really mean for Native American students? If freedom means the right to learn without undue obstructions, how much freedom did they have when early missionary educators took them away from their families and communities, and forced them to "look" like European Americans, accept their religion, and ascribe to their values. Where is the freedom in this? And what about today? How unrestricted are the opportunities for Native Americans to learn, practice, and celebrate their cultural heritages in modern schools?

Student 2: I'm concerned about Filipinos and other immigrant or first-generation U. S.-born students who may not be fluent in English. What does freedom to learn and the right to equal educational opportunities mean for them? Where is the equality when teachers in schools don't speak Tagalog, Thai, Cambodian, Spanish, or some other languages, and these students have to try to function in a language system that is alien to them. Do they have opportunities for educational mastery comparable to children who are competent in the language of instruction? People may say, as they often do, that "these children are now in the United States and they must learn to speak English." I'm not opposed to this, but I am still left wondering, What about the possibility of loss of language? How might this loss affect students' cultural affiliation and sense of identity? How does having to learn in an unfamiliar language affect achievement level? What is the connection between "freedom to learn" and "equalizing opportunities"? Where do bi- or multilingualism and cultural diversity fit into the equal opportunity equation?

Student 3: It seems to me that public education as the "great equalizer" really meant Anglicizing all students from non-European origins. I think schools have done much more to homogenize culturally di-

verse students than to make the educational experience a true amal-
gamation of contributions from all the different ethnic groups and
cultures that make up the United States. If this had happened
years ago, there would be no grounds for current appeals for ethnic studies, women's studies, multicultural education, and bilingualism to be included in school programs.

Student 4: I don't think there is much equality in never seeing your
own ethnic group's contributions represented in textbooks, or having them depicted in biased and stereotypical ways. Imagine what
African American students must have felt being told over and over
that they are descendants of slaves, chattel, unintelligent buffoons,
who were treated almost like animals. Or Native Americans being
portrayed as uncivilized heathens and murdering savages. Or, for
that matter, the ego inflation potential of the notion of "manifest
destiny" for European Americans. These seem to me far, far removed from educational freedom and equality. They sound more
like "psychological and cultural imperialism." Can students from
diverse ethnic backgrounds perform to the best of their intellectual
ability under these conditions? I think not.

Student 5: The whole idea is a hustle, a myth. Education has never
been free and equal in this country. Children who have the least
have always had to make the greatest sacrifices, pay the highest
prices, and get the lowest benefits. Look at the desegregation experiment. Who were on those buses going where? Look at the condition of city schools compared to suburban ones. Where are the best
teachers assigned? The best buildings and materials? The best programs? Where is the most money for education being spent? If true
equality had existed from the beginning, we would not have the
kind of achievement disparities we currently have.

Student 6: I think we need to take a closer look at who came up with
these ideas, and what did *they* mean by them. Their conceptions
probably were quite different from ours. If we knew this, we
would be better able to make better sense of them conceptually,
and decide whether to continue to accept them on blind faith or to
revise them so that they are more appropriate for today's realities.
I guess I am proposing here that we do what one of my other professors means by "positionality analyses."

Student 7: (*Laughing in response to the comments made by Student 6*) Girl,
we know who *they* be. *They* most definitely ain't *us*. If *we* had made
glib statements like that, *you* wouldn't be wondering what *we*
meant, 'cause *we* would have told you explicitly and up front what
was what.

Several other students: Uh, huh (*and other signs of endorsement of Student 7's comments*)

Instructor: This is good. You are questioning, critiquing, deconstructing, evoking a variety of points of reference, seeking out specific cultural grounding of applicability of general pedagogical ideas. Continue to "think about."

Symboling

The kindergarten class Lois teaches is comprised of immigrant and first-generation U. S. students from many countries, as well as a mixture of different native ethnic groups. Consequently, there is a lot of ethnic, racial, cultural, and linguistic diversity present. Looking into her classroom provides a glimpse of how culturally responsive teaching can be accomplished through the use of visual imagery and symbols. The school year has been in session for a little more than 4 months. Lois has established some clear routines with her students for embracing and celebrating each other's cultural diversity. As we take a quick tour of this classroom, we witness the following:

Attached to the entrance door is a huge welcome sign brightly decorated with the children's own art. The sign reads "Welcome to Our Academic Home." This message is accompanied by a group photograph of the members of the class and "welcome" in different languages (Spanish, Japanese, German, French, various U. S. dialects, etc.). Stepping inside the room, one is bombarded with an incredibly rich and wide range of ethnically and culturally diverse images. Maps of the world and the United States are prominently displayed on the front wall, under the heading "We Come from Many Places." Strings connect different parts of the world to the United States. They represent the countries of origin of the families and/or ethnic groups of the students in the class. A display in another corner of the room is labeled "Our Many Different Faces." It includes a montage of close-up facial photographs of the members of the class. These are surrounded by pictures of adults from different ethnic groups in ceremonial dress for various rites of passage (e.g., marriage, adulthood, baptism) and occupations (clergy, doctors, construction workers, dancers).

The room's "Reading Center" is a prototype of multicultural children's literature—a culturally responsive librarian's dream! Many different ethnic groups, topics, and literary types are included. Books, poems, comics, song lyrics, posters, magazines, and newspapers beckon the students to discover and read about the histories, families, myths, folktales, travels, troubles, triumphs, experiences, and daily lives of a wide variety of Asian, African, European, Middle Eastern, Latino, Native American, and Pacific Islander groups and individuals. Audio- and videotapes are liberally sprinkled among these items, including music, books on tape, storytelling, and television programs. Others look like student productions. In the midst of all these media materials, a video camera and a tape recorder stand in readiness for use. Another curious item captures the attention. It is a pile of tattered, well-used photo albums. These resources invite students to explore the past, to reflect on the present, to imagine the future.

The extent and quality of this collection of materials prompt the question, "Lois, how did you come by all of this?" She credits parents for the accomplishment. At the beginning of the academic year, she gets the parents of the students to make a contractual agreement to donate two books or other forms of media to the class collection. One of these books is to be about their own ethnic group and the other about some other group that they either use with their children at home or would like their children to learn about in school. The families are given credit for their contributions by having each item stamped "Donated by _____." When the collection becomes too large to be easily accommodated in the classroom, or the students "outgrow it," some of the items are donated to the school library or community agencies. This is a class project, with the students deciding which items they will keep and which they will give away. Only one stipulation is attached to the gifts. The recipients must agree to acknowledge the donors with the credit line "Donated by the Kindergarten Class of Room _____ at _____ Elementary School."

Lois is a strong believer in "representative ethnic imagery." She is very conscientious about ensuring that the visual depictions of ethnic groups and individuals in her classroom are accurate, authentic, and pluralistic. She explains that she wants students to readily recognize who the ethnic visuals represent rather than having to wonder what they are supposed to be. She also wants the students to be exposed to a wide variety of images within and among groups to avoid ethnic stereotyping. To assist the students with this identification, all of the pictures of ethnic individuals displayed throughout the classroom include personal and ethnic identities. These read, "My name is _____; I am _____ [ethnic group]. Lois justifies this protocol by simply saying, "Students need to know that it's OK to recognize other people's ethnicity and to expect others to acknowledge theirs. Ethnicity is an important feature of our personal identities."

Two other permanent culturally pluralistic displays exist in this stimulating, intellectually invigorating, and culturally diverse classroom. One is entitled "We Can Do Many Things." Here are images, samples, and symbols of the contributions and accomplishments of different ethnic groups, such as crafts, arts, science, technology, medicine, and music. They include children and adults of different ages, famous and common folks, profound achievements and regular, daily occurrences. For example, there is one photograph of three students who have been especially helpful to classmates from other ethnic groups and another of six great-grandparents who are 75 years of age or older. The master tape representing different ethnic groups' contributions to music includes excerpts from operas, jazz, rap, spirituals, movie sound tracks, country, pop, and children's songs. The names of other individuals are accompanied by miniature samples of their contributions. There is the athlete with a little basketball, but it's refreshing to see that she is a member of the 1996 U. S. Olympic team, and Venus and Serena are there with their little tennis rackets. Some kernels of corn appear next to Native Americans, and a little make-believe heart operation kit is connected to African Americans.

The other permanent display is a multicultural alphabet streamer. Different ethnic groups and contributions are associated with each of the letters in the alphabet. For example, "Jamaican" and "Japanese American," as well as "jazz" appear under the letter J, and "lasso" and "Latino" appear under L.

The tour of this classroom also offers a glimpse into how Lois incorporates the ethnically diverse symbols into her formal instruction. Small groups of students are working on different skills. As Lois circulates among them, activities in the reading and math groups are riveting. It is Carlos's turn to select the book to be read for storytime. He chooses one about a Japanese American family. Lois asks him to tell the group why he made this choice. Carlos explains that he had seen Yukiko (a classmate) at McDonald's over the weekend, and he wanted to do something nice for her by reading "her" book. He also said he saw some other people like those in the book, and he wanted to know more about them because they don't look like people where he lives.

Before Lois begins to read the story, she tells the students a little about this ethnic group, like the proper name, its country of origin, some symbol of its culture (they eat a lot of different kinds of noodles), and where large numbers of its members live in the United States. She asks if anyone can find Japan and California on the maps. She helps the group locate these places. As the students return to their places and settle down for the story, we hear Lois asking, "If we wanted to go to the places where there are a lot of Japanese Americans, how would we get there? Who would like to go?" Several hands pop up quickly at the thought of such an imagined journey. Incidentally (maybe not!), the book Carlos chose to read is about a little boy taking his first airplane ride with his parents to go visit his grandparents, who live far away. Once this "context setting" is completed, Lois proceeds through a dialogic reading of the book. She pauses frequently to probe the students' understanding of associated meaning prompted by the

narrative text, to examine their feelings, and to predict upcoming developments in the story.

In math, the students are practicing bilingual counting. They already
know how to count in English and to associate the number with the appropriate word. On this occasion, they are learning to count to 10 in Spanish.
Under Lois's supervision, the students go through an oral exercise using the
Spanish words for the numbers. One student points to the words as the
others say them aloud. After some giggling and gentle consternation about
their pronunciation, Lois compliments the students' efforts, while sympathiz-
ing with their concerns and reminding them that people who are learning a
language do not sound like those who are native speakers. Tamika reminds
everyone that Rosita speaks Spanish at home and announces, with conviction, "I bet she can say those words real good." Lois asks Rosita if she
would like to give it a try. After a little encouragement from other members
of the group, she agrees. Lois tells the group that Rosita is now the teacher
and the other students are to practice saying the words as she does. After
this is done, the students are asked to sit quietly, listen, and observe another
native Spanish speaker counting. This is presented in the form of a video-
tape, using a motif similar to "Sesame Street."

Symbols are powerful conveyers of meaning, as Lois's classroom
attests. Her students are inundated with positive images and interactions
with ethnic and cultural diversity. They learn about and celebrate their
own and one another's identities and abilities, while simultaneously being
invited to extend the boundaries of their knowledge and skills. All of
this occurs in a warm, supportive, affirming, and illuminating classroom
climate, in which the use of culturally diverse referents in teaching and
learning is habitual. This type of instruction is very conducive to high
levels of many different kinds of achievement for students from all ethnic
groups.

ROLES AND RESPONSIBILITIES OF TEACHERS

Implicit in these mandates, attributes, and personifications of culturally
responsive pedagogy are some key roles and responsibilities for teachers.
Diamond and Moore (1995) have organized them into three major categories: *cultural organizers, cultural mediators,* and *orchestrators of social contexts
for learning.* Gentemann and Whitehead (1983) combined these tasks into
the single role of *cultural broker.* As *cultural organizers,* teachers must understand how culture operates in daily classroom dynamics, create learning
atmospheres that radiate cultural and ethnic diversity, and facilitate high

academic achievement for all students. Opportunities must be provided for students from different ethnic backgrounds to have free personal and cultural expression so that their voices and experiences can be incorporated into teaching and learning processes on a regular basis. These accommodations require the use of various culturally centered ways of knowing, thinking, speaking, feeling, and behaving.

As *cultural mediators*, teachers provide opportunities for students to engage in critical dialogue about conflicts among cultures and to analyze inconsistencies between mainstream cultural ideals/realities and those of different cultural systems. They help students clarify their ethnic identities, honor other cultures, develop positive cross-ethnic and cross-cultural relationships, and avoid perpetuating prejudices, stereotypes, and racism. The goal is to create communities of culturally diverse learners who celebrate and affirm each other and work collaboratively for their mutual success, where empowerment replaces powerlessness and oppression.

As *orchestrators of social contexts* for learning, teachers must recognize the important influence culture has on learning and make teaching processes compatible with the sociocultural contexts and frames of reference of ethnically diverse students. They also help students translate their cultural competencies into school learning resources. Spring's (1995) definition of a cultural frame of reference can be helpful in achieving these teaching–learning synchronizations. He defines it as "those elements that cause a cultural group to interpret the world . . . in a particular manner" (p. 5), or the filter through which impressions of, experiences with, and knowledge of the outside world are ordered and made meaningful.

CONCLUSION

To recapitulate, culturally responsive pedagogy simultaneously develops, along with academic achievement, social consciousness and critique, cultural affirmation, competence, and exchange; community building and personal connections; individual self-worth and abilities; and an ethic of caring. It uses ways of knowing, understanding, and representing various ethnic and cultural groups in teaching academic subjects, processes, and skills. It cultivates cooperation, collaboration, reciprocity, and mutual responsibility for learning among students and between students and teachers. It incorporates high-status, accurate cultural knowledge about different ethnic groups into all subjects and skills taught.

Culturally responsive teachers have unequivocal faith in the human dignity and intellectual capabilities of their students. They view learning as having intellectual, academic, personal, social, ethical, and political dimensions, all of which are developed in concert with one another. They scaffold instruction and build bridges between the cultural experiences of ethnically diverse students and the curriculum content of academic subjects to facilitate higher levels of learning. These teachers use a variety of approaches to all aspects of the educational process, including curriculum, instruction, and assessment, embedded in multicultural contexts. They consider critical and reciprocal dialogue and participatory engagement as central to the acquisition and demonstration of learning. Academic success is a non-negotiable goal for everyone and the responsibility of all participants in the teaching–learning process. In their interpersonal relationships with students, culturally responsive teachers are warm, supportive, personable, enthusiastic, understanding, and flexible (Shade, Kelly, & Oberg, 1997), yet rigorous in demanding high-quality academic performance from both themselves and their students.

Thus, culturally responsive pedagogy validates, facilitates, liberates, and empowers ethnically diverse students by simultaneously cultivating their cultural integrity, individual abilities, and academic success. It is anchored on four foundational pillars of practice—teacher attitudes and expectations, cultural communication in the classroom, culturally diverse content in the curriculum, and culturally congruent instructional strategies.

If the potential of culturally responsive pedagogy is to be realized, then widespread instructional reform is needed, as well as major changes in the professional development, accountability, and assessment of teaching personnel. It requires teachers who have (1) thorough *knowledge* about the cultural values, learning styles, historical legacies, contributions, and achievements of different ethnic groups; (2) the *courage* to stop blaming the victims of school failure and to admit that something is seriously wrong with existing educational systems; (3) the *will* to confront prevailing educational canons and convictions, and to rethink traditional assumptions of cultural universality and/or neutrality in teaching and learning; (4) the *skills* to act productively in translating knowledge and sensitivity about cultural diversity into pedagogical practices; and (5) the *tenacity* to relentlessly pursue comprehensive and high-level performance for children who are currently underachieving in schools. Hopefully, then, schooling experiences like those of Amy and Aaron, described in Chapter 1, will be historical memories, not everyday occurrences, and their children will have more successful stories to tell about their learning encounters and academic achievement.

CHAPTER 3

The Power of Caring

She routinely begins her classes with declarations to the effect that "I believe in collaborative teaching and successful learning for all students. This course is designed to ensure these. We are going to work hard; we are going to have fun doing it; and we are going to do it together. I am very good at what I do, and since you are going to be working in partnership with me, you are going to be good, too. In fact, as my students, you have no choice but to be good." These declarations are at once a promise and a mandate, an ethic and an action. They set in motion an esprit de corps, an ambiance, an instructional style, a set of expectations that are directed toward high-level student achievement. The message intended for students is "I have faith in your ability to learn, I care about the quality of your learning, and I commit myself to making sure that you will learn."

INTRODUCTION

These declarations set the tone and contours for the discussions of caring presented in this chapter. They also meet Webb, Wilson, Corbett and Mordecai's (1993) criteria that caring is a value and a moral imperative that moves "self-determination into social responsibility and uses knowledge and strategic thinking to decide how to act in the best interests of others. Caring binds individuals to their society, to their communities, and to each other" (pp. 33–34). The interest of concern here is improved achievement, and the "community" is underachieving students of colors and their teachers.

This kind of caring is one of the major pillars of culturally responsive pedagogy for ethnically diverse students. It is manifested in the form of teacher attitudes, expectations, and behaviors about students' human value, intellectual capability, and performance responsibilities. Teachers demonstrate caring for children as *students* and as *people*. This is expressed in concern for their psychoemotional well-being and academic success; personal morality and social actions; obligations and celebrations; communality and individuality; and unique cultural connections and universal human bonds. In other words, teachers who really care about students honor their humanity, hold them in high esteem, expect high performance from them, and use strategies to fulfill their expectations. They also model academic, social, personal, and moral behaviors and values for students to emulate. Students, in kind, feel obligated to be worthy of being so honored. They rise to the occasion by producing high levels of performance of many different kinds—academic, social, moral, and cultural.

Conventional wisdom, personal experience, theoretical assertions, research findings, and best practices attest to the effect of genuine teacher caring on student achievement. They suggest that the heart of the educational process is the interactions that occur between teachers and students. These interactions are major determinants of the quality of education children receive (U. S. Civil Rights Commission, 1973). Unfortunately, all teachers do not have positive attitudes toward, expectations of, and interactions with students of color. Racial biases, ethnic stereotyping, cultural ethnocentrism, and personal rejections cause teachers who don't care to devalue, demean, and even fear some African American, Latino, Native American, and Asian American students in their classrooms. These devaluations are accompanied by low or negative expectations about their intellectual abilities, which have deleterious effects on student achievement (Good & Brophy, 1994; Harry, 1992; Oakes, 1985).

While most teachers are not blatant racists, many probably are cultural hegemonists. They expect all students to behave according to the school's cultural standards of normality. When students of color fail to comply, the teachers find them unlovable, problematic, and difficult to honor or embrace without equivocation. Rather than build on what the students have in order to make their learning easier and better, the teachers want to correct and compensate for their "cultural deprivations." This means making ethnically diverse students conform to middle-class, Eurocentric cultural norms.

Because positive and negative teacher attitudes and expectations have profound effects on student achievement (Good & Brophy, 1978, 1994), attention is given to both in the analysis below. This seems a reasonable direction to take because culturally responsive teaching should first confront existing instructional presumptions and practices before it proceeds with the more regenerative aspects of reform. It should simultaneously deconstruct and transform, critique and create, correct and direct, reflect and project. Therefore, this chapter examines four key topics: (1) the concept of caring; (2) predominant teacher attitudes and expectations toward ethnically and culturally different students; (3) how teacher expectations affect their instructional behaviors and students' achievement; and

(4) how negative attitudes and expectations can be modified to make them more compatible with the mandates of culturally responsive pedagogy. Ideas and insights gleaned from research, theory, and practice are woven together throughout these discussions. These are further augmented by personal experiences of teachers who cared and students who were cared for.

CONCEPT OF CARING

Caring interpersonal relationships are characterized by patience, persistence, facilitation, validation, and empowerment for the participants. Uncaring ones are distinguished by impatience, intolerance, dictations, and control. The power of these kinds of relationships in instructional effectiveness is expressed in a variety of ways by educators, but invariably the message is the same. Teachers who genuinely care about students generate higher levels of all kinds of success than those who do not. They have high performance expectations and will settle for nothing less than high achievement. Failure is simply unacceptable to them, so they work diligently to see that success for students happens.

Caring Is Concern for Person and Performance

Mercado's (1993) research illustrates how beliefs about students shape the instructional behaviors of teachers. She is convinced that the academic accomplishments of the middle school Latino students with whom she and her colleagues worked resulted as much from the ethic of caring the instructional team demonstrated as from promoting literacy and academic learning. A common theme that emerged from interviews with African American students about their experiences in segregated schools was the interpersonal caring of the teachers and administrators. They remembered these schools as "homes away from home," places where they were nourished, supported, protected, encouraged, and held accountable. The students recalled their teachers having faith and conviction in the students' abilities; being demanding, yet supportive and encouraging; and insisting that students have high aspirations to be the best that they could be. The teachers and administrators did not limit their interactions with students to merely teaching subject matter. They demonstrated concerns for the students' emotional, physical, economic, and interpersonal conditions as well. In so doing, a *consistently* caring climate was created that made students more willing to participate in learning tasks and encouraged higher levels of achievement (Jones, 1981; Siddle-Walker, 1993; Sowell,

1976). Consequently, "the psychological and tangible attention revealed in the interpersonal relationships . . . contributed strongly to [the students'] academic and life success" (Siddle-Walker, 1993, p. 75).

Results of research in more contemporary classroom settings (M. Foster, 1994, 1995, 1997; Howard, 1998; Ladson-Billings, 1994) indicate that effective teachers of African American students demonstrate the same kind of beliefs, attitudes, and behaviors. M. Foster (1995) found that these teachers "concern themselves with the complete development of children" (p. 576) and model multidimensional caring in their personal behaviors and instructional practices. They are explicit about teaching and modeling personal values that they view as foundations of learning and living. These include patience, persistence, and responsibility to self and others. They also foster the development of student interests, aspirations, self-confidence, and leadership skills. Their instructional practices incorporate skills for self-determination in a society that perpetuates institutional racism while proclaiming equality for all (M. Foster, 1995).

Caring Is Action-Provoking

As these descriptions indicate, there is much more to interpersonal caring than teachers merely exhibiting feelings of kindness, gentleness, and benevolence toward students, or expressing some generalized sentiments of concern. In fact, these attitudes without concomitant competence-producing actions constitute a form of academic neglect. When teachers fail to demand accountability for high-level performance from ethnically diverse students under the guise that "I don't want to put them on the spot in case they don't know how to do the academic tasks," they really are abdicating their pedagogical responsibilities. This is not real caring. A most effective way to be uncaring and unconcerned is to tolerate and/or facilitate academic apathy, disengagement, and failure. To avoid doing this, teachers must thoroughly understand their own and their students' perspectives and experiences (Noddings, 1992, 1996). Learning is contingent on their cultural inclusion and confirmation in the educational process. The attitude that drives this kind of caring "accepts, embraces, and leads upward. It questions, it responds, it sympathizes, it challenges, it delights" (Noddings, 1996, p. 29). Thus, caring in education has dimensions of emotion, intellect, faith, ethics, action, and accountability.

These attributes are further refined by Tarlow's (1996) study of caring in families, schools, and voluntary agencies. She describes caring as an ongoing, action-driven process of "supportive, affective, and instrumental interchanges embedded in reciprocal relationships" (p. 81). A caring person is sensitive to, emotionally invested in, and attentive to the needs and interests of others. Caring has elements of both reciprocity and community because the "caring process . . . confronts the person cared for, calling out to him or her to reciprocate . . . [and is] an acknowledgment of and respect for the meaning of the group" (pp. 80–81).

Ladson-Billings (1994) found evidence of the kind of caring Tarlow describes in her study of successful teachers of African American students in an urban elementary school. When she asked the students in one of the classes what they liked about it, they responded, "the teacher." In elaborating on this choice, they explained that she listened to and respected them, encouraged them to express their opinions, and was friendly toward them both in and out of class. The African American students in Hanley's (1998) study of knowledge construction through dramatic preparation and performance spoke with similar convictions. They unanimously and enthusiastically declared that good teachers are respectful of them, care about them, provide choices, and are tenacious in their efforts to make the information taught more understandable for them. Conversely, poor teachers are those who don't listen, don't care, are too hurried and harried to persist in facilitating learning, and are unconcerned about the general well-being of students. These are very revealing comments. The students feel a need to have a personal connection with teachers. This happens when teachers acknowledge their presence, honor their intellect, respect them as human beings, and make them feel like they are important. In other words, they empower students by legitimizing their "voice" and visibility.

Caring Prompts Effort and Achievement

Personal anecdotes of individuals in many walks of life, reflecting on their school days, provide variations of the same theme of the importance of teacher caring to student achievement reported by Ladson-Billings, Foster, Hanley, and other researchers. Long after leaving school, they remember fondly, and in graphic detail, those teachers who cared, and painfully those who did not. They may not recall the content these teachers taught, but their human impact is indelibly imprinted in their minds. Thirty-five years after high school, Johnny is still fond of telling how much he feared, but respected, his eleventh-grade social studies teacher because "she was hard on you, and you couldn't run no game on her. She knew everybody, and she didn't make you feel stupid even if you didn't know the answers. That's why I made sure I got her homework done even when I wouldn't do it for anybody else." This teacher and Johnny had the same last name, and she would often tell him, "People with our name always do the best they possibly can." This connection further motivated him to exert greater efforts on learning tasks than he otherwise might have. His cousin Betty, who attended the same school at the same time as Johnny, has very different memories of another teacher. Many years later, this teacher's name still provokes negative responses from her, such as, "That dog. I hated him. He was evil, and didn't care nothing about nobody. You couldn't talk to him. He thought he was bad, and acted like he was a king or something. All he wanted to do was flunk everybody."

These stories add other important dimensions to caring—or the lack thereof—as a necessary feature of effective teaching for students of color. In addition to respecting the cultural backgrounds, ethnic identity, and humanity of students, teachers who care hold them accountable for high-quality academic, social, and personal performance, and ensure that this happens. They are demanding but facilitative, supportive and accessible, both personally and professionally. And they do not have to be of the same ethnic groups as students to do this well. Some of the teachers in Ladson-Billings study were European Americans. So were Johnny's and Betty's teachers, while they are African Americans. St. John (1971) described these kind of teachers as "child-oriented" and "interpersonally competent." This orientation was expressed in the instructional interactions as kindliness, adaptability, and optimism. These teachers also had little faith is test scores as good indicators of student ability; they used other indicators of success. They produced greater gains in reading improvement, attendance, and classroom conduct for African American students than teachers who were more task-oriented.

Kleinfeld (1973, 1974, 1975) found similar characteristics among the effective teachers of rural Athabascan Eskimo and Indian students she studied. She described these teachers as "warm demanders." They created classroom climates of emotional warmth; consistently and clearly demanded high-quality academic performance; spent time establishing positive interpersonal relationships between themselves and students, and among students; extended their relationships with and caring for students beyond the classroom; and communicated with students through nonverbal cues, such as smiles, gentle touch, teasing, and establishing a "kinesthetic feeling of closeness" (1975, p. 322). Academic demands were complemented with emotional support and facilitative instruction, a coaching and cajoling rather than a dictatorial style of teaching was used, and reciprocal responsibility for learning was developed. This emotionally warm, personally caring, and interpersonally supportive instructional style had a substantial positive effect on the intellectual performance of students, as indicated by increases in verbal participation in classroom discourse and improved levels of cognitive understanding. Kleinfeld attributes the success of the teachers in her studies to two major factors: (1) congruency between their styles of teaching and the cultural socialization and interactional styles of rural Eskimo and Indian students, and (2) the instructional style of the teachers, not their ethnic-group membership.

Vida Hall's success with African American students in an urban high school further validates Kleinfeld's conclusions and illuminates the power of caring in teaching. She was one of those "warm demanders," as confirmed by former students and her own personal reflections. Vida achieved levels of performance with students other teachers thought were almost unteachable long before multicultural education or culturally responsive teaching was initiated. A high school social studies teacher, she taught students in the full spectrum of "A," "R," and "L" (advanced, regular, and low-achieving) classes. She was notorious for "taking no stuff" and for being "hard but fair." Vida insisted that students in her classes perform to the best of their abilities and consistently conveyed to them that they were capable of doing much more than they imagined. She refused to accept unfounded excuses for incomplete or undone work. "I can't do" was taboo in her classes.

When this explanation was offered by students, Vida responded with gentle but firm insistence, "Of course you can. Now, tell me what I need to do to help you out. Do I need to review the instructions or go over the content again? Do you and I need to spend some time one-on-one together? Do you need to work with another student in class? Or do I need to let the coach know that you are spending so much time with athletics that it's interfering with you completing your social studies assignments?" These were not threats or intimidations; rather, Vida was proposing different avenues to take to remove obstacles to student achievement. And she stood in readiness to aggressively pursue any or all of them to ensure that her students were successful. When they succeeded she applauded them, while simultaneously cajoling them to reach for even higher levels of achievement.

Concern for and commitment to helping students be the best they could did not end at the threshold of Vida Hall's classroom door. She held similar high expectations for their social behavior and personal decorum outside the classroom. Many times she diffused potentially confrontational situations among her students in the hallways and cafeteria by stepping up to them and saying, "Aren't you in my _____-period class? Using fisticuffs to solve problems is beneath your dignity. You are better than that." Nor was she above setting some boundaries for her students about how young men and women were expected to "carry themselves." A frequent comment of hers, upon observing behaviors in students she considered socially unacceptable, was "Young men [or women] don't behave that way." In more than 40 years of teaching, she recalled few occasions when students became belligerent and hostile in the face of these chastisements.

Both Vida and her former students attribute this incredible record to the fact that the students knew what she expected of them and that she was "in their corner." As their teacher, she deserved to be honored as she honored them. They worked hard to meet her expectations. The result was reciprocal and complementary achievement for the students and the teacher. The achievements were of many different kinds. Some of her greatest success did not get the best grades in class, or the highest scores on standardized tests, but they shone brightly in other ways—by demonstrating good manners, being respectful, having high positive self-concepts, persisting in their academic efforts, and even improving their school attendance.

Caring Is Multidimensional Responsiveness

Obviously, then, caring is a multidimensional process. Its essence, according to Berman (1994), is *responsiveness*, which is contingent on understanding people in context. Speaking more specifically about teaching, Bowers and Flinders (1990) suggest that being responsive is understanding and acting on, in educationally constructive ways, cultural influences on the behaviors and mental ecology of the classroom. Hence, for teachers to do culturally responsive teaching, they must be competent in cultural diversity and committed to its inclusion in the educational process. Sullivan (1974) made this observation 25 years ago when he proposed that it is not enough for teachers merely to like ethnically different students. Instead, "the challenge is to effectively teach them within a cultural context" (p. 56). To do this well, they must have *commitment, competence, confidence,* and *content* about cultural pluralism. These five C's (as Sullivan called them) are as applicable today as they were then.

Within the context of culturally responsive teaching, when acted upon these various aspects of caring place teachers in an ethical, emotional, and academic partnership with ethnically diverse students, a partnership anchored in respect, honor, integrity, resource sharing, and a deep belief in the possibility of transcendence; that is, an unshakable belief that marginalized students not only can but *will* improve their school achievement under the tutelage of competent and committed teachers who *act* to ensure that this happens. Marva Collins (1992) developed a "creed of caring" that helped to guide her interactions with students at the Westside Preparatory School in Chicago, which she founded. Called "Into My Heart," it is a personification of the ethics and power of caring. Part of it is quoted to illustrate how general principles of caring are manifested in Collins's personal creed of behavior with students. It may inspire readers to give expression to their own commitment to caring for culturally diverse students. Collins says, in part:

> I discourage being average. I believe all of my students can learn if I do not teach them too thoroughly that they cannot . . .
> I will teach them to think for themselves . . .
> I will teach them to have the fortitude to build their own bridges . . . to be courageous enough not to run from everything that is difficult, but to face unflinchingly the problems of life and see them . . . as challenges of living.
> I shall encourage them to never rest on their past laurels . . . to [know] that excellence is a non-ending process, and that they will never arrive in the land of the done.
> I [believe] . . . my students will become like stars that will light the world with excellence, with self-determination, with pride. (pp. 260–262)

TEACHER EXPECTATIONS MATTER

Before a genuine ethos of caring can be developed and implemented on a large scale, educators must identify and understand current noncaring attitudes and behaviors, and how they can obstruct student achievement. This understanding will help to locate places and spaces in classroom interactions that need to be changed and to determine which aspects of caring will be most appropriate to expedite student achievement.

By virtue of being unilaterally in charge of the classrooms, teachers control and monopolize academic interactions. They decide who will participate in what, when, where, and how (Goodlad, 1984). These decisions, and their consequences, are direct reflections of teacher attitudes and expectations. As Page (1987) explains, teachers' "perceptions are potent and assume a life of their own: they furnish a rationale for curriculum decisions and thereby provide the conditions for their own re-creation" (p. 77). Students who are perceived positively are advantaged in instructional interactions. Those who are viewed negatively or skeptically are disadvantaged, often to the extent of total exclusion from participation in substantive academic interactions.

Influences on Expectations

Disparities in classroom interactional opportunities are affected by many different variables, most of which have little to do with the intellectual abilities of students. Of utmost importance among them are racial identity, gender, ethnicity, social class, and home language. Even physical appearance can affect teacher expectations of students. In their meta-analysis of pertinent research, Ritts, Patterson, and Tubbs (1992) found that physically attractive students received higher grades, higher scores on standardized tests, and more academic assistance; they were also considered to be more friendly, attentive, popular, and outgoing, as well as better-behaved. The effects were greater on social than academic skills assessments. However, distinctions among these domains of schooling are not clearly demarcated, and effects in one can easily influence the other.

Culture also influences student and teacher expectations as well as how they engage in classroom interactions (Boggs et al., 1985; Boykin, 1994; Pai, 1990; Philips, 1983; Shinn, 1972). Social etiquette and rules of decorum about appropriate interactions with teachers and other students can hinder participation for some students and expedite it for others. Consider the following three examples of impediments. Immigrant students from traditional cultures with a rather rigid hierarchical social structure enter U.S. classrooms. They have been socialized to be passive and deferential in interactions with teachers and to treat teachers with respect at all times. U.S. education promotes a more fluid relationship, with students encouraged to engage actively with teachers. The immigrant students may appear to be overly quiet, accommodating, and reluctant to engage freely in instructional interactions, despite repeated invitations and enticements. In reality, these expectations may be very disconcerting and baffling to students new to the United States. They also may be overwhelmed by the gregarious style of other students. After their efforts to pull them into the interactions continue to fail, teachers stop trying and leave these students alone. Their learning opportunities and achievement potential are thus minimized because of a mismatch in cultural expectations about student–teacher relationships and interactional styles.

Another compelling example of cultural intrusion on quality interactions between students and teachers involves African Americans. The energy and exuberance with which highly culturally affiliated African Americans invest their interactions (what Boykin [1986] calls "verve") is troublesome to many teachers. They may view this behavior as impulsive, overemotional, and out of control. Consequently, much of their classroom interaction with these students is of a disciplinary and controlling manner, directed toward getting them to "settle down" and "spend more time on task." The students are often reprimanded for undesirable behaviors more than they are instructed on academic learning. High-level achievement is seriously constrained under these conditions.

The third example is a personal one, and more positive. Its cultural nuances are subtle, but the achievement results are somewhat more explicit. The situation occurred while I was an undergraduate. The instructor of one of my classes had the reputation of being a "grill king." He would select a student to probe and keep him or her on the "hot seat" for the entire duration of the class, except for an occasional diversion here and there to allow others to make brief comments about something the targeted student had said. He told us repeatedly that he wanted us to think about what we were learning rather than merely regurgitating textbook information. His teaching style lived up to this expectation, for he probed, cajoled, and, with rapid-fire questions, challenged us to critique, analyze, interpret, explain, reflect, extend. Today we would probably say he was a liberator, transformative, or constructivist teacher because he was committed to freeing our minds from the restraints of rote memory and helping us become articulate critical thinkers. At the time, I was too consumed with dread at the prospect of my time in the hot seat to think about this. I agonized for the greater portion of the semester about what would happen when I was called on. Would I be able to think? What did thinking mean? Would I be able to say anything? Would I sound and look stupid?

This was the first time I could recall any teacher demanding that I think and refusing to let me abdicate this responsibility. I needed to be prepared, so I tried to practice thinking beforehand. But I was trying so hard to get myself to think that I couldn't think about anything but thinking. I was traumatized as much by how the professor went about probing and prompting students as by the prospect of this thing called thinking. If two or three other students could have joined me in the spotlight, they would have deflected some of the attention away from me and made everything easier to bear. But that was not to be. This professor believed firmly in students being "lone riders" through the thinking journey. Finally, my time came. I don't know what I said, but evidently I did *think*. I met the professor's expectations. The conversation flowed rather smoothly, and he complimented me on being so well pre-pared and clear in my explanations. I was in a state of shock that I had pulled it off—I had actually *thought* about something. This was a teacher who genuinely cared about his students' learning; he insisted that we think; he held us accountable for demonstrating critical thinking; and he was diligent in his facilitation of this skill development.

Holliday (1981, 1985) used a "transactional, theoretical perspective" to explain how disjunctures in the frames of reference of schools and the home cultures of ethnically different students can generate negative teacher expectations, which in turn can compromise academic achieve-ment. She contends that social competence is a prerequisite for academic opportunities; that is, students must be able to comply with the procedural or managerial rules and regulations that surround the educational process before they are granted permission to participate in its substantive dimensions. An example of this is denying students an opportunity to read or participate in story-time because they did not raise their hands or wait for permission from the teacher before speaking out. In this situation, the speaking out is a management issue, while reading is an academic opportunity. The punishment does not fit the crime.

Over time, negative teacher attitudes and low expectations can cultivate "learned helplessness" among African American students (Holliday, 1981, 1985). If told too often for too long that their contributions and competencies are not worthy, students will stop being intellectually engaged in classroom interactions. Philips (1983) found similar results for Native Americans at the Warms Spring Reservation in Oregon. Many of the achievement problems of the students in her study derived from the interactional and procedural protocols of teaching rather than the substantive content of what was taught. How teachers talked to students interfered more with their academic engagement than the topics being discussed. Biklen and Pollard (1993), Klein (1985), the AAUW Report (1995), and Grossman and Grossman (1994) report that teacher expectations are also affected by the gender of students, leading to disparities in the quality of learning opportunities provided to males and females. Gender interactions, then, are other crucial "sites" where academic achievement is either facilitated or obfuscated.

Good and Brophy (1994) have compiled one of the most comprehensive summaries of research on teacher expectations and related classroom behaviors, and the effects of these on student achievement. In an earlier edition of this review, these authors noted that "many students in most classrooms are not reaching their potential because their teachers do not expect much from them and are satisfied with poor or mediocre performance when they could obtain something better" (1978, p. 70). Goodlad's (1984) national study of schooling, and Oakes's (1985, 1986a, 1986b) analyses of the effects of tracking on learning opportunities substantiate these findings and provide additional explanations.

An important ingredient for achievement that is missing in most of the classrooms Goodlad observed was the kind of engagement in learning activities demanded by Vida Hall's, Marva Collins's, and my undergraduate college professor's ethos of caring described earlier in this chapter. He characterized the classes as being void of intellectual energy and excitement, lacking "exuberance, joy, laughter, abrasiveness, praise and corrective support of individual student performance, punitive teacher behavior, or high interpersonal tension" (Goodlad, 1984, p. 112). Students' interactions with each other and with teachers were characterized by "neutrality . . . considerable passivity . . . and emotional flatness" (p. 113).

Another problem in effectively teaching students of color is the discrepancy in the quality of instruction that occurs in high and low curriculum tracks, as revealed by Oakes. This is particularly troubling because of the overrepresentation of Latinos, African Americans, and Native Americans in low-track curriculum options and low-status classes. These "emotionally flat" and "intellectually dull" classrooms result from instructional strategies that emphasize teacher dominance, didactic and large-group teaching, a narrow range of learning activities, workbook assignments, and very little interactive dialogue (Good & Brophy, 1994; Goodlad, 1984).

Persistent Trends in Expectations

Five other specific trends in teacher expectations have emerged from research and practice that support and explicate these general conclusions. They offer some important insights for the changes needed to improve the achievement of ethnically different students. First, *teacher expectations significantly influence the quality of learning opportunities provided to students.* Values and beliefs do not necessarily translate to behavior, but expectations do. Many teachers profess to believe that all students can learn, but they do not expect some of them to do so (Good & Brophy, 1978, 1994). Therefore, they allow students to sit in their classes daily without insisting on and assisting their engagement in the instructional process. This behavior is justified with statements to the effect that "you can't teach these students because they are not motivated to learn."

Teachers may believe in gender and ethnic equity yet do nothing to promote it in their classroom instruction. This lack of action is justified on the basis of not having enough time and the issues not being appropriate to the subjects they teach. They may bemoan the inadequacies of textbooks' information on the contributions of women and ethnic groups but continue to use them without providing any compensating material. Some teachers are adamant about the individual differences of students, while simultaneously declaring intentions to treat all of them the same and disavowing the importance of ethnicity, culture, and gender in pedagogical decision making.

If teachers *expect* students to be high or low achievers, they will act in ways that cause this to happen. Good and Brophy (1994) refer to this as the "self-fulfilling prophecy effect." This concept was popularized by Rosenthal and Jacobson in their 1968 landmark study (*Pygmalion in the Classroom*) of teacher expectations on the learning opportunities and outcomes of students. It means that teachers' assumptions about students' intellect and behavior affect how they treat students in instructional interactions. Over time, these treatments strongly influence the extent of student learning.

The mere existence of a generalized expectation does not lead to the self-fulfilling prophecy, nor is it something that happens incidentally or instantaneously. It requires *focused beliefs* and *deliberate and systematic action* over a period of time. According to Good and Brophy (1994), six steps are involved in the creation of a self-fulfilling prophecy: (1) The teacher expects specific achievement from specific students; (2) the teacher behaves toward students according to these expectations; (3) the teacher's behaviors convey to the students what is expected of them and are consistent over time; (4) students internalize teachers' expectations, and these affect their self-concepts, achievement motivations, levels of aspiration, classroom conduct, and interactions with teachers; (5) over time students' behavior becomes more and more attuned to what the teacher expects, unless they engage in deliberate resistance and change strategies; and (6) ultimately, students' academic achievement and other outcome measures are affected.

A second trend indicates that *teacher expectations about students are affected by factors that have no basis in fact and may persist even in the face of contrary evidence.* And teachers are" more likely to be affected by information leading to negative expectations than information leading to positive expectations" (Good & Brophy, 1994, p. 95). This is true even when the information derives from prejudices or stereotypes. Thus, some students are more susceptible to negative teacher expectations than others because of biases associated with the ethnic groups to which they belong.

Two of my friends tell a gripping story about a situation involving their teenage son that illustrates this point. Randy is African American, a high school senior well over 6 feet tall. He routinely meets four of his male friends (also African Americans) in the schoolyard at the end of the day to visit and socialize as they wait to be picked up by their parents. One day, while waiting for him to end his visit, Randy's father watched a teacher approach the group. He threatened the young men with disciplinary action and police intervention if they didn't disperse immediately. The students were baffled by these reactions since they were simply visiting, not doing anything wrong. In fact, all were good students and had no disciplinary records, and some were on the school's basketball team. What prompted this teacher's reactions? Randy's parents were convinced the motivation was negative attitudes toward and expectations about African American young men. The father speculated, "In his mind, that teacher saw potential gang members and a bunch of Black troublemakers. He didn't bother to see that these guys were team members and were exhibiting good behavior. They weren't even being loud or rambunctious."

Assumptions about connections among the intellectual capability, ethnicity, gender, and classroom adjustment of students attest to the tenacity of teacher expectations, even in the face of contrary evidence. This third trend was partially demonstrated by Rosenthal and Jacobson (1968) in their study *Pygmalion in the Classroom.* They told teachers some students had higher IQs than others when, in reality, there were no differences. The teachers expected the students with the supposed higher IQs to perform better in reading, and they did. In situations where teachers expect boys and girls to perform equally as well, they do, even though there are real ability differences between them. Palardy (1969) found this to be the case with reading achievement. Some teachers expect the schoolwork of students who speak African American and working-class dialects to be of lower quality than that of students who speak mainstream Standard English, and they tend to assess their performance accordingly (Bowie & Bond, 1994; Grossman & Grossman, 1994).

Many teachers expect Japanese, Chinese, and Korean American youth to always be studious, high-achieving, and obedient students. They are surprised to find that some individuals from these groups having serious learning difficulties (Osajama, 1991; Wong, 1980, 1995). Conversely, many teachers expect Latinos and African Americans to be low achievers and disciplinary problems. When they demonstrate high performance, teachers who expected otherwise are awed, suspicious, or declare them to be "overachievers." Some African American professionals lament being complimented with "you speak so well" or "you are so articulate" in circumstances in which coherent speech is a normal occurrence, not deserving of special note. Their response, in thought if not deed, is, "Why is my competence surprising? What did you expect?"

Classroom discipline is often expected to correlate strongly with student ethnicity, gender, and intellectuality. For instance, some teachers expect students of color and males to create more classroom management problems than European Americans and females, and for reverse correlations to exist between discipline and achievement (McFadden, Marsh, Price, & Hwang, 1992; Mickelson, 1990). Low achievers are expected to create more disciplinary problems than high achievers. Sheets (1995b) found that high school teachers sometimes behaved in ways that instigated disciplinary problems for African Americans and, to a lesser degree, Latinos. This was done by not allowing students to explain potentially problematic situations, giving them harsher punishments, and punishing them for some infractions that were ignored when committed by European and Asian Americans.

The achievement effects of these expectations are exponential. As teachers' expectations for higher achievers increase, so does student performance, while the performance of low achievers becomes even worse when teachers have low expectations. This cycle is particularly dangerous for low achievers because it can "confirm or deepen the students' sense of hopelessness and cause them to fail even where they could have succeeded under different circumstances" (Good & Brophy, 1994, p. 114). This process may explain what Holliday (1985) means by "learned helplessness" and account for the cumulative failure that some students experience in schools.

A fourth pattern of expectations that emerges from educational research, theory, and practice is that *teachers tend to have higher universal academic achievement expectations for European Americans than for students of color, with the exception of some Asian Americans.* Students from these ethnic groups are expected to do better in *all* subjects, tasks, and skills. These expectations are apparent as early as preschool and continue through college. In a study of teachers in 144 elementary and secondary schools in San Francisco, Wong (1980) found that teachers expected Asian American students to be more academically capable, emotionally stable, and cheerful compared to European American students. These expectations were the same for the third-, sixth-, eighth-, and eleventh-grade teachers who participated in the study. Washington (1982) studied teacher perceptions of the ethnicity and gender of students in grades 1 and 4. Both African and European American teachers viewed Black males most negatively and White females most positively. Black males and, to a lesser degree, Black females were perceived as being uncooperative, immature, and destructive; as not applying themselves; as having academic and social adjustment problems, and as needing to improve their physical appearance. By comparison, White female students were perceived as being cooperative, high-achieving, well adjusted to school, physically attractive, and possessed of winning personalities. When individual students do not conform to these expectations, they are acknowledged as "exceptions to the rule," but no modifications are made in the rule itself.

Finally, *teachers' expectations and sense of professional efficacy are interrelated.* Teaching efficacy stems from the beliefs teachers hold about their abilities to positively affect the academic achievement of particular students. It influences teachers' choices of activities, the efforts they exhibit, and their persistence in the face of obstacles and challenging situations (Ashton & Webb, 1986; Miller, 1991; Pang & Sablan, 1995). Teachers who have low performance expectations for students do not feel very efficacious about their own competencies with those students. But they attribute student failure to lack of intellectual ability and poor home environments rather than to the quality of their teaching. They also spend little time helping low-achieving students and may even ignore them entirely. These behaviors are justified on the basis that the students are unteachable anyway. Ashton and Webb (1986) explain further that teachers with a low sense of efficacy avoid learning activities they feel incapable of facilitating and are consumed with thoughts about their own inadequacies or limitations. These preoccupations create stress, divert attention from instructional to personal issues, and further reduce teaching effectiveness.

Conversely, teachers with strong self-confidence and feelings of efficacy in their teaching abilities have high achievement expectations for students. Furthermore, their teaching behaviors reflect these expectations. They use a greater variety and range of teaching strategies; hold themselves and their teaching accountable for the achievement of difficult learners; are more persistent in their efforts to facilitate learning; and spend more time in planning for instruction and professional development activities to improve their teaching quality than low-efficacy teachers (Miller, 1991). Teachers with a strong sense of efficacy also "choose challenging activities and are motivated to try harder when obstacles confront them. They become engrossed in the teaching situation itself, are not easily diverted, and experience pride in their accomplishments when the work is done" (Ashton & Webb, 1986, p. 3).

A significant number of the pre- and inservice teachers in the Pang and Sablan (1995) study felt they could not effectively teach or influence African American students in their classrooms. These attitudes were supported by beliefs that poor discipline in the home and lack of interest in academic success are the main reasons for the achievement gaps that exist between African and European American students. Ashton and Webb's (1986) research revealed positive correlations between teachers' sense of efficacy and the mathematics and communications, but not reading, skills of low-achieving students. They attributed these results to teachers' feeling more efficacious about teaching some subjects than others, thereby affirming their contention that teacher attitudes about efficacy are situation-specific. The "situations" to which they are directly connected include subjects or skills to be taught, as well as the ethnic identity and ability level of students. These troubling results led Pang and Sablan (1995) to posit that "teacher efficacy is an important construct in student achievement, and teacher educators need to seriously examine what teachers believe about their ability to teach children from various underrepresented groups" (p. 16).

These studies suggest that some part of the failure to learn that unsuccessful teachers attribute to students results from their own low levels of efficacy (Ashton & Webb, 1986). This is as much of a deterrent to effective teaching as students who consider themselves incapable of learning, whether that perception is based in fact or the distorted impositions of others. Thus, changing teachers' attitudes, expectations, and feelings of efficacy is as imperative to the design and implementation of effective culturally responsive teaching as is increasing their knowledge about and commitment to cultural diversity and mastery of related pedagogical skills.

THE ABSENCE OF CARING

Caring teachers are distinguished by their high performance expectations, advocacy, and empowerment of students as well as by their use of pedagogical practices that facilitate school success. The reverse is true for those who are noncaring. Their attitudes and behaviors take the form of low expectations, personal distance and disaffiliation from students, and instructional behaviors that limit student achievement. Just as caring is a foundational pillar of effective teaching and learning, the lack of it produces inequities in educational opportunities and achievement outcomes for ethnically different students. These are apparent in the disparities in teachers' instructional interactions in classrooms. Unfortunately, many students of color encounter too many uncaring teachers at all levels of education from preschool to college. The consequences of this "pedagogical noncaring" are so profound and numerous that they need to be exposed as a necessary part of the process of implementing culturally responsive teaching.

Quantitative and qualitative variables are used in research and practice to examine relationships between teachers' instructional expectations of and interactions with ethnically different students. Common among them are the number and kind of contacts with students initiated by teachers; the types of academic questions and intellectual tasks given to whom; amount of wait-time allowed for student participation; praise and criticism, cues and prompts, and elaborations teachers apply to student responses; and contacts students initiate with teachers. The results of these analyses indicate that significant discrepancies exist in favor of European Americans in both the quantity and quality of interactions uncaring teachers have with students by race, ethnicity, gender within ethnic groups, social class of individuals and schools, and intellectual ability.

Research on tracking (Anyon, 1981, 1988; Good & Brophy, 1994; Goodlad, 1984; Oakes, 1985, 1986a, 1986b; Oakes & Guiton, 1995; Persell, 1977; Rist, 1970), or the assignment of students to courses and curriculum options by ability grouping, has been especially helpful in revealing differential patterns of teacher interactions with students. These patterns are established early and persist largely unchanged over time and circumstances of schooling thereafter. They are powerful barriers to academic success for the students who are not perceived positively. Differential teacher interactions with ethnically different students should be understood as both obstacles to and opportunities for culturally responsive pedagogical interventions.

Teacher Interactions and Student Ethnicity

The patterns of teachers' interactions with African Americans, Latinos, and Native Americans are similar enough to allow for a composite presentation. The only major difference among them is in the magnitude, not the kind, of treatment. Teacher interactions with various Asian American groups are less clear because of the overall paucity of research on them. Students of color, especially those who are poor and live in urban areas, get less total instructional attention; are called on less frequently; are encouraged to continue to develop intellectual thinking less often; are criticized more and praised less; receive fewer direct responses to their questions and comments; and are reprimanded more often and disciplined more severely. Frequently, the praise given is terse, ritualistic, procedural, and social rather than elaborate, substantive, and academic. General praise of personal attributes is less effective than that which is related to task-specific performance in improving the learning efforts and outcomes of students (Damico & Scott, 1988; Good & Brophy, 1994; Grossman & Grossman, 1994; U. S. Civil Rights Commission, 1973).

Jackson and Cosca (1974, p. 227) observed that Mexican American students in the Southwest "receive substantially less of those types of teacher behavior presently known to be most strongly related to gains in student achievement" (p. 227). In a study of teachers working with preschoolers, Guilmet (1979) made similar observations. He concluded that "a situation exists in which Navajo children, who are more in need of the teachers' and aides' help, receive less attention than the Caucasian children who are more prepared for learning in the public school environment" (p. 262).

The middle- or upper-class status and specific ethnic identity sometimes produce more positive learning opportunities for students. One case of this is the "model minority" status ascribed to many Japanese, Korean, and Chinese Americans. These students are exposed to instructional opportunities and interactions that are directed toward higher-quality academic achievement. Schneider and Lee (1990) studied the relationship among sociocultural factors, interpersonal interactions, and academic success among East Asian middle schoolers. Their results indicated that East Indian students were assigned to top-level classes and thus academically advantaged. Teachers tended to challenge these students with more intellectually demanding and exploratory topics, creative homework assignments, and engaging classroom work. Students in top-level classes also were less likely to be academically distracted or off-task because of disruptive behaviors from their classmates. The combination of these factors produces high levels of achievement.

When qualitative analyses are added to negative quantitative teacher expectations and interactions with students of color, results are even more devastating. African, Latino, and Native American students routinely are asked lower-order cognitive questions; given answers more frequently instead of being encouraged and prompted to find solutions for themselves; and have more managerial than substantive interactions with teachers (Grant, 1984; Oakes, 1985; Oakes & Guiton, 1995). For example, European American students may be asked to answer divergent, thought-provoking questions in instructional discourses, while African American and Latino students are asked single-answer, convergent ones. Or their engagements are limited to exchanges such as, "Did you understand the answer _____ gave?" and "Do you have any questions about the instructions for doing the assignment?" Another difference in the quality of instructional discourse is the amount of probing teachers use with students from various ethnic groups. European American students, especially males, are encouraged more to try harder at answering questions and explaining their ideas more clearly; they are given hints and cues to facilitate this performance; and they are rewarded for their intellectual pursuits (Sadker & Sadker, 1982; AAUW, 1995). Ethnic-minority students tend to be applauded more for following procedures, for adapting to institutional rules and regulations, and for being "nice" (Grossman & Grossman, 1994; Oakes, 1985).

Teachers who exhibit these kinds of behaviors offer several justifications for not being as pedagogically persistent and intellectually focused with students of color as with European Americans. One is that they do not want to embarrass students who do not know answers to questions. Another is that students who have limited English proficiency are hard to understand, and probing them too much might make them reluctant to participate in, or cause them to withdraw from, classroom discussions. They also take so much time to formulate responses that other students become impatient and rude. Some teachers claim lack of prior experience and not knowing how to relate to students of color. They are intimidated by these students' presence in their classrooms. Other teachers pose "distribution of limited resources" arguments for not engaging certain students in instructional interactions. If too much teaching time and effort are devoted to poorly prepared and unmotivated students, the more intellectually capable ones who are interested in learning will be short-changed. Consequently, some students are simply ignored, as long as they are not disruptive. When disruptions do occur, the easiest course of action is taken by removing these students from the classroom.

Anecdotal reports are replete with stories of disproportionate numbers of Latino, Native, African, and some Asian American students sitting in hallways or principals' offices. Or they are socializing, grooming themselves, and sleeping in classrooms when instruction is going on, without some teachers being concerned about the inappropriateness of these behaviors. Ignoring, silencing, and physically removing students from the "sites" where teaching occurs epitomizes noncaring.

Teacher Interactions and Student Gender

Research on the education of girls and women indicates that teachers interact differently with male and female students but that ethnicity is a critical intervening variable. Stated differently, male and female students from the same ethnic groups do not receive comparable opportunities to participate in classroom instruction. When the unit of analysis is all girls, European Americans have better-quality interactions with teachers than Latinos, Native Americans, and African Americans.

Most of the research available that substantiates these general interactional patterns involves European American students. It reveals that males are treated preferentially. They have more interactions with teachers regardless of type—academic or social, intellectual or managerial, positive or negative, verbal or nonverbal, student- or teacher-initiated. As Streitmatter (1994) explains, "Males dominate the classrooms both in the positive sense as learners, as well as in a negative sense as behavioral problems" (p. 128). The magnitude of this ratio varies somewhat by the nature of the communication. It is greatest in disciplinary encounters and smallest in instructional interactions (Good & Brophy, 1994). European American males also initiate more contacts with teachers; receive more encouragement, feedback, and praise; are cued, prompted, and probed more; are rewarded more for academic accomplishments; are asked more complex, abstract, and open-ended questions; and are taught how to become independent thinkers and problem solvers. By comparison, females initiate less; receive less academic encouragement, praise, prompts, rewards, and expectations for success; have less total interactional time with teachers; are asked more simple questions that require descriptive and concrete answers; are disciplined less frequently and less severely; and are rewarded more for social than for academic accomplishments (Good & Brophy, 1994; Grossman & Grossman, 1994; Sadker & Sadker, 1982; E. Scott & McCollum, 1993; AAUW, 1995).

Given the magnitude of these academic disadvantages, Masland's (1994) reaction to them is understandable. She declares, "It is nothing short of amazing that females succeed in school at all. After reading the research and studying the reports from female students themselves, one is struck by the resiliency and tenacity that it takes to persevere in an environment that is so demeaning and adverse" (p. 22). The same can be said, with even greater reason, about Native Americans, African Americans, Latinos, and female students of color, especially those who are poor.

Teacher interactions with African American females are similar to those with African American males, but more negative when compared to their European American counterparts. Even when their actual achievement is equal to or greater than that of African American males, they still receive less and lower-quality opportunities to engage in instructional interactions (Damico & Scott, 1988). For example, in the assignment of classroom managerial tasks, European American females receive "trusted lieutenant duties and special high prestige assignments" (Grossman & Grossman 1994, p. 90), but African American females are given duties that involve low-status social responsibilities. In their study of peer-assisted instruction, Damico and Scott (1988) observed teachers asking African American females to help other students with nonacademic tasks, while European American females were directed to give academic assistance.

These types of instructional disparities can have long-term negative consequences on achievement. They create a kind of intellectual dependency that causes females to be less assertive, confident, and skillful in the kind of analytical thinking, problem solving, and decision making that are associated with academic success in higher education, careers, and adult leadership roles. An additional negative effect occurs for African American females. They develop low self-esteem and strong feelings of powerlessness and hopelessness about being able to control their academic destinies. These feelings, in turn, diminish learning efforts and time-on-task, which subsequently leads to low academic achievement (Grant, 1984; E. Scott & McCollum, 1993).

Informal classroom observations conducted in 1996 and 1997 by a group of students enrolled in the teacher education program at the University of Washington, Seattle, indicate that many of the traditional patterns of classroom interactions with students by ethnicity and gender still prevail. In some instances, the teachers were unaware of discrepancies in their instructional behaviors and were inclined to deny any existed. In other situations, efforts were made to counteract traditional trends, but by merely reversing the discrepancy patterns. Girls were then given more pedagogical attention than boys to accomplish "gender equity" in learning opportunities. Some teachers were oversolicitous toward ethnic-minority students, especially when the subject of instruction was something about the ethnic group to which they belonged, because they wanted to make them feel "accepted."

Neither of these strategies is desirable or effective in meeting the criteria of culturally responsive teaching and improving academic achievement. Male students dislike being ignored, excluded, or "bashed"; female students may develop inflated notions of self-importance; and students of color may resent and resist being put in the spotlight by having to be experts on themselves. Simply "reversing the order of things" in teacher interactions may backfire and cause the students it is intended to benefit to become even further marginalized. As a result, academic achievement, social development, and classroom discipline can suffer.

Teacher Interactions and Student Ability

The interactions of uncaring teachers with low-achieving and high-achieving students are consistent with trends established for ethnicity and gender. High achievers are offered instructional opportunities similar to those offered European American males, and the treatment of low-achievers is similar to that of students of color and females. Research on teachers' instructional interactions with low- and high-achieving students in reading, English, and math provide specific support for these general conclusions. Brown, Palincsar, and Purcell (1986) report that teachers interrupt poor readers more often than good readers and give mostly graphemic/ phonemic helping cues to poor readers while giving semantic/syntactical ones to good readers. Instruction with good readers emphasizes comprehension skills, such as inferring meaning from, thinking about, criticizing, and evaluating text. Much of the teaching time with poor readers is devoted to drills on pronunciation and decoding, as well as establishing procedural rituals such as turn-taking and hand-raising.

In her studies of 300 high- and low-track English and math classes in 38 schools, Oakes (1985) found instructional discrepancies between high- and low-ability classes similar to those reported by Brown and colleagues. In the high-level English classes students were taught how to analyze narrative texts, write thematic essays and research papers, think critically, and expand their vocabularies. Teaching in the low-track classes emphasized grammar, rote drill and memorization of facts, simplistic workbook exercises, filling out application forms, and memorizing facts and other low-level comprehension skills. The high-track math classes focused on concept mastery, problem solving, and mathematical reasoning, while low-track ones taught basic facts and computational skills. Similar instructional differences by social class in social studies teaching were revealed by Anyon (1981). In the working- and middle-class schools she studied, students were taught blind patriotism, obedience to laws, and uncontested compliance to the decisions of leaders. In upper-middle-class and wealthy schools, students were taught critical and analytical intellectual skills, as well as how to be social and political change agents to create the kind of society they desired rather than merely adjusting to the existing one.

Instructional interactions at the school level have also been used as the unit of analysis in examining relationships between teaching behaviors and student achievement. This was the focus of research conducted by Page (1987) and by Oakes and Guiton (1995). Their findings paralleled those of Anyon. Page's ethnographic study of regular and low-track classes in two high schools—one characterized as having an ethos of academic excellence, the other as promoting "pedestrian competence" (p. 87)—revealed significant differences in curriculum and instruction, both by class and school. The student population in the schools was almost totally European American. In the regular classes in the first school, students were perceived by teachers as high achievers and were taught to think critically, broadly, and enthusiastically about traditional academic subjects considered to be important to their present and future educational success.

The resulting instruction was focused, purposive, academically demanding, exploratory, spontaneous, and engaging. In comparable classes in the "pedestrian" school, the teachers were more perfunctory in performing their jobs and showed little enthusiasm or investment of self. They placed more emphasis on discipline, keeping order and control, punctuality, and practical education than academic pursuits. Students in low-track classes in the pedestrian school were treated more like their peers in the regular classes than like those in the low-track of the "academic" school. The differences were more a matter of degree than kind. At the academic school, low-track students were seen as "troubling anomalies" to the norm, were considered "irremediably basic" (p. 94), were entertained with a curriculum of puzzles and games; their teachers acted more as caretakers than as instructors. Although academic neglect was apparent for the low-achieving classes at both schools, it was somewhat more genteel for the "academics" than the "pedestrians."

In their study of tracking decisions in three comprehensive high schools, Oakes and Guiton (1995) found patterns of teacher expectations and instructional behaviors virtually identical to those reported by Page. However, the sites where their study took place were quite different. At one the students were racially and socioeconomically diverse; at another they were primarily middle- and upper-middle-class European and Asian Americans; at the third the students were mostly low-income African Americans and Latinos. Oakes and Guiton observed schools with many high achievers providing greater access to a better quality and variety of courses, as well as an overall atmosphere of high academic performance expectations.

This general pattern of expectations and behaviors by kind of school was further evident in four more specific practices:

- Academically able students took vocational courses that taught keyboarding or accounting, skills considered beneficial for college preparatory students, while students in low-achieving schools took mechanically orientated vocations courses, such as auto and wood shop.
- The school with predominately Asian and European American students was perceived to be highly motivated and achieving. To accommodate the students, it offered a college-oriented curriculum. By comparison, the curriculum offerings in the school with the high African American and Latino population were disproportionally vocational.
- Teacher perceptions of students' suitability for different curriculum tracks were influenced by race, ethnicity, and social class. Asian American students, considered to be highly motivated and academically capable, were identified with high track, college-prep, and advanced-placement academic courses. Latinos were perceived to be best suited for low-track academic and remedial courses and vocational programs. Performance expectations for European Americans were lower than those for Asian Americans but higher than those for students of color. African Americans were considered slightly more academically capable than Latinos.
- Students in schools where high achievement was expected had the best-planned curricula and the best-qualified teachers, and they were given more time and consideration by counselors.

These disparities in quality of instructional expectations and interactions are perceived by uncaring teachers as a consequence of variability in student intellectual ability. They find it difficult to tease out distinguishing attributes of ethnicity, gender, social class, and intellect. In some instances, teachers are not consciously aware of discrepancies in their expectations for and interactions with ethnically different students. To move from "noncaring" to "caring" pedagogical philosophy and practice, more teach-

ers need to develop a heightened awareness of their instructional dispositions.

MOVING TOWARD CULTURALLY RESPONSIVE CARING

In working with students of color, more teachers need to exhibit culturally
responsive caring and to be "tough" and "take no stuff," like the individuals introduced earlier in this chapter; that is, "tough" and intractable
in the sense of having high performance expectations and diligence in
facilitating their achievement. This style of teaching is anchored in caring,
commitment, cultural competence, and an understanding that school performance takes place within a complex sociocultural ecology and is filtered
through cultural screens both students and teachers bring to the classroom. Caring (in the form of teacher expectations and their attendant
instructional behaviors) is too pivotal in shaping the educational experiences and outcomes of ethnically different students to be taken for granted
or left to chance. Nor should it be assumed that constructive caring about,
and pedagogical responsiveness to, cultural diversity will emerge natu-
rally from the professional ethics or personal altruism of teachers. Instead,
it must be deliberately cultivated.

Acquiring a Knowledge Base

Teachers need to begin the process of becoming more caring and culturally
competent by acquiring a *knowledge base about ethnic and cultural diversity
in education*. This can be derived from the rich bodies of social science,
educational, and literary scholarship on ethnic groups' histories, heritages,
cultures, and contributions. A recent publication by G. Smith (1998), *Common Sense About Uncommon Knowledge*, may expedite the identification of
this knowledge base even more so. He has culled from the scholarship
13 wide-ranging components of multicultural education that he considers
essential for inclusion in teacher education. Among these are ideological
foundations; learning styles; sociocultural contexts of human growth and
development; essentials of culture; experiential knowledge; and principles
of culturally responsive curriculum design and classroom instruction.
Another valuable resource in reconceptualizing and transforming the
professional preparation of teachers for culturally responsible pedagogy
is *Preparing Teachers for Cultural Diversity*, edited by J. King, Hollins, and
Hayman (1997). The contributing authors to this book place cultural diversity in historical perspective; identify critical dimensions of cultural diver-

sity for teacher education; and suggest a variety of culturally sensitive pre- and inservice teaching processes and strategies.

Personal and Professional Self-Awareness

The recommendations suggested by Smith (1998) and King and colleagues (1997) include a wide range of content and pedagogical knowledge that teachers need to become competent and caring culturally responsive instructors for ethnically diverse students. However, this knowledge alone is not sufficient. It should be complemented with careful *self-analyses* of what teachers believe about the relationship among culture, ethnicity, and intellectual ability; the expectations they hold for students from different ethnic groups; and how their beliefs and expectations are manifested in instructional behaviors. These examinations are necessary and viable if Good and Brophy's (1994) contention is correct that most teachers are unaware, in any systematic way, of what they do while in the act of teaching. One cannot start to solve a problem until it is identified and understood. If teachers do not know how their own cultural blinders can obstruct educational opportunities for students of color, they cannot locate feasible places, directions, and strategies for changing them. Therefore, a critical element of culturally responsive teaching is *cultural self-awareness* and *consciousness-raising* for teachers.

Spindler and Spindler (1993, 1994) and Bennett (1995b) offer models that are useful in facilitating the development of this awareness. They are techniques for teachers to study their own classroom behaviors as they are occurring. The Spindler and Spindler model is called "cultural therapy." It is a process for bringing individuals' own cultural identities to a level of cognitive consciousness; deconstructing one's cultural embeddedness (Bowers & Flinders, 1991; Schram, 1994) in perceptions; analyzing why the cultural behaviors of others are perceived as objectionable, irritating, or shocking; and making explicit unequal power relationships and interactions in classrooms. Its purpose is to empower teachers through self-knowledge, the creation of a systematic basis for self-renewal, and the development of greater appreciation for the fallibility of presumed cultural universality.

Cultural therapy combines personal awareness with professional analysis and cultural knowledge with instructional action. It includes explicating culturally patterned assumptions, values, and roots that drive expectations, communications, and behaviors; identifying culturally determined mechanisms for the expression, defense, and protection of "the enduring self"; recognizing cultural conflicts in the classroom between diverse students and teachers; and understanding the various kinds of *instrumental competencies* and *situational self-efficacy* required for school success for students, such as social etiquette, study skills, interactional rules, bureaucratic protocols, and high-level achievement in high-status subjects and skills.

Cultural therapy is beneficial to the implementation of culturally responsive teaching because it helps teachers to "see" more clearly the imprints of culture in their own and their students' behaviors—or to understand that "behavior is largely a matter of communicating in culturally prescribed ways" (Bowers & Flinders 1990, p. xi) and that people internalize patterns of thinking and behaving prescribed by their own cultural socialization. Cultural therapy also makes teachers more receptive to the notion that they may misread some of the behaviors of their culturally different students and, as a result, mistreat or disempower them, personally and pedagogically (Spindler & Spindler, 1994). For example, they come to realize that students who do not rise eagerly to expectations of individual competition in academic tasks are not necessarily unmotivated and uninterested in learning. They may simply be culturally cued to demonstrate motivation and academic competition in other ways, such as in cooperative group arrangements. These "cracks" in the sense of certainty about their own cultural claims and mechanisms, or what Bowers and Flinders (1990) call "taken-for-granted" assumptions of reality, are windows of opportunity for acknowledging the presence and legitimacy of cultural frames of reference in the classroom other than those of the teacher. Therefore, the purpose of cultural therapy is to alleviate the suffering caused when one's cultural biases are implicitly or explicitly forced upon others.

Bennett's (1995b) model emerged from the Teacher as Decision Maker Program at Indiana University, which emphasizes decision making and reflective practice in preservice teacher preparation. Both of these emphases are prominent in caring, culturally responsive teaching. Referred to as the "Teacher Perspective Framework," it is designed to develop skills in pedagogical self-awareness, self-analysis, and self-reflection. Preservice teachers are asked first to declare their personal perspectives on teaching philosophies by selecting from among seven conceptual options, and then to study their instructional actions to determine if assumed and actual behaviors are congruent. Self-recorded observations of teaching behaviors are accompanied by periodic self-reflections and interviews to further heighten awareness and understanding of teaching modes. If in congruencies are apparent, the teachers are challenged to explain and resolve them. This resolution may require making another conceptual choice or adapting behaviors to fit better with ideals. Although the Teaching

Perspective Framework was not designed specifically for analyzing the perspectives of teachers on the cultural behaviors of self and others, it can be adapted for this purpose.

Dialogues About Culturally Diversity

In addition to engaging in self-reflections about their expectations and interactions with cultural diversity in classrooms, teachers need to discuss them with others. These dialogues should be informative and analytical, and they should involve individuals who are in positions of authority and/or expertise to help teachers make better sense of their behaviors and improve them. Ideally, they will include professional peers and supervisors, as well as students, and participants in the dialogues will be multiethnic. The discussions should be inquiring and collaborative in nature, with the participants working together to share perceptions and expose their deep thinking on the topics under consideration. In this instance, the focus of analysis will be teacher expectations for and interactional styles with students from different ethnic groups and how these affect performance. The purpose of these dialogues is not merely to engage in cathartic "emotional massaging" or "psychological bashing," but for the participants to learn how to talk about ethnic and cultural differences, acquire a heightened level of cultural sensitivity and critical consciousness, reevaluate cultural assumptions underlying behavior, and identify themes, ideas, and issues that have generative potential for pedagogical renewal. Intergroup dialogues can be used to facilitate these discussions.

Schoem, Frankel, Zuniga, and Lewis (1993) describe how dialogues were developed and used in the Program on Intergroup Relations and Conflict at the University of Michigan. The intent was to help college students learn about different ethnic groups' cultures and experiences, deconstruct racial myths and stereotypes, and combat racism. The technique involves several different progressional stages of learning. Zuniga and Nagda (1993) identify these as (1) creating a learning atmosphere conducive to cross-racial discussions and the constructive confrontation of misinformation and conflict; (2) examining ethnic-group membership and cultural identity; (3) critically analyzing impressions and stereotypes people from different ethnic and racial groups have about each other; (4) exploring connections among attitudes, feelings, values, and behaviors; and (5) building alliances, coming to closure, and engaging is action for social change.

These kinds of examinations and dialogues can be both intimidating and empowering. They should be led by individuals skilled in conducting group discussions about ethnic and racial issues. One of the major challenges for the facilitator is getting the participants talking in constructive and mutually supportive ways. Many participants may want to find safety in silence and may resist sharing genuine beliefs and feelings for fear that they will be accused of being racists. Group leaders may overcome this hurdle by creating some "personal distance" for the members to begin to actively engage with the issues. Educational and commercial films and videos that depict issues of ethnic and cultural diversity in education can provide this stimulus and opportunity. There are many excellent examples on the market. Among them are *The Color of Fear* (Mun Wah, 1994), *Rosewood* (Peters & Barone, 1997), *Eye of the Storm* (1970) and its sequel *A Class Divided* (1986), *Stand and Deliver* (Menendez, 1988), *Something Strong Within* (Nakamura, 1994), *Ethnic Notions* (Biggs, 1987), *Eyes on the Prize* (Hampton, 1987), *Ruby Bridges* (Palcy, 1998), *Skin Deep* (Reed, 1995), *Race the Sun* (Kanganis, 1996), *Valuing Diversity* (1987), *The Wedding* (Burnett, 1998), and *Smoke Signals* (Estes & Rosenfelt, 1998).

Written stories and scenarios, as well as films and videos, can be very provocative prompts to initiate and focus intergroup dialogues among teachers on ethnic diversity. They are available in various genres, including fiction and nonfiction, essays and novels, poetry and prose, autobiographical and biographical documents. Illustrative of these are *The Joy Luck Club* (Tan, 1989), *A Man's Life* (Wilkins, 1982), *Let the Circle Be Unbroken* (M. Taylor, 1981), "Incident" (Cullen, 1970), *Father Song: Testimonies of African-American Sons and Daughters* (Wade-Gayles, 1997), *Tearing the Silence: On Being German in America* (Hegi, 1997), *I Am Joaquin* (Gonzales, 1972), and *Fitting In* (Bernardo, 1996).

Teachers also can use video recordings of their own classroom behaviors to develop awareness and understanding of how they interact with ethnically different students. After recording segments of instruction, they can view the tapes critically and analytically to discern differences in their expectations and behaviors by the gender and ethnicity of students. These analyses should be both quantitative and qualitative. In the first category teachers might simply count the number of times they have any kind of verbal and nonverbal contact with students from different ethnic and gender groups during the course of a lesson. These contacts could include how many questions asked of whom; praise, prompts, or guidance given; and discipline imposed. The qualitative assessments will require deeper analyses and may be more challenging and disconcerting.

In conducting these analyses, teachers might consider working with a colleague, supervisor, or external consultant who is more informed about cultural influences on classroom behaviors. The focus of attention should be on discrepancies in the *quality* of interactions teachers have with different students by ethnicity and gender. These might include what kinds of questions are asked of boys and girls, of Latino, African, Native, Asian, and European Americans; who is praised and who is criticized; to what extent experiences and perspectives of different ethnic groups are woven into instruction; which students are encouraged to think deeper and extend, clarify, or refine their verbal contributions; which students are ignored by the teacher; what subtle ways teachers signal students that they are, or are not, expected to be masterful, high-level achievers? Once these interactional patterns are discerned and clearly understood, teachers can begin to design strategies for changing them, the first of which is to abort the negative and accelerate the positive. The next step will be to learn how to modify instructional interactions so that they are responsive to some of the cultural orientations of students from different ethnic groups. Some strategies for doing this can be gleaned from the information presented in Chapters 4–7.

CONCLUSION

Out of these processes of self-awareness and self-renewal, reflection and introspection, deconstruction and reconstruction should emerge teachers with expectations and interactions, knowledge and skills, values and ethics that exhibit the power of caring, individuals like those introduced earlier in this chapter. They will be more inclined toward and effective in implementing culturally responsive teaching because they now know that this is an unavoidable moral mandate for educating ethnically different students. And they will join the ranks of other teachers who are already moving forward on this agenda with conviction and effectiveness, such as those M. Foster (1997) writes about in *Black Teachers on Teaching* and embodied by Mable Bette Moss, who says:

> My students know that they have to learn something every day, even if it's just a little bit. . . . They also know that if they don't know something or didn't learn something it's not their fault. . . . When the children tell me they can't do something, . . . I will say, 'I know you can't do it now, but we'll work together and soon you will be able to do it on your own.' . . . I want them to just keep persevering until they can. I have a lot of patience. (quoted in M. Foster, 1997, pp. 172–173).

Genuinely caring teachers are academic taskmasters. All students are held accountable for high academic efforts and performance. It is not uncommon to hear these teachers making declarations to students to the effect that "there is no excuse for not trying to learn," "you will never know what you can do unless you try," and "'I can't do' is unacceptable in my classroom." Their performance expectations are complemented with uncompromising faith in their students and relentless efforts in helping them meet high academic demands. The results are often phenomenal. Students who others feel can only reach minimal levels of academic and social achievement produce stellar performance for caring, culturally sensitive teachers. The success of these teachers demonstrates that the idea of caring as essential to instructional effectiveness is not merely a truism; it is a fact. When combined with pedagogical competence, caring becomes a powerful ideological and praxis pillar of culturally responsive pedagogy for students.

CHAPTER 4

Culture and Communication
in the Classroom

A semiotic relationship exists among communication, culture, teaching and, learning, and it has profound implications for implementing culturally responsive teaching. This is so because "what we talk about; how we talk about it; what we see, attend to, or ignore; how we think; and what we think about are influenced by our culture . . . [and] help to shape, define, and perpetuate our culture" (Porter & Samovar, 1991, p. 21). Making essentially the same argument, Bruner (1996) states that "learning and thinking are always situated in a cultural setting and always dependent upon the utilization of cultural resources" (p. 4). Culture provides the tools to pursue the search for meaning and to convey our understanding to others. Consequently, communication cannot exist without culture, culture cannot be known without communication, and teaching and learning cannot occur without communication or culture.

INTRODUCTION

The discussions in this chapter explicate some of the critical features and pedagogical potentials of the culture–communication semiotics for different ethnic groups of color. The ideas and examples presented are composites of group members who strongly identify and affiliate with their ethnic group's cultural traditions. They are not intended to be descriptors of specific individuals within ethnic groups, or their behaviors in all circumstances. If, how, and when these cultural characteristics are expressed in actual behavior, and by whom, are influenced by many different factors, some of which were discussed in Chapter 1. Therefore, the ethnic interactional and communication styles described in this chapter should be seen as *general and traditional referents of group dynamics* rather than static attributes of particular individuals.

Students of color who are most traditional in their communication styles and other aspects of culture and ethnicity are likely to encounter more obstacles to school achievement than those who think, behave, and express themselves in ways that approximate school and mainstream cultural norms. This is the case for many highly culturally and ethnically affiliated African Americans. In making this point, Dandy (1991) proposes that the language many African Americans speak "is all too often degraded or simply dismissed by individuals both inside and outside the racial group as being uneducated, illiterate, undignified or simply nonstandard" (p. 2). Other groups of color are "at least given credit for having a legitimate language heritage, even if they are denied full access to American life" (p. 2).

Much of educators' decision-making on the potential and *realized* achievement of students of color is dependent on communication abilities (their own and the students'). If students are not very proficient in school communication, and teachers do not understand or accept the students' cultural communication styles, then their academic performance may be misdiagnosed or trapped in communicative mismatches. Students may know much more than they are able to communicate, or they may be communicating much more than their teachers are able to discern. As Boggs (1985, p. 301) explains, "The attitudes and behavior patterns that have the most important effect upon children . . . [are] those involved in communication." This communication is multidimensional and multipurposed, including verbal and nonverbal, direct and tacit, literal and symbolic, formal and informal, grammatical and discourse components.

The discussions of culture and communication in classrooms in this chapter are organized into three parts. The first outlines some key assertions about culture and communication in teaching and learning in general. These help to anchor communication within culturally responsive teaching. The controversy prompted by the 1996 Oakland, California, school district policy on using Ebonics (African American communication style) to teach mainstream English language and literacy skills to African American students is summarized in the second part. This "case" is presented to illustrate the promises and perils of responding to the communication systems of ethnic groups of color in classroom instruction. In the third part of the chapter, some of the major characteristics of the communication *modes* of African, Native, Latino, Asian, and European Americans are presented. The focus throughout these discussions is on discourse dynamics; that is, who participates in communicative interactions and under what conditions, how these participation patterns are affected by cultural socialization, and how they influence teaching and learning in classrooms.

RELATIONSHIP AMONG CULTURE,
COMMUNICATION, AND EDUCATION

In analyzing the routine tasks teachers perform, B. Smith (1971) declares that "teaching is, above all, a linguistic activity" and "language is at the very heart of teaching" (p. 24). Whether making assignments, giving directions, explaining events, interpreting words and expressions, proving propositions, justifying decisions and actions, making promises, dispersing praise and criticism, or assessing capability, teachers must use language. And the quality of the performance of these tasks is a direct reflection of how well they can communicate with their students. Smith admonishes educators for not being more conscientious in recognizing the importance of language in the performance and effectiveness of their duties. He says, "It could be that when we have analyzed the language of teaching and investigated the effects of its various formulations, the art of teaching will show marked advancement" (p. 24). Dandy (1991) likewise places great faith in the power of communication in the classroom, declaring that "teachers have the power to shape the future, if they communicate with their students, but those who cannot communicate are powerless" (p. 10). These effects of communication skills are especially significant to improving the performance of underachieving ethnically different students.

Porter and Samovar's (1991) study of the nature of culture and communication, the tenacious reciprocity that exists between the two, and the importance of these to intercultural interactions provides valuable information for culturally responsive teaching. They describe communication as "an intricate matrix of interacting social acts that occur in a complex social environment that reflects the way people live and how they come to interact with and get along in their world. This social environment is culture, and if we are to truly understand communication, we must also understand culture" (p. 10). Communication is dynamic, interactive, irreversible, and invariably contextual. As such, it is a continuous, ever-changing activity, that takes place between people who are trying to influence each other; its effects are irretrievable once it has occurred, despite efforts to modify or counteract them. Communication is also governed by the rules of the social and physical contexts in which it occurs (Porter & Samovar, 1991). Culture is the rule-governing system that defines the forms, functions, and content of communication. It is largely responsible for the construction of our "individual repertoires of communicative behaviors and meanings" (p. 10). Understanding connections between culture and communication is critical to improving intercultural interactions. This is so because "as cultures differ from one another, the communication practices and behaviors of individuals reared in those cultures will also be different," and "the degree of influence culture has on intercultural communication is a function of the dissimilarity between the cultures" (p. 12).

Communication entails much more than the content and structure of written and spoken language, and it serves purposes greater than the mere transmission of information. Sociocultural context and nuances, discourse logic and dynamics, delivery styles, social functions, role expectations, norms of interaction, and nonverbal features are as important as (if not more so than) vocabulary, grammar, lexicon, pronunciation, and other linguistic structural dimensions of communication. This is so because the "form of exchange between child and adult and the conditions in which it occurs will affect not only what is said, but how involved the child will become" (Boggs 1985, p. 301). Communication is the quintessential way in which humans make meaningful connections with each other, whether as caring, sharing, loving, teaching, or learning. Montagu and Matson (1979, p. vii) suggest that it is "the ground of [human] meeting and the foundation of [human] community."

Communication is also indispensable to facilitating knowing and accessing knowledge. This is the central idea of the Sapir–Whorf hypothesis about the relationship among language, thought, and behavior. It says that, far from being simply a means for reporting experience, language is a way of defining experience, thinking, and knowing. In this sense, language is the semantic system of meanings and modes of conveyance that people habitually use to code, analyze, categorize, and interpret experience (Carroll, 1956; Hoijer, 1991; Mandelbaum, 1968). In characterizing this relationship, Sapir (1968) explains that "language is a guide to 'social reality' . . . [and] a symbolic guide to culture. . . . It powerfully conditions all of our thinking about social problems and processes" (p. 162). People do not live alone in an "objectified world" or negotiate social realities without the use of language. Nor is language simply a "mechanical" instrumental tool for transmitting information. Instead, human beings are "very much at the mercy of the particular language which has become the medium of expression for their society" (p. 162). The languages used in different cultural systems strongly influence how people think, know, feel, and do.

Whorf (1952, 1956; Carroll, 1956), a student of Sapir, makes a similar argument that is represented by the "principle of linguistic relativity." It contends that the structures of various languages reflect different cultural patterns and values, and, in turn, affect how people understand and respond to social phenomena. In developing these ideas further, Whorf (1952) explains that "a language is not merely a reproducing instrument for voicing ideas but rather is itself the shaper of ideas, the program and guide for the individual's mental activity, for his analysis of impressions, for his synthesis of his mental stock in trade" (p. 5). Vygotsky (1962) also recognizes the reciprocal relationship among language, culture, and thought. He declares, as "indisputable fact," that "thought development is determined by language . . . and the sociocultural experience of the child" (p. 51).

Moreover, the development of logic is affected by a person's socialized speech, and intellectual growth is contingent on the mastery of social means of thought, or language. According to Byers and Byers (1985), "The organization of the processes of human communication in any culture is the template for the organization of knowledge or information in that culture" (p. 28). This line of argument is applied specifically to different ethnic groups by theorists, researchers, and school practitioners from a wide variety of disciplinary perspectives, including social and developmental psychology, sociolinguistics, ethnography, and multiculturalism. For example, Ascher (1992) applied this reasoning to language influences on how mathematical relationships are viewed in general. Giamati and Weiland (1997) connected it to Navajo students' learning of mathematics, concluding that the performance difficulties they encounter are "a result of cultural influences on perceptions rather than a lack of ability" (p. 27). This happens because of the reciprocal interactions among language, culture, and perceptions. Consistently, when these scholars refer to "language" or "communication," they are talking more about discourse dynamics than structural forms of speaking and writing.

Thus, *languages and communication styles are systems of cultural notations and the means through which thoughts and ideas are expressively embodied.* Embedded within them are cultural values and ways of knowing that strongly influence how students engage with learning tasks and demonstrate mastery of them. The absence of shared communicative frames of reference, procedural protocols, rules of etiquette, and discourse systems makes it difficult for culturally diverse students and teachers to genuinely understand each other and for students to fully convey their intellectual abilities. Teachers who do not know or value these realities will not be able to fully access, facilitate, and assess most of what these students know and can do. Communication must be understood to be more than a linguistic system.

SYMBOL OF SIGNIFICANCE: AFRICAN AMERICAN EBONICS

The 1996–1997 attempt of the school board and the superintendent of the Oakland, California, school district to institute a policy of using Ebonics to better teach African American students caused a major controversy. It is a graphic example of the promise and peril of incorporating cultural communication into transformed educational practices for some ethnically diverse students. The term "Ebonics" derives from "ebony" and "phonics." It was coined in 1973 to refer to the linguistic and paralinguistic features of the communication styles of many African Americans (R. Williams, 1997). E. Smith (1998) suggests that it conveys their underlying psychological and cultural thought processes as well. The importance of the Ebonics debate is underscored by the fact that African American culture is grounded so heavily in an oral–aural tradition, which gives high priority to the development and delivery of communicative competence in the socialization of children (Asante, 1998; Harrison, 1972; Smitherman, 1977).

Supporters of using Ebonics in teaching reasoned that since language produces and structures thought, to better facilitate the thinking and learning capabilities of African American students, teachers need to know well their cultural ethos and communication styles. This can be a challenging task because socialization in different cultural systems produces different modes of speaking and thinking. It is complicated further by attitudes and assumptions to the effect that Ebonics is an undesirable form of communication for academic purposes, inappropriate for discourse in public arenas, and/or symptomatic of racial and intellectual inferiority (Haskins & Butts, 1973, p. 40).

The Controversy

The resolution adopted by the Oakland, California, board of education on Ebonics (on which the policy statement was based) stated, in part, that African American students possess a recognizable language system discrete from mainstream Standard English. It is grounded in their African-based origins, history, and culture, and its principles, laws, and structures should be applied in appreciating these students' inherent language skills, as well as helping them to master English-language skills. The policy also declared that no students, including African Americans, who come from backgrounds or environments where a language other than English is dominant should be dehumanized, stigmatized, discriminated against, or denied opportunities to learn because of the language they speak (Perry & Delpit, 1998).

The Linguistic Society of America passed a resolution supporting this position and commending the actions of the Oakland school board. Its decision was based on research evidence that children who speak a language or dialect different from the dominant one used by a society and its schools can be helped to learn the mainstream standard by pedagogical approaches that recognize the legitimacy of other varieties of a language (e.g., Cummins, 1989; E. Garcia, 1999). The society added that "from this perspective, the Oakland school board's decision to recognize the vernacular of African-American students in teaching them Standard English is linguistically and pedagogically sound" (quoted in Perry & Delpit, 1998, p. 161).

The good intentions of the policy on Ebonics in Oakland were quickly and effectively derailed by critics whose tactics involved distortions and distractions. The controversy pitted African Americans against European Americans, and African Americans against each other. Age, generational differences, social class, and degree of assimilation into mainstream society added other complexities (see, for example, Perry & Delpit, 1998; *Journal of Black Psychology*, 1997; *Black Scholar*, 1997). Research conducted by Koch and Gross (1997) indicating that African American youth and adults have reverse preferences toward Ebonics may explain why some high-profile African Americans, who were otherwise supporters of African American causes, opposed the Oakland proposal. When exposed to samples of Black English (BE) and Standard English (SE) speaking, the 12- to 16-years-olds who participated in the Koch and Ross study rated the BE speaker more likable (e.g., friendly, pleasant, considerate, open-minded, etc.) and competent (e.g., honest, intelligent, socially responsible, confident, creative, etc.) than the SE speaker. Other research (Doss & Gross, 1994) indicates that middle-class African American adults who are active participants in mainstream society are more positive toward Standard English.

This "positionality" may have caused Jesse Jackson and Maya Angelou to be among the most vocal opponents of the Oakland policy. During a news conference, Jackson declared the policy was an "unacceptable surrender" in the struggle to ensure quality education for African American students that bordered on disgrace. Jackson later retreated from his initial position. Still, Maulana Karenga (a longstanding advocate of Afrocentricism and professor of African American Studies at California State University, Long Beach) found Jesse Jackson's "intemperate remarks" about Ebonics unfortunate and ironic given that he is a frequent speaker of Ebonics himself (Boyd, 1997).

Media sensationalism quickly overshadowed the logic of a group of educational policy makers seeking ways to improve the academic achievement of African American students. After reviewing more than 2,500 articles, editorials, columns, and letters to the editor published in different newspapers during the first few weeks after the Ebonics resolution was released, Jackson (1997) concluded the media reactions were disdainful and demeaning. For the most part newspaper, magazine, television, and radio commentators found the idea of Ebonics imprudent, dubious, and even laughable; it quickly became the object of ridicule, condescending jokes, and mockery (Marlowe, 1997). These sentiments prevailed long after the proposal was announced in December 1996. They are illustrated by comments made in a *Washington Post* story (Sanchez, 1998) more than a year later. The author referred to the Oakland proposal as the "ebonics campaign," which provoked "immense outrage among many whites and blacks." In a tone of relief, but using pejorative language, the staff writer added, "the board has removed that incendiary term from its policies, its separatist rhetoric about a black language has subsided, and the notion of even seeking federal bilingual education funds for black students has been abandoned" (Sanchez, 1998, p. A10).

Attack on the Ebonics Proposal

Many of the individuals who spoke vehemently against Oakland's policy were woefully uninformed about the definition and characteristics of Ebonics. They often confused Ebonics with slang, "rap," illiteracy, and incorrect or "broken" English (Hoover, 1998; Smitherman, 1998a, 1998b, 1998c; Smitherman & Cunningham, 1997; R. Williams, 1997). Others assumed that the proponents of this policy were stereotyping African American students by implying that all of them speak Ebonics. They failed to recognize or acknowledge the variability that is inherent to all languages, including Ebonics. Individuals use their cultural language systems with varying degrees of frequency and fluency. This facility is influenced by many factors, including age, education, residence, social class, situation, and ethnic identity and affiliation. Of course, some African Americans are very adept in and comfortable with speaking Ebonics while others are not. Some speak it virtually all the time, others on rare occasions. Some speakers depend almost exclusively on Ebonics for communication, others speak Standard English as well as Ebonics. This variability of use obviously applied, to some degree, to the students in the Oakland schools.

Some critics misread or misinterpreted the Oakland policy to mean that Ebonics would be taught *instead* of Standard English and that it would be imposed on all African American students. The proponents of the reform were very clear about targeting those students who spoke Ebonics and were not performing very well academically. Students who did not speak Ebonics or who spoke Ebonics, but were academically successfully were not their primary concern. Others critics appeared to deliberately distort the wording of the policy to compromise its integrity. For example, rather than dealing with the overall merits of the proposal, these opponents focused on the unfortunate use of the phrase in the resolution that African American language is "genetically based." These critics seemed to be suggesting that claiming language is biologically determined was ludicrous and therefore made the credibility of the entire policy suspect.

Other opponents were incensed by the audacity of the Oakland board of education in elevating Ebonics to the status of a language and assuming it deserved comparable quality treatment in teaching children who speak it. Their opposition may have been prompted by negative values, perceptions, and stereotypes they attached to the communication styles of African Americans, especially those who are poor, minimally educated, inner-city or rural residents. For example, Education Secretary Richard Riley declared that elevating Black English to the status of a language was not the way to raise the achievement standards of students (Boyd, 1997). McWhorter (1997) and Hutchinson (1997) took similar positions. They viewed claims that Ebonics is a discrete language and teaching through it will improve the academic performance of African American students as highly contestable. McWhorter thought they amounted to wasting energy on illusions, and Hutchinson deemed these claims a "slavish bow to fringe Afrocentricism, political correctness, . . . [and] a flat-out fallacy" (p. 37). Still other critics distracted attention from the pedagogical intents of the policy statement to engage in theoretical debates about whether Ebonics is a language or a dialect.

Response to the Criticism

Many supporters of the Oakland policy in particular and using African American language as a tool of classroom instruction in general tried to counter the arguments of the critics. Some recalled a statement made several years earlier by James Baldwin that was applicable to the Oakland situation and to the challenge of culturally responsive teaching. Baldwin said the real issue in the debate over the use, status, or reality of Black English is not about language itself but about the role of language and the validity of African American students' experiences. He adds that "a child cannot be taught by anyone whose demand, essentially, is that the child repudiate his experience and all that gives him sustenance, and enter into a limbo in which he will no longer be black" (Baldwin 1997, p. 6).

Baldwin's arguments make sense in view of the relationship between language and culture discussed earlier. It is reiterated by Burnett, Burlew, and Hudson (1997) in their explanation that language is the quintessential cultural form through which people express group values and behavioral norms, and reveal themselves. Williams (1997) probed further by asking, "Why is it so overwhelmingly, even colorfully comprehensible in some contexts, particularly in sports and entertainment, yet deemed so utterly incapable of effective communication when it comes to finding a job as a construction worker?" (p. 7). This query can be easily extended to include, "Why can Ebonics be used in the mainstream marketplace to sell products and make money but not in the classroom to improve the achievement of African Americans students? Why is one arena of use considered creative while proposals for use in the other are thought by some to be catastrophic?"

The superintendent of the Oakland schools (Getridge, 1998) responded to the barrage of opposition to the Ebonics proposal by emphasizing the goal of building bridges between the language, culture, and communication of African American students and those of schools for the purpose of improving literacy achievement. She declared that something significantly different needed to be done in teaching African American students in Oakland because their achievement levels were "dismal," "mind-numbing and a cause for moral outrage" (p. 158). The Ebonics policy was an attempt to find a solution to these performance problems. Superintendent Getridge (1998) cautioned the critics that "the question is not whether or not we must act; rather we are confronted with questions about how best to act, and how quickly can we act? The answers to these questions are not simple and they are not comforting. . . . [They] challenge some of the most fundamental assumptions we have about the purpose and design of education" (p. 158). Central to this challenge is acknowledging that communication in classrooms between culturally diverse students and teachers is not just about the linguistic structure of speech acts. It is about how teaching and learning, thinking, knowing, and conveying meaning are exemplified in symbolic systems and discourse dynamics that are not necessarily mutually intelligible for teachers and students of color.

A simple but profound lesson was reinforced by this controversy; that is, recognizing the importance of language and culture to personal identity and honoring personal identity in educating students of color. Robert Williams (1997), the creator of the term "Ebonics," underscored this connection when he explained, "My language is me. It is an extension of my being, my essence. It is a reflection and badge of my culture. Criticism of my language is essentially a direct attack on my self-esteem and cultural identity" (p. 209). Geneva Smitherman (1998c), an African American sociolinguist, offered a similar argument in suggesting that African American communication styles are "the Black experience made manifest in verbal form" (p. 171). Dell Hymes (1985), a communication ethnographer, adds that educational reform is more likely to succeed for ethnically diverse students if educators accept their language systems. He says, "If one rejects a child's speech, one . . . probably is throwing away the chance of change. In accepting what one wishes to change . . . for what it is to the child, one probably is maximizing one's opportunity for change" (p. xxxiii).

Effects of Ebonics on Achievement

There is some research support for the claims made by the Oakland proposal that incorporating elements of cultural discourse into teaching would improve the academic performance of African American students. Some of this research is discussed here to illustrate the kind of evidence that is available. R. Williams (1997) reviewed three projects of the early 1970s that successfully used Ebonics to improve student achievement. One translated items on the Boehm Test of Basic Concepts into Ebonics and then administered it to K–2 students. The children scored significantly higher on the Ebonics version. In another project, a translated version of the Peabody Picture Vocabulary Test produced major improvements in the IQ scores of African Americans. The third study dealt with the Bridge reading program. It began instruction by using the students' own language skills and then gradually shifted to Standard English. After 4 months of this instruction, the Bridge students showed an increase of 6.2 months in their reading scores on the Iowa Test of Basic Skills.

M. Foster (1989) did an ethnographic analysis of the effects of an African American community college teacher's use of cultural communication styles on the achievement of her students. As the cultural nuances in her instructional discourse increased, so did the students' performance. Improvements occurred in attending behaviors, time-on-task, participation in classroom dialogue, concept mastery, recall of factual information with greater accuracy, and more enthusiasm in and confidence about learning. Similar findings have been reported for young children by Piestrup (1973), W. Hall, Reder, and Cole (1979), and Howard (1998). These researchers found that using African American communication styles with students in Headstart programs and in the early elementary grades improved their reading literacy skills. The communication features used in teaching included dramatic presentation styles, conversational and active participatory discourse, dialect, gestures and body movements, rapidly paced rhythmic speech, metaphorical imagery, and reading materials about African American culture and experiences. Improvements occurred in students' interest and task engagement, recall of more factual details from stories told, greater word recognition and accuracy of meanings, and higher scores on standardized reading test accuracy.

Even more impressive are the results Lee (1991, 1993) and Delain, Pearson, and Anderson (1985) obtained from using cultural discourse techniques prominent among African Americans to teach higher-order literary skills to high school and middle school students. Lee used *signifying* as the entrée to teaching high school seniors skills in critical thinking, textual analysis, and literary criticism. According to Smitherman (1977), *signifying* is the verbal art of insult in which speakers use humor, insinuation, and exaggeration to put down and talk about each other. Lee (1993) adds that it is a discourse heuristic for problem solving that requires analogical reasoning. Metaphor, irony, symbolism, and innuendo are critical tools of signifying. Sounding is similar to signifying in content, technique, and effect. Both Lee and Delain and associates hypothesized that using these discourse techniques in classroom instruction will help African American students who are familiar with them to improve their mastery of some literary skills commonly taught in schools.

Lee tested this hypothesis with 109 students, two-thirds of whom had performed in the lowest two quartiles of the local school district– and state-mandated standardized tests of reading achievement. She designed a 6-week experimental intervention that was implemented in four phases. First, the students in the experimental group analyzed samples of signifying dialogues to become consciously aware of their own personal and social communicative competence. Second, two articles written by recognized experts on the meaning and characteristics of signifying were analyzed. Third, students worked in small groups to create their own signifying dialogues. Fourth, the conceptual knowledge acquired about signifying was applied to tasks of literary criticism. The students had to interpret figurative language, ironic verbal constructions, and complex implied relationships in the literary texts of Zora Neale Hurston's *Their Eyes Were Watching God* and Alice Walker's *The Color Purple*. An inquiry mode of instruction was employed throughout the intervention to conduct close text analyses of the novels, allow small groups of students to talk about questions related to the readings, and allow students to write about their ideas and opinions related to the questions posed. Students in the control group received no specific instruction beyond what normally occurred in their literature classes.

At the end of the intervention, both groups had made improvements in their literary criticism skills, but those of the experimental group were substantially greater than the control group. Of the eight specific reading categories of literary analysis skills examined, the experimental group

made significant improvements in five (key detail, simple implied relationships, application, structural generalizations, complex implied relationships). The control group improved in three of these skills (key detail,
simple implied relationships, and structural generalizations). The greatest
difference occurred in the ability to infer different types of relationships
(stated, simple implied, and complex implied) embedded in literary texts.
Students in the experimental group who began the experience at the
lowest level of achievement made the greatest gains. Lee attributes this
to higher levels of congruency between their prior social knowledge of
and skills in signifying, and the metaphors and irony embedded in the
literary texts used in the study.

The quality of classroom discourse also differed by treatment groups.
Discussions in the experimental classes were more student-initiated, as
well as consistently focused on difficult, inferential questions and figurative or metaphorical aspects of the narrative text of the novels being
studied; in addition, the students routinely referenced literary texts explaining concepts, principles, and skills. In the control classes, discussions
were teacher-dominated, concentrated on students' personal opinions
about themes in the texts, and emphasized literal renditions of plots.
These students did not engage with the words, images, and ironies in the
literary texts, nor were they challenged to analyze their multiple meanings
(Lee, 1993).

Delain and associates (1985) used "sounding" as their target of analysis. The participants in their study were 157 seventh-graders (107 African
Americans and 50 European Americans) in two schools. Data were gath-
ered on the students' general verbal ability, figurative language comprehension, skill in sounding, and general skill in Black language. Nine
measures were used to collect these data. They included the Stanford
Diagnostic Reading Test; the Anderson–Freebody vocabulary test; a comprehension test of Standard English double-function words, such as idi-
oms, metaphors, and similes; five different assessments of sounding skills
(peer ratings, word completion and translation comprehension measures,
a recognition measure, and open-ended "come-back" responses to sounding prompts); and knowledge of double-function items used in Black
English only.

The results of the study revealed significant differences between the
abilities of the African and European American students on the various
experimental tasks. Only general language ability accounted for the White
students' figurative language comprehension. The figurative language
comprehension of the African American students was influenced by a
combination of general verbal ability, sounding, and Black-language skills.
In other words, their general language ability was significantly related

to figurative language comprehension, and their Black-language facility influenced their sounding abilities, which in turn affected their comprehension of figurative language. These findings led Delain and associates (1985) to recommend that since "skills acquired 'in the streets,' so to speak, do transfer to school settings, teachers need to develop a respect for, rather than a bias against, the use of such language" (p. 171). Teachers can recognize and even employ the home language of culturally diverse students while simultaneously teaching them mainstream Standard English.

CULTURALLY DIFFERENT DISCOURSE STRUCTURES

In conventional classroom discourse students are expected to assume what Kochman (1985) calls a *passive–receptive* posture. They are told to listen quietly while the teacher talks. Once the teacher finishes, then the students can respond in some prearranged, stylized way—by asking or answering questions; validating or approving what was said; or taking individual, teacher-regulated turns at talking. Individual students gain the right to participate in the conversation by permission of the teacher. The verbal discourse is accompanied by nonverbal attending behaviors and speech-delivery mechanisms that require maintaining eye contact with the speaker and using little or no physical movement. Thus, students are expected to be silent and look at teachers when they are talking and to wait to be acknowledged before they take their turn at talking. Once permission is granted, they should follow established rules of decorum, such as one person speaking at a time, being brief and to the point, and keeping emotional nuances to a minimum (Kochman, 1981; Philips, 1983).

These structural protocols governing discourse are expressed in other classroom practices as well. Among them are expecting students always to speak in complete sentences that include logical development of thought, precise information, appropriate vocabulary, and careful attention to grammatical features such as appropriate use of vocabulary and noun–verb tense agreement. Student participation in classroom interactions is often elicited by teachers asking questions that are directed to specific individuals and require a narrow range of information-giving, descriptive responses. It is important for individuals to distinguish themselves in the conversations, for student responses to be restricted to only the specific demands of questions asked, and for the role of speaker and audience to be clearly separated.

In contrast to the passive–receptive character of conventional classroom discourse, some ethnic groups have communication styles that

Kochman (1985) describes as *participatory–interactive*. Speakers expect listeners to engage them actively through vocalized, motion, and movement responses *as they are speaking*. Speakers and listeners are action-provoking partners in the construction of the discourse. These communicative styles have been observed among African Americans, Latinos, and Native Hawaiians. As is the case with other cultural behaviors, they are likely to be more pronounced among individuals who strongly identify and affiliate with their ethnic groups and cultural heritages. For example, low-income and minimally educated members of ethnic groups are likely to manifest group cultural behaviors more thoroughly than those who are middle class and educated. This is so because they have fewer opportunities to interact with people different from themselves and to be affected by the cultural exchanges and adaptations that result from the intermingling of a wide variety of people from diverse ethnic groups and varied experiential backgrounds.

ETHNIC VARIATIONS IN COMMUNICATION STYLES

Among African Americans the participatory–interactive style of communicating is sometimes referred to as *call–response* (Asante, 1998; Baber, 1987; Kochman, 1972, 1981, 1985; Smitherman, 1977). It involves listeners giving encouragement, commentary, compliments, and even criticism to speakers *as they are talking*. The speaker's responsibility is to issue the "calls" (making statements), and the listeners' obligation is to respond in some expressive, and often auditory, way (e.g., smiling, vocalizing, looking about, moving around, "amen-ing") (Dandy, 1991; Smitherman, 1977). When a speaker says something that triggers a response in them (whether positive or negative; affective or cognitive), African American listeners are likely to "talk back." This may involve a vocal or motion response, or both, sent directly to the speaker or shared with neighbors in the audience. Longstreet (1978) and Shade (1994) describe the practice as "breaking in and talking over." This mechanism is used to signal speakers that their purposes have been accomplished or that it is time to change the direction or leadership of the conversation. Either way, there is no need for the speaker to pursue the particular discourse topic or technique any further.

African Americans "gain the floor" or get participatory entry into conversations through personal assertiveness, the strength of the impulse to be involved, and the persuasive power of the point they wish to make, rather than waiting for an "authority" to grant permission. They tend to invest their participation with personality power, actions, and emotions.

Consequently, African Americans are often described as verbal performers whose speech behaviors are fueled by personal advocacy, emotionalism, fluidity, and creative variety (Abrahams, 1970; Baber, 1987). These
communication facilities have been attributed to the oral–aural nature of
African American cultural and communal value orientations (Pasteur &
Toldson, 1982; Smitherman, 1977). Many teachers view them negatively,
as "rude," "inconsiderate," "disruptive," and "speaking out of turn," and
they penalize students for them.

Native Hawaiian students who maintain their traditional cultural
practices use a participatory–interactive communicative style similar to
the call–response of African Americans. Called "talk-story" or "co-narration," it involves several students working collaboratively, or talking together, to create an idea, tell a story, or complete a learning task (Au,
1980a, 1993; Au & Kawakami, 1985, 1991, 1994; Au & Mason, 1981; Boggs
et al., 1985). After observing these behaviors among elementary students,
Au (1993) concluded that "what seems important to Hawaiian children
in talk story is not individual . . . but group performance in speaking" (p.
114). These communication preferences are consistent with the importance
Native Hawaiian culture places on individuals' contributing to the well-
being of family and friends instead of working only for their own betterment (Gallimore, Boggs, & Jordan, 1974; Tharp & Gallimore, 1988).

A communicative practice that has some of the same traits of call–response and talk-story has been observed among European American females. Tannen (1990) calls it "cooperative overlapping" and describes it
as women "talking along with speakers to show participation and support" (p. 208). It occurs most often in situations where talk is casual and
friendly. This *rapport-talk* is used to create community. It is complemented
by other traditional women's ways of communicating, such as the following:

- Being "audience" more often than "speaker" in that they are recipients
  of information provided by males
- Deemphasizing expertise and the competitiveness it generates
- Focusing on individuals in establishing friendships, networks, intimacy,
  and relationships more than exhibiting power, accomplishment, or con-
  trol
- Negotiating closeness in order to give and receive confirmation, sup-
  port, and consensus
- Avoiding conflict and confrontation (Tannen, 1990; Belensky, Clinchy,
  Goldberger, & Tarule, 1986; Klein, 1982; Maltz & Borker, 1983)

While these habits of "communal communication and interaction"
are normal to the users, they can be problematic to classroom teachers.
On first encounter, they may be perceived as "indistinguishable noise

and chaos" or unwholesome dependency. Even after the shock of the initial encounter passes, teachers may still consider these ways of communicating socially deviant, not conducive to constructive intellectual engagement, rude, and insulting. They see them as obstructing individual initiative and preempting the right of each student to have a fair chance to participate in instructional discourse. These assessments can prompt attempts to rid students of the habits and replace them with the rules of individualistic, passive–receptive, and controlling communication styles that predominate in classrooms. Teachers may not realize that by doing this they could be causing irreversible damage to students' abilities or inclinations to engage fully in the instructional process. Hymes (1985) made this point when he suggested that rejecting ethnically different students' communication styles may be perceived by them as rejection of their personhood. Whether intentional or not, casting these kinds of aspersions on the identity and personal worth of students of color does not bode well for their academic achievement.

Problem Solving and Task Engagement

Many African American, Latino, Native American, and Asian American students use styles of inquiry and responding different from those employed most often in classrooms. The most common practice among teachers is to ask convergent (single-answer) questions and use deductive approaches to solving problems. Emphasis is given to details, to building the whole from parts, to moving from the specific to the general. Discourse tends to be didactic, involving one student with the teacher at a time (Goodlad, 1984). In comparison, students of color who are strongly affiliated with their traditional cultures tend to be more inductive, interactive, and communal in task performance. The preference for inductive problem solving is expressed as reasoning from the whole to parts, from the general to the specific. The focus is on the "big picture," the pattern, the principle (Boggs et al., 1985; Philips, 1983; Ramírez & Castañeda, 1974; Shade, 1989).

Although these general patterns of task engagement prevail across ethnic groups, variations do exist. Some teachers use inductive modes of teaching, and some students within each ethnic group of color learn deductively. Many Asian American students seem to prefer questions that require specific answers but are proposed to the class as a whole. While many Latino students may be inclined toward learning in group contexts, specific individuals may find these settings distracting and obstructive to their task mastery.

In traditional African Americans and Latino cultures, problem solving is highly contextual. One significant feature of this contextuality is creating a "stage" or "setting" prior to the performance of a task. The stage setting is invariably social in nature. It involves establishing personal connections with others who will participate as a prelude to addressing the task. In making these connections, individuals are readying themselves for "work" by cultivating a social context. They are, in effect, activating their cultural socialization that an individual functions better within the context of a group. Without the group as an anchor, referent, and catalyst, the individual is set adrift, having to function alone.

These cultural inclinations may be operating when Latino adults begin their task interactions with colleagues by inquiring about the families of the other participants and their own personal well-being or when African American speakers inform the audience about their present psychoemotional disposition and declare the ideology, values, and assumptions underlying the positions they will be taking in the presentation (i.e., "where they are coming from"). This "preambling" is a way for the speakers to prime the audience and themselves for the subsequent performance. Students of color in classrooms may be setting the stage for their engagement with learning tasks (e.g., writing an essay, doing seatwork, taking a test) when they seem to be spending unnecessary time arranging their tests, sharpening pencils, shifting their body postures (stretching, flexing their hands, arms, and legs, etc.), or socializing with peers rather than attending to the assigned task. "Preparation before performance" for these students serves a similar purpose in learning as a theater performer doing yoga exercises before taking the stage. Both are techniques the "actors" use to focus, to get themselves in the mood and mode to perform.

For those Asian Americans who prefer to learn within the context of groups, it is accomplished through a process of *collaborative and negotiated problem solving*. Regardless of how minor or significant an issue is, they seek out opinions and proposed solutions from all members of the constituted group. Each individual's ideas are presented and critiqued. Their merits are weighed against the ones suggested by every other member of the group. Discussions are animated and expansive so that all parties can participate and understand the various elements of the negotiations. Eventually, a solution is reached that is a compromise of several possibilities. Then more discussions follow to ensue that everyone is in agreement with the solution and understands who is responsible for what aspects of its implementation. These discussions proceed in a context of congeniality and *consensus building* among the many, not with animosity, domination, and the imposition of the will of a few.

A compelling illustration of the positive effects of this process on student achievement occurred in Treisman's (1985; Fullilove & Treisman, 1990) Mathematics Workshop Program at the University of California, Berkeley. He observed the study habits of Chinese Americans to determine why they performed so well in high-level mathematics classes and to see if he could use their model with Latinos and African Americans. He found what others have observed more informally—the Chinese American students always studied in groups, and they routinely explained to each other their understanding of the problems and how they arrived at solutions to them. Treisman attributed their high achievement to the time they devoted to studying and to talking through the solution processes with peers. When he simulated this process with African Americans and Latinos, their achievement improved radically. Treisman was convinced that "group study" made the difference. Given other evidence that compatibility between cultural habits and teaching–learning styles improves student performance, this is probably what occurred. Communal problem solving and the communicative impulse were evoked, thus producing the desired results.

These are powerful but challenging pedagogical lessons for all educators to learn and emulate in teaching students of color. Collective and situated performance styles require a distribution of resources (timing, collective efforts, procedures, attitudes) that can collide with school norms; for instance, much of how student achievement is assessed occurs in tightly scheduled arrangements, which do not accommodate stage setting or collective performance. Students of color have to learn different styles of performing, as well as the substantive content to demonstrate their achievement. This places them in potential double jeopardy—that is, failing at the level of both procedure and substance. Pedagogical reform must be cognizant of these dual needs and attend simultaneously to the content of learning and the processes for demonstrating mastery. It also must be bidirectional—that is, changing instructional practices to make them more culturally responsive to ethnic and cultural diversity, while teaching students of color how to better negotiate mainstream educational structures.

Organizing Ideas in Discourse

In addition to mode, the actual process of discourse engagement is influenced by culture and, in turn, influences the performance of students in schools. Several elements of the dynamics of discourse are discussed here to illustrate this point. They are how ideas are organized, taking positions, conveying imagery and affect through language, and gender variations in conversational styles. How ideas and thoughts are organized in written and spoken expression can be very problematic to student achievement. Two techniques are commonly identified—*topic-centered* and *topic-associative* or *topic-chaining* techniques. European Americans seem to prefer the first, while Latinos, African Americans, Native Americans, and Native Hawaiians (Au, 1993; Heath, 1983) are inclined toward the second.

In *topic-centered* discourse speakers focus on one issue at a time; arrange facts and ideas in logical, linear order; and make explicit relationships between facts and ideas. In this process, cognitive processing moves deductively from discrete parts to a cumulative whole with a discernible closure. Quality is determined by clarity of descriptive details, absence of unnecessary or flowery elaboration, and how well explanations remain focused on the essential features of the issue being analyzed. The structure, content, and delivery of this discourse style closely parallel the expository, descriptive writing, and speaking commonly used in schools. A classic example of topic-centered discourse is journalistic writing, which concentrates on giving information about who, what, when, where, why, and how as quickly as possible. Its purpose is to convey information and to keep this separate from other speech functions, such as persuasion, commentary, and critique. Another illustration is the thinking and writing associated with empirical inquiry, or critical problem solving. Again, there is a hierarchical progression in the communication sequence, beginning with identifying the problem, collecting data, identifying alternative solutions and related consequences, and selecting and defending a solution. There is a clear attempt to separate facts from opinions, information from emotions.

A *topic-associative style* of talking and writing is episodic, anecdotal, thematic, and integrative. More than one issue is addressed at once. Related explanations unfold in overlapping, intersecting loops, with one emerging out of and building on others. Relationships among segments of the discourse are assumed or inferred rather than explicitly established (Cazden, 1988; Lee & Slaughter-Defoe, 1995). Thinking and speaking appear to be circular and seamless rather than linear and clearly demarcated. For one who is unfamiliar with it, this communication style sounds rambling, disjointed, and as if the speaker never ends a thought before going on to something else.

Goodwin (1990) observed topic-chaining discourse at work in a mixed-aged (4- to 14-year-olds) group of African Americans in a Philadelphia neighborhood as they told stories, shared gossip, settled arguments, and negotiated relationships. She noted the ease and finesse with which a child could switch from a contested verbal exchange to an engaging story and dramatically reshape dyadic interactions into multiparty ones. Using a single utterance, the children could evoke a broad history of events, a complex web of identities and relationships that all participants understood without having elaborate details on any of the separate segments. The talk-story discourse style among Native Hawaiian operates in a similar fashion, which explains why Au (1993) characterizes it as a "joint performance, or the cooperative production of responses by two or more speakers" (p. 113).

Two other commonplace examples are indicative of a topic-chaining or associative discourse style. One is used by many African Americans who literally try to attach or connect the sentences in a paragraph to each other through the prolific use of conjunctive words and phrases; for example, frequently beginning sentences with "consequently," "therefore," "however," "thus," "moreover," "additionally," and "likewise." These sentences are in close proximity to each other—sometimes as often as four of every five or six.

The second example illuminates the storytelling aspect of topic-chaining discourse. African Americans (Kochman, 1981, 1985; Smitherman, 1977) and Native Hawaiians (Boggs, 1985) have been described as not responding directly to questions asked. Instead, they give narratives, or tell stories. This involves setting up and describing a series of events (and the participants) loosely connected to the questions asked. It is as if ideas and thoughts, like individuals, do not function or find meaning in isolation from context. A host of other actors and events are evoked to assist in constructing the "stage" upon which the individuals eventually interject their own performance (i.e., answer the question). This narrative-response style is also signaled by the attention given to "introductions" and preludes in writing. They are extensive enough to prompt such comments from teachers as, "Get to the point?" or "Is this relevant?" or "More focus needed" or "Too much extraneous stuff" or "Stick to the topic." The students simply think that these preludes are necessary to setting the stage for the substantive elements of the discourse.

Storytelling as Topic-Chaining Discourse

Speaking about the purposes and pervasiveness of storytelling among African Americans, Smitherman (1977) surmises that they allow many different things to be accomplished at once. These include relating information, persuading others to support the speaker's point of view, networking, countering opposition, exercising power, and demonstrating one's own verbal aestheticism. She elaborates further:

> An ordinary inquiry [to African American cultural speakers] is likely to elicit an extended narrative response where the abstract point or general message will be couched in concrete story form. The reporting of events is never simply objectively reported, but dramatically acted out and narrated. The Black English speaker thus simultaneously conveys the facts and his or her

personal sociopsychological perspective on the facts. . . . This meandering away from the "point" takes the listener on episodic journeys and over tributary rhetorical routes, but like the flow of nature's rivers and streams, it all eventually leads back to the source. Though highly applauded by blacks, this narrative linguistic style is exasperating to whites who wish you'd be direct and hurry up and get to the point. (pp. 161, 148)

It takes African American topic-chaining speakers a while to get to the point—to orchestrate the cast of contributors to the action. The less time they have to develop their storylines, the more difficult it is for them to get to the substantive heart of the matter. Frequently in schools, the time allocated to learning experiences lapses while African Americans are still setting up the backdrop for "the drama"—their expected task performance—and they never get to demonstrate what they know or can do on the proposed academic task.

Posed to an African American student who routinely uses a topic-chaining discourse style, a simple, apparently straightforward question such as, "What did you do during summer vacation?" might prompt a response such as the following:

Sometimes, especially on holidays, you know, like July 4, or maybe when a friend was celebrating a birthday, we go to the amusement park. It's a long ways from where I live. And, that is always a big thing, because we have to get together and form car caravans. Jamie and Kelly are the best drivers, but I preferred to ride with Aisha because her dad's van is loaded, and we be just riding along, chilling, and listening to tapes and stuff. Going to the amusement park was a kick 'cause we had to drive a long way, and when we got there people would stare at us like we were weird or something. And we would just stare right back at them. All but Dion. He would start to act crazy, saying things like, "What you lookin' at me for? I ain't no animal in no zoo. I got as much right to be here as you do." You see, Dion gets hyped real quick about this racist thing. And we be telling him, "Man, cool it. Don't start no stuff. We too far from home for that." Then, we just go on into the park and have us a good time. We try to get all the rides before everything closes down for the night. Then, there's the trip home. Everybody be tired but happy. We do this three or four times in the summer. Different people go each time. But, you know something—we always run into some kind of funny stuff, like people expecting us to make trouble. Why is that so? All we doing is out for a good time. Dion, of course, would say it's a racist thing.

The narrator does eventually answer the question, but it is embedded in a lot of other details. In fact, there are stories within stories within stories (e.g., celebration rituals, friendships, drivers, the drive, racism, risk taking, activities at the amusement park, similarities and differences, continuity and change, etc.). These elaborate details are needed to convey the full meaning of the narrator's answer to the initial question. But to culturally uninitiated listeners or readers (such as many classroom teachers), the account sounds like rambling and unnecessarily convoluted information, or Smitherman's (1977) notion of "belabored verbosity" (p. 161).

Teachers seeking to improve the academic performance of students of color who use topic-associative discourse styles need to incorporate a storytelling motif into their instructional behaviors. This can be done without losing any of the substantive quality of academic discourses. Gee (1989) believes topic-associative talking is inherently more complex, creative, literary, and enriching than topic-centered speech. The assertions are verified by the success of the Kamehameha Early Elementary Program, which produced remarkable improvement in the literacy achievement of Native Hawaiian students by employing their cultural and communication styles in classroom instruction. Boggs (1985) found the performance of Native Hawaiian students on the reading readiness tests correlated positively with narrative abilities. The children who told longer narratives more correctly identified the picture prompts than those who responded to individually directed questions from adults.

Yet topic-associative discourse is troubling to many conventional teachers. Michaels and Cazden's (1986) research explains why. The European American teachers who participated in their study found this discourse style difficult to understand and placed little value on it. African American teachers gave equal positive value to topic-centered and topic-associative discourse. We should not assume that this will always be the case. Some African American teachers are as troubled by topic-chaining discourse among students as teachers from other ethnic groups. The ethnicity of teachers is not the most compelling factor in culturally responsive teaching for ethnically diverse students. Rather, it is teachers' knowledge base and positive attitudes about cultural diversity, as well as their ability to teach ethnically diverse students, contributions, experiences, and perspectives effectively.

Taking Positions and Presenting Self

In addition to significant difference in the *organization* of thinking, writing, and talking, many ethnically diverse students *relate* differently to the materials, issues, and topic discussed or analyzed. Most of the information available on these patterns deals with African and European Americans. Not much research has been done on the discourse dynamics of Latinos and Native Americans. Deyhle and Swisher (1997) concluded their histori-cal review of research conducted on Native Americans with a strong conviction that there are fundamental and significant linkages among culture, communication, and cognition that should help shape classroom instruction for ethnically diverse students. But they do not provide any descriptions of the discourse dynamics of various Native American groups. Fox (1994) examined the thinking, writing, and speaking behav-iors of international students from different countries in Africa, Asia, Latin America, and the Middle East studying in U. S. colleges and universi-ties. She found that their cultural traditions valued indirect and holistic communication, wisdom of the past, and the importance of the group. Their cultural socialization profoundly affects how these students interact with professors and classmates, reading materials, problem solving, and writing assignments. How they write is especially important to their academic performance because, according to Fox (1994), "writing touches the heart of a student's identity, drawing its voice and strength and meaning from the way the student understands the world" (p. xiii).

Personalizing or Objectifying Communications

Kochman (1972, 1981, 1985), Dandy (1991), and Smitherman (1977) point out that African Americans (especially those most strongly affiliated with their ethnic identity and cultural heritage) tend to take positions of advo-cacy and express personal points of view in discussions. Facts, opinions, emotions, and reason are combined in presenting one's case. The worth of a particular line of reasoning is established by challenging the validity of oppositional ideas and by the level of personal ownership of the individ-uals making the presentations. Declaring one's personal position on issues, and demanding the same of others, is also a way of recognizing "the person" as a valid data source (Kochman, 1981). Publication is not enough to certify the authority of ideas and explanations, or the expertise of the people who author them. They must stand the test of critical scrutiny and the depth of personal endorsement.

Consequently, Kochman (1981) proposes that African Americans are more likely to challenge authority and expertise than students from other ethnic groups. He suggests the following reason for this:

> Blacks . . . consider debate to be as much a contest between individuals as a test of opposing ideas. Because it is a contest, attention is also paid to perfor-

mance, for winning the contest requires that one outperform one's opponents: outthink, outtalk, and outstyle. It means being concerned with art as well as argument. . . . [B]lacks consider it essential for individuals to have personal positions on issues and assume full responsibility for arguing their validity. Otherwise, they feel that individuals would not care enough about truth or their own ideas to want to struggle for them. And without such struggle, the truth value of ideas cannot be ascertained. (pp. 24–25)

According to Kochman (1981), the discourse dynamics of European Americans are almost the opposite of African Americans. He says they relate to issues and materials as spokespersons, not advocates, and consider the truth or merits of an idea to be intrinsic, especially if the person presenting it has been certified as an authority or expert. How deeply individuals personally care about the idea is irrelevant. Their responsibility is to present the facts as accurately as possible. They believe that emotions interfere with one's capacity to reason and quality of reasoning. Thus, European Americans try to avoid or minimize opposition in dialogue (especially when members of ethnic-minority groups are involved) because they assume it will be confrontational, divisive, and lead to intransigence or the further entrenchment of opposing viewpoints. They aim to control impulse and emotions, to be open-minded and flexible, and to engage a multiplicity of ideas. Since no person is privy to all the answers, the best way to cull the variety of possibilities is to ensure congeniality, not confrontation, in conversation. As a result of these beliefs and desires, the European American style of intellectual and discourse engagement "weakens or eliminates those aspects of character or posture that they believe keep people's minds closed and make them otherwise unyielding" (Kochman, 1981, p. 20).

"Playing with and on" Words

African American cultural discourse uses repetition for emphasis and to create a cadence in speech delivery that approximates other aspects of cultural expressiveness such as dramatic flair, powerful imagery, persuasive effect, and polyrhythmic patterns (Baber, 1987; Kochman, 1981; Smitherman, 1977). Some individuals are very adept at "playing on" and "playing with" words, thereby creating a "polyrhythmic character" to their speaking. It is conveyed through the use of nonparallel structures, juxtaposition of complementary opposites, inclusion of a multiplicity of "voices," manipulation of word meanings, poetic tonality, creative use of word patterns, and an overall playfulness in language usage. Although decontextualized, this statement written by a graduate student illustrate some

of these tendencies: "The use of culturally consistent communicative competencies entails teachers being able to recognize the multitude of distinct
methods of communication that African American students bring to the
classroom." Another example of these discourse habits is the frequent
use of verb pairs. Following are some samples selected from the writings
of students:

- a number of public issues to be explored and represented . . .
- numerous factors have impacted and influenced . . .
- make an attempt to analyze and interpret . . .
- no model is available to interpret and clarify . . .
- many ways of explaining and understanding . . .
- a framework that will enable and facilitate . . .
- validity was verified and confirmed . . .
- he will describe and give account . . .

Two other examples are helpful in illustrating the dramatic flair and
poetic flavor of playing with words that characterize African American
cultural discourse. One comes from Smart-Grosvenor (1982), who describes African American cultural communication as "a metaphorical con-
figuration of verbal nouns, exaggerated adjectives, and double descrip-
tives" (p. 138). She adds (and in the process demonstrates that which she
explains) that "ours is an exciting, practical, elegant, dramatic, ironic,
mysterious, surrealistic, sanctified, outrageous and creative form of verbal
expression. It's a treasure trove of vitality, profundity, rhythm—and, yes,
style" (p. 138). Smitherman (1972) provides a second example of African
American discourse style and aestheticism. She writes:

> The power of the word lies in it enabling us to translate vague feelings and
> fleeting experiences into forms that give unity, coherence, and expression
> to the inexpressible. The process of composing becomes a mechanism for
> discovery wherein we may generate illuminating revelations about a particu-
> lar idea or event. (p. 91)

Ambivalence and Distancing in Communication

Classroom experiences and personal conversations with Asian international and Asian American college students and professional colleagues
reveal some recurrent communication features. These individuals tend
not to declare either definitive advocacy or adversarial positions in either
oral or written discourse. They take moderate stances, seek out compro-

mise positions, and look for ways to accommodate opposites. They are rather hesitant to analyze and critique but will provide factually rich descriptions of issues and events. They also use a great deal of "hedges" and conciliatory markers in conversations; that is, "starts and stops," affilitative words, and apologetic nuances interspersed in speech, such as "I'm not sure," "maybe . . . ," "I don't know, but . . . ," "I may be wrong, but . . . " These behaviors give the appearance of tentative, unfinished thinking, even though the individuals using them are very intellectually capable and thoroughly prepared academically. And many Asian and Asian American students are virtually silent in classroom discussions.

I have observed Asian and Asian American students frequently interjecting "ritualistic laughter" into conversations with me about their academic performance. This happens in instructional and advising situations in which the students are having difficulty understanding a learning task that is being explained by the teacher. Rather than reveal the full extent of their confusion, or lack of understanding, students will interject laughter into the conversations. It functions to diffuse the intensity of their confusion and give the impression that the problem is not as serious as it really is. Teachers who are unaware of what is going on may interpret these behaviors to mean the students are not taking their feedback or advice seriously. Or they may assume that the students understand the issue so completely that they have reached a point in their intellectual processing where they can relax and break the mental focus (signaled by laughter). When queried about this practice, students invariably say "it's cultural" and often add an explanation for it that invokes some rule of social etiquette or interpersonal interaction that is taught in their ethnic communities. Interestingly, Japanese, Chinese, Korean, Taiwanese, and Cambodians offer similar explanations about the motivation behind and meaning of this shared behavior. These students explain that "ritualized laughter" is a means of maintaining harmonious relationships and avoiding challenging the authority or disrespecting the status of the teacher.

These communication behaviors among students of Asian origin are consistent with those reported by Fox (1994). Hers were gleaned from observations, interviews, and working with students from non-Western cultures and countries (Fox refers to them as "world majority students") on their analytical writing skills in basic writing courses at the Center for International Education at the University of Massachusetts. Data were collected over 3 years. Sixteen graduate students from several different disciplines participated in the formal interviews. They represented twelve countries: Korea, Japan, the People's Republic of China, Nepal, Indonesia, Brazil, India, Chile, Sri Lanka, Côte d'Ivoire, Somalia, and Cape Verde. Faculty members who worked closely with these students were also interviewed. Additional information was derived from informal conversations and interactions with other students; analyzing writing samples; the teacher's notes about how she and the students worked through writing difficulties; and students' explanations about what they were trying to say in their writing, why assignments were misunderstood, and connections among language, culture, and writing.

Several common writing habits among these students from different countries emerged that conflict with formal writing styles of academe, known variously as academic argument, analytical or critical writing, and scholarly discourse (Fox, 1994). The characteristics and concerns included:

- Much background information and imprecise commentary
- Exaggeration for effect
- Prolific use of transitional markers, such as "moreover," "nevertheless," and "here again"
- Preference for contemplative instead of action words
- Much meandering around and digressions from the primary topic of discussion
- Emphasis on surrounding context rather than the subject itself
- Being suggestive and trying to convey feelings instead of being direct and concise and providing proof or specific illustrations, as is the expectation of academic writing in the United States
- Tendency to communicate through subtle implications
- Great detail and conversational tonality
- Elaborate and lengthy introductions
- Reticence to speak out, to declare personal positions, and to make one's own ideas prominent in writing

Although these communication tendencies were shared by all the students Fox (1994) studied, how they were expressed in actual behaviors varied widely. Culturally different meanings of "conversational tone" illustrates this point. Fox notes:

> In Spanish or Portuguese . . . speakers and writers may be verbose, rambling, digressive, holistic, full of factual details, full of feeling, sometimes repetitious, sometimes contradictory, without much concern for literal meanings. In many Asian and African languages and cultures, metaphor, euphemism, innuendo, hints, insinuation, and all sorts of subtle nonverbal strategies—even silence— are used both to spare the listeners possible embarrassment or rejection, and to convey meanings that they are expected to grasp. (p. 22)

These descriptions of Asian American and non-Western student discourse are based on observations and conversations with a small number of people, in college classes and professional settings. How widespread they are across other educational settings, ethnic groups, generations of immigrants, and social circumstances is yet to be determined. Much more description and substantiation of these communicative inclinations are needed.

The explanations of Asian students that their discourse styles are cultural is elaborated by S. Chan (1991), Kitano and Daniels (1995), and Nakanishi (1994). They point to traditional values and socialization that emphasize collectivism, saving face, maintaining harmony, filial piety, interdependence, modesty in self-presentation, and restraint in taking oppositional points of view. Leung (1998) suggests some ways these values translate to behavior in learning situations, which underscore the observations made by Fox. Students socialized this way are less likely to express individual thoughts, broadcast their individual accomplishments, and challenge or disagree with people in positions of authority, especially in public arenas. These interpretations echo the connections between Asian American culture and communicative styles provided by B. Kim (1978). She suggests that one of their major functions is to promote social harmony and build community. Consequently, many Asian American students may avoid confrontations as well as the expression of negative feelings or opinions in classroom discourse.

GENDER VARIATIONS IN DISCOURSE STYLES

Most of the detailed information on gender variations in classroom communication involves European Americans. Some inferences can be made about probable gender discourse styles among African, Latinos, Native, and Asian Americans from their cultural values and gender socialization, since culture and communication are closely interrelated.

Females Communicate Differently from Males

Lakoff (1975) was among the first to suggest that different lexical, syntactical, pragmatic, and discourse features existed for females and males. She identified nine speech traits prolific among females that are summarized by L. Crawford (1993) as specialized vocabulary for homemaking and caregiving, mild forms of expletives, adjectives that convey emotional reactions but no substantive information, tag comments that are midway between questions and statements, exaggerated expressiveness, superpolite forms, hedges or qualifiers, hypercorrect grammar, and little use of humor.

Other research indicates that European American females use more affilitative, accommodative, and socially bonding language mechanisms, while males are more directive, managing, controlling, task-focused, and action-oriented in their discourse styles. Girls speak more politely and tentatively, use less forceful words, are less confrontational, and are less intrusive when they enter into conversations. By comparison, boys inter-rupt more; use more commands, threats, and boast of authority; and give information more often (Austin, Salehi, & Leffler, 1987; M. Crawford, 1995; Grossman & Grossman, 1994; Hoyenga & Hoyenga, 1979; Maccoby, 1988; Simkins-Bullock & Wildman, 1991; Tannen, 1994). Because of these gender patterns, Maccoby (1988) concludes that "speech serves more ego-istic functions among boys and more socially binding functions among girls" (p. 758).

These general trends were substantiated by Johnstone (1993) in a study of spontaneous conversational storytelling of men and women among friends. The women's stories tended to be about groups of people (women and men) engaged in supportive relationships and the impor-tance of community building. The men's stories were more about con-quests (physical, social, nature) in which individuals acted alone. Invari-ably, the characters were nameless men who did little talking but engaged in some kind of physical action. More details were given about places, times, and things than about people. Based on these findings, Johnstone suggests that women are empowered through cooperation, interdepen-dence, collaboration, and community. For men, power comes from indi-viduals "conquering" and acting in opposition to others.

Research by Gray-Schlegel and Gray-Schlegel (1995/1996) on the cre-ative writing of third- and sixth-grade students produced similar results. They examined 170 creative writing samples of 87 students to determine if differences existed in how control, outcomes, relationships, and violence were used. Clear gender patterns emerged. Both boys and girls placed male characters in active roles more often than females, but this tendency increased with age only for the males. Females were more optimistic about the fate of their characters, while males were inclined to be cynical. Boys usually had their protagonists acting alone, while girls had them acting in conjunction with others. Regardless of age or the gender of the story character, boys included more crime and violence in their narrative than girls.

Gender Communication Patterns Established Early in Life

These kind of gender-related discourse patterns are established well be-fore third grade, as research by Nicolopoulou, Scales, and Weintraub (1994) revealed. They examined the symbolic imagination of 4-year-olds as expressed in the kinds of stories they told. The girls' stories included more order and social realism. These were conveyed through the use of coherent plots with stable characters, continuous plot lines, and social and familial relationships as the primary topics of and contexts for problem solving. Their stories emphasized cyclical patterns of everyday domestic life, along with romantic and fairytale images of kings and queens, princesses and princes. They were carefully constructed, centered, and coherent, with elaborate character and theme development, and were invariably directed toward harmonious conflict resolution. Whenever threatening or disruptive situations occurred, the girls were careful to reestablish order before concluding their stories. The boys' stories contained much disorder and a picaresque, surrealistic aesthetic style. These traits were apparent in the absence of stable, clearly defined characters, relationships, and plots; large, powerful, and frightening characters; violence, disruption, and conflict; and a series of loosely associated dramatic images, actions, and events. The boys were not concerned with resolving conflicts before their stories ended. Instead, their plots were driven by action, novelty, excess, defiance, destruction, and often escalating and startling imagery.

In summarizing differences between how boys and girls construct stories, Nicolopoulou and associates (1994) made some revealing observations that should inform instructional practices. They noted that the stories produced by girls focused on "creating, maintaining, and elaborating structure." In comparison, the stories boys told emphasized "action and excitement" and involved a restless energy that is often difficult for them to manage (p. 110). Furthermore, the boys and girls dealt with danger, disorder, and conflict very differently. The girls' strategy was *implicit avoidance* while the boys' techniques was *direct confrontation*.

Another fascinating verification of theorized gender differences in communication is provided by Otnes, Kim, and Kim (1994). They analyzed 344 letters written to Santa Claus (165 from boys and 179 from girls). Although the age of the authors was not specified, they were probably 8 years old or younger, since children stop believing in Santa Claus at about this time. The content of the letters was analyzed to determine the use of six kinds of semantic units, or meaning phrases: (1) polite or socially accepted forms of ingratiation, (2) context-oriented references, (3) direct requests, (4) requests accompanied by qualifiers, (5) affectionate appeals, and (6) altruistic requests of gifts for someone other than self. For the most part, results of the study confirmed the hypothesized expectations. Girls wrote longer letters, made more specific references to Christmas, were more polite, used more indirect requests, and included more expressions of affection. By comparison, boys made more direct requests. There were no differences between boys and girls in the number of toys requested or the altruistic appeals made. Findings such as these provide evidence about the extent and persistence of patterns of culturally socialized communicative behaviors.

Early gender patterns of communication may transfer to other kinds of social and educational interactions. They also can entrench disadvantages that will have long-term negative effects on student achievement. Interventions to achieve more comparable communications skills for male and female students should begin early and continue throughout the school years. Efforts also should be undertaken in both research and classroom practices to determined if or how communicative styles are differentiated by gender in ethnic groups other than European Americans. Undoubtedly some differences do exist, since discourse styles are influenced by cultural socialization, and males and females are socialized differently in various ethnic groups.

Problems with Gendered Communication Styles

The "gendered" style of communication may be more problematic than the gender of the person per se doing the communicating. If this is so, then a female who is adept at using discourse techniques typically associated with males will not be disadvantaged in mainstream social interactions. Conversely, males who communicate in ways usually ascribed to females will lose their privileged status. Hoyenga and Hoyenga (1979) offer some support for this premise. In their review of research on gender and communication, they report that "feminine communication styles" are associated with less intelligence, passivity, and submissiveness, while "masculine styles" evoke notions of power, authority, confidence, and leadership.

However, M. Crawford (1995) suggests that some of the claims about female–male communication differences need to be reconsidered. For example, indirectness and equivocation in communication are not inherently strategies of female subordination or dominance. They can be tools of power or powerlessness as well. Interpretations of speech behaviors may depend more on the setting, the speaker's status and communicative capability, and relationship to listeners than the person's gender per se (Tannen, 1994). Sadker and Sadker (1994) propose that males may be at greater *emotional risk* than females because of their role socialization. Girls are encouraged to be caring and emotionally expressive, but boys are taught to deny their feelings and to be overly cautious about demonstrating how deeply they care. Thus, male advantages in conventional conceptions of academic discourse may be countered somewhat by the psychoemotional and social advantages that females have in interpersonal relations.

CONCLUSION

Communication is strongly culturally influenced, experientially situated, and functionally strategic. It is a dynamic set of skills and performing arts whose rich nuances and delivery styles are open to many interpretations and instructional possibilities. Ethnic discourse patterns are continually negotiated because people talk in many different ways for many different reasons. Sometimes the purpose of talking and writing is simply to convey information. It is also used to persuade and entertain; to demonstrate sharing, caring, and connections; to express contentment and discontentment; to empower and subjugate; to teach and learn; and to convey critical reflections and declare personal preferences. In imagining and implementing culturally responsive pedagogical reform, teachers should not merely make girls talk more like boys, or boys talk more like girls, or all individuals within and across ethnic groups talk like each other. Nor should they assume that all gender differences in communication styles are subsumed by ethnicity or think that all ethnic nuances are obliterated by gender, social class, and education. Instead, we must be mindful that communication styles are multidimensional and multimodal, shaped by many different influences. Although culture is paramount among these, other critical influences include ethnic affiliation, gender, social class, personality, individuality, and experiential context.

The information in this chapter has described some of the patterns, dynamics, and polemics of the discourse styles of different ethnic and gender groups. Since communication is essential to both teaching and learning, it is imperative that it be a central part of instructional reforms designed to improve the school performance of underachieving African, Latino, Native, Asian, and European American students. The more teachers know about the discourse styles of ethnically diverse students, the better they will be able to improve academic achievement. Change efforts should attend especially to discourse dynamics as opposed to linguistic structures. The reforms should be directed toward creating better agreement between the communication patterns of underachieving ethnically diverse students and those considered "normal" in schools.

Knowledge about general communication patterns among ethnic groups is helpful, but it alone is not enough. Teachers need to translate it to their own particular instructional situations. This contextualization might begin with some self-study exercises in which teachers examine their preferred discourse modes and dynamics, and determine how students from different ethnic groups respond to them. They should also learn to recognize the discourse habits of students from different ethnic groups. The purposes of these analyses are to identify: (1) habitual discourse features of ethnically diverse students; (2) conflictual and complementary points among these discourse styles; (3) how, or if, conflictual points are negotiated by students; and (4) features of the students' discourse patterns that are problematic for the teacher. The results can be used to pinpoint and prioritize specific places to begin interventions for change.

Whether conceived narrowly or broadly, and expressed formally or informally, communication is the quintessential medium of teaching and learning. It also is inextricably linked to culture and cognition. Therefore, if teachers are to better serve the school achievement needs of ethnically diverse students by implementing culturally responsive teaching, they must learn how to communicate differently with them. To the extent they succeed in doing this, achievement problems could be reduced significantly.

CHAPTER 5

Ethnic and Cultural Diversity in Curriculum Content

The fundamental aim of culturally responsive pedagogy is to *empower* ethnically diverse students through academic success, cultural affiliation, and personal efficacy. Knowledge in the form of curriculum content is central to this empowerment. To be effective, this knowledge must be accessible to students and connected to their lives and experiences outside of school. Sleeter and Grant (1991a) explain that knowledge has no intrinsic power. Information and skills that are potentially powerful become so only through interaction with the interests, aspirations, desires, needs, and purposes of students. Almost 90 years earlier Dewey (1902) made essentially the same case in disavowing the notion of an inherent dichotomy between the child and the curriculum, meaning teachers must prioritize one or the other, but not both. He suggested that this is an artificial division detrimental to quality teaching. Curriculum content should be seen as a tool to help students assert and accentuate their present and future powers, capabilities, attitudes, and experiences.

These explanations emphasize the importance of "student relevance and participation" in curriculum decision making. Because of the dialectic relationship between knowledge and the knower, interest and motivation, relevance and mastery, Native Americans, Latinos, African Americans, and Asian Americans must be seen as co-originators, co-designers, and co-directors (along with professional educators) of their education. If the "creator, producer, and director" roles of students of color are circumscribed and they are seen as only "consumers," then the levels of their learning will also be restricted. This is too often true of present educational conditions. To reverse these trends, ethnically diverse students and their cultural heritages must be the sources and centers of educational programs. In the words of Dewey (1902), their curricula must be "psychologized" if they are to be relevant, interesting, and effective to their learning. This does not mean students should be taught only those things in which they have a personal interest. Nor should they be involved in every decision made about curriculum. Rather, curriculum content should be chosen and delivered in ways that are directly meaningful to the students for whom it is intended. In some instances, this means validating their personal experiences and cultural heritages; in others, it means teaching content entirely new to students but in ways that make it easy for them to comprehend.

INTRODUCTION

Discussions in this chapter elaborate this line of thinking as it relates to the importance of multicultural curriculum content in improving the school achievement of marginalized ethnic students. Five key observations provide the conceptual contours and organizational directions for these discussions:

- Curriculum content is crucial to academic performance and is an essential component of culturally responsive pedagogy.
- The most common source of curriculum content used in classrooms is textbooks. Therefore, the quality of textbooks is an important factor in student achievement and culturally responsive teaching.
- Curriculum content that is meaningful to students improves their learning.
- Relevant curriculum content for teaching African American, Latino, Asian American, and Native American students includes information about the histories, cultures, contributions, experiences, perspectives, and issues of their respective ethnic groups.
- Curriculum content is derived from various sources, many of which exist outside the formal boundaries of schooling.

The chapter is divided into five sections. The first three examine important sources of curriculum content for culturally responsive teaching. These include textbooks, literary and trade books, and mass media. Some suggestions for improving the quality of multicultural curriculum content are presented in the fourth section of the chapter. In the last part of the chapter some documented effects of ethnic content on student achievement are presented. Achievement is conceived broadly to include indicators of performance other than scores on standardized tests and grades. As is the case elsewhere in this book, descriptions, principles, and proposals derived from theory, research, and practice are woven throughout the discussions.

IMPORTANCE OF TEXTBOOKS AS CURRICULUM CONTENT

Textbooks are the basis of 70% to 95% of all classroom instruction (Apple, 1985; Davis, Ponder, Burlbaw, Garza-Lubeck, & Moss, 1986; Tyson-Bernstein & Woodward, 1991; Wade, 1993). As levels of education advance from kindergarten through high school, this dominance increases. Another testament to the power of textbooks is the fact that most students consider their authority to be incontestable and the information they present always to be accurate, authentic, and absolute truth (Gordy & Pritchard, 1995). School level has little if any effect on these perceptions. When called upon to defend the validity of their explanations and understandings of issues, students often respond, "Because the book said so."

While the dominance of textbooks is apparent in all subject areas, it is even more so in some than in others (Tyson-Bernstein & Woodward, 1991). Teaching kindergarten without textbooks is far more possible than third, seventh, or twelfth grade; and art, music, and physical education are more easily taught without textbooks than math, science, or social studies. Textbooks are often thought to be a foolproof means of guaranteeing successful teaching and learning. These practices and associated attitudes are so strongly entrenched in the minds of students that the value of courses without textbooks is sometimes suspect.

Furthermore, most textbooks used in schools are controlled by the dominant group (European Americans) and confirm its status, culture, and contributions. European American subjective experiences and interpretations of reality are presented as objective truth. These representations are entrenched further by the exclusion of certain information about the various racial minorities and social classes in the United States (Sleeter & Grant, 1991b). The largely uncontested authority and pervasiveness of textbooks are important reasons why understanding their treatment of ethnic and cultural diversity and their effects on student learning is essential to culturally responsive teaching.

ETHNIC AND CULTURAL DIVERSITY IN TEXTBOOKS

Over the years a great deal of research has been done to determine if textbooks are dealing adequately with groups of color and cultural diversity issues. The variables studied include narrative text, visuals, language, and overall tone. These have been filtered through different assessment criteria such as quantitative inclusion, accuracy of information, placement of diversity features, authenticity, and significance (Davis et al., 1986; Tetreault, 1985; AAUW, 1995; Sadker & Sadker, 1982).

Progress but Some Problems Remain

Analyses of textbooks produced in the 1980s and 1990s for a variety of subjects and across different grade levels indicate that blatant ethnic stereotypes, exclusions, and racist depictions have been eliminated (Anyon, 1988; Davis et al., 1986; Deane, 1989; Gordy & Pritchard, 1995; Wade, 1993). Still, the overall quality of the treatment of culturally diverse groups and experiences continue to be inadequate.

Textbooks give little attention to different groups of color interacting with each other. Typically they are presented interacting only with European Americans and various segments of mainstream society. Sleeter and Grant (1991b) found these patterns of treatment of diversity to be the case with 47 textbooks used in grades 1–8 to teach social studies, mathematics, reading and language arts, and science that they examined. All the books were published between 1980 and 1988. A six-part analysis was applied that included visuals, topics and issues discussed, "people to study," language, portrayals and role functions of characters, and miscellaneous (features unique to particular books). Sleeter and Grant were particularly interested in how these books treated different racial groups, both sexes, social classes, and people with disabilities.

Textbooks continue to be flawed with respect to their treatment of ethnic and cultural diversity for several reasons. First, there is an imbalance across ethnic groups of color, with most attention given to African Americans and their experiences. This disparity is consistent across types of instructional materials, subjects, and grade levels. Second, the content included about ethnic issues is rather bland, conservative, conformist, and "safe." It tends to emphasize harmonious relations among racial groups. Contentious issues and individuals are avoided, and the unpleasant sides of society and cultural diversity are either sanitized or bypassed entirely. Third, gender and social-class disparities prevail within the representations of ethnic groups, with preference given to males, the middle class, and events and experiences that are closely aligned with mainstream European American values, beliefs, and standards of behavior. Fourth, textbook discussions about ethnic groups and their concerns are not consistent across time, with contemporary issues being overshadowed by historical ones.

A study conducted by Gordy and Pritchard (1995) illustrates how these general trends were demonstrated in a specific sample of textbooks. They analyzed 17 fifth-grade social studies textbooks used in Connecticut schools to determine how they represented the perspectives of diverse women and men during slavery and Reconstruction. None of the authors provided thorough critiques of the slave trade, the reduction of Africans to commodities for that trade, or the values and beliefs used to justify slavery. All the texts discussed the living conditions under enslavement, but they excluded the sexual exploitation of female slaves, made no connections between slavery and the present living conditions of African and European Americans, and ignored the role that other ethnic groups, such as Native Americans and Mexicans, played in slavery.

A similar emphasis on description instead of interpretative and critical analysis characterized the treatment of Emancipation and Reconstruction. Because the perspectives of diverse groups were not presented, these textbooks gave partial and incomplete analyses of these critical events in U. S. history and their effects. They continued the long-established tradition of giving mostly European American and male perspectives on sociopolitical issues. Consequently, students using them "will not be given a full understanding of the racial and gender discrimination inherent in the slave system and the consequences of this discrimination on generations of Americans, both African American and White" (Gordy & Pritchard, 1995, p. 213).

Gwen, who is a veteran second-grade teacher, draws attention to another major inconsistency in the quality of many contemporary textbooks. She works in a large urban school district (32,000 students) and has taught many different types of students—African and European American, center-city and suburban, middle- and lower-class, academically able and intellectually challenged—in her career. Her district uses a literature approach to teaching reading. The second-grade text is rich in ethnic and cultural diversity. Its content represents a wide variety of literary genres (poetry, short stories, fiction, realistic descriptions, mythology), cultural themes, and ethnic male and female authors and illustrators.

Unfortunately, these strengths are compromised by repeated inappropriateness in the substantive content of the text for second-graders. Gwen explains that many of the stories are simply too complex for 7-year-olds. The vocabulary is often too advanced, as are many of the literary techniques (such as simile, metaphor, analogy) used in the narrative text. The topics of the stories are often irrelevant to the experiences and perspectives of the urban students she teaches. Gwen bemoans these dilemmas by observing that "much age-appropriate and good ethnic children's literature already exists that will be interesting to students like mine. Why aren't we allowed to use it to teach reading?" One indeed wonders why not, especially when her school district and others throughout the United States claim to be searching for ways to improve reading achievement by using instructional materials that have high interest appeal and cultural relevance to students.

Analyses of how gender issues are addressed in textbooks, such as those conducted by Powell and Garcia (1985) and the American Association of University Women (AAUW, 1995) and others reviewed by Grossman and Grossman (1994), reveal patterns of progress similar to those of ethnic diversity. Blatant gender biases have been eliminated, and females are depicted in less traditional roles and relationships. But males still appear more frequently than females. Men still dominate careers, positions, and images of action, power, leadership, and decision making. Although they are now portrayed in a wider variety of activities, females continue to be overrepresented in supportive and caregiving roles, suggesting that those who behave closer to traditional expectations are preferred.

The extent to which progress has been made in achieving gender equity in instructional materials is a function of subject areas, ethnic groups, and type of resource. The presentation of females in social studies, language arts, and literature instructional materials comes closer to being egalitarian than in math, science, and computer education. More gender balance exists in supplementary materials—especially those of a literary nature, such as children's picture books—than in required textbooks. As is the case with ethnic group representation in textbooks, there are major imbalances in the treatment of women from different ethnic groups and sociocultural backgrounds. The progress tends to be much better for middle-class and European American females than those who are poor and from different groups of color. Obviously, then, improvements are still needed in how males and females from different ethnic groups are presented in curriculum content resources routinely used by students.

Effects of Multicultural Textbook Content

Little systematic empirical research is currently available on how biased textbooks affect the achievement of ethnically diverse students. But personal stories from students of various ages and circumstances abound. Students, like Amy and Aaron from Chapter 1, tell of being insulted, embarrassed, ashamed, and angered when reading and hearing negative portrayals of their ethnic groups or not hearing anything at all. Some challenge these inaccuracies and exclusions, and intimidate teachers by doing so. Others recall being put on the spot when isolated events and individuals from their ethnic groups are singled out for special attention. On other occasions students are excited and amazed to learn new information about different ethnic groups, to discover what they have endured and accomplished, even though it is introduced in the classroom sporadically. This was the reaction of Amy and Aaron when they first watched *Roots*, the televised series of Alex Haley's (1976) book of the same title, and read *The Autobiography of Malcolm X* (Malcolm X & Haley, 1966). A group of European American college students were rendered speechless after viewing *Something Strong Within* (Nakamura, 1994), a video composite of home movies taken by Japanese Americans in internment camps during World War II. Finally, after a long silence, one student said, "I never even thought of the people having regular lives in the camps. The video made me 'see them as human beings." This reaction represented the sentiments of many others in the class, and it was echoed in comments to the effect that the students felt their education had shortchanged them through information voids, thereby further dehumanizing and marginalizing Japanese Americans.

The observations Chun-Hoon (1973) made more than 25 years ago about the effects of these textbook inadequacies on the perceptions of ethnic groups are still applicable today. Omissions and myopic analyses of ethnically diverse peoples, issues, cultures, and experiences imply that they are irrelevant and even expendable. Although Chun-Hoon was concerned specifically about Asian Americans, his observations can be easily extended to other groups of color, as Sleeter and Grant (1991b) have done. They recommended that authors and publishers reorient their focus to deal with more authentic and substantial human experiences and contextualize specific subject-matter skills in more meaningful multicultural content. This is a better route to improving student achievement than using bland and fictitious stories, teaching decontextualized skills, and repeating excessive numbers of adventure stories about European American males.

The inadequacies of textbook coverage of cultural diversity can be avoided by including accurate, wide-ranging, and appropriately contextualized content about different ethnic groups' histories, cultures, and experiences in classroom instruction on a regular basis. The efforts need not be constrained by lack of information and materials. Plenty of resources exist about most ethnic groups and in such variety that all subjects and grades taught in schools can be served adequately. Since this information is not always in textbooks, teachers need to develop the habit of using other resources to complement or even replace them. Students also should be taught how to critique textbooks for the accuracy of their multicultural content and how to compensate for the voids these analyses reveal.

ETHNIC DIVERSITY IN LITERARY AND TRADE BOOKS

The inclusion of information about ethnic and cultural diversity in supplementary instructional materials, such as children's picture books and fiction written by ethnic authors about ethnic groups, is both encouraging and discouraging. Six studies are presented here to explain why. They deal with portrayals of African Americans, Asian Americans, Native Americans, Mexican Americans, and multiethnic groups in children and adolescent literature.

The importance of including ethnic literature as curriculum content has been recognized by E. Kim (1976). She says fiction can provide valuable and otherwise unavailable insights into the social consciousness, cultural identity, and historical experiences of ethnic groups. Ramírez and Dowd (1997) add that high-quality authentic multicultural literature can help children "make connections to their personal experiences, provide role models, and expand their horizons" (p. 20). It also is a powerful way to expose students to ethnic groups, cultures, and experiences different from their own to which they may not have access in their daily life. Making explicit connections between instructional resources used in classrooms and lived experiences of students outside of school improves the mastery of academic skills as well as other dimensions of learning, such as interest, motivation, and time-on-task. Ethnic literature and trade books are conduits for achieving these goals, as well as reducing fear of and prejudices toward "unfamiliar others."

Biases Persist in Children and Adolescent Literature

A study conducted by Deane (1989) of approximately 300 popular children's fiction books poses some serious questions about their progress in including ethnically diverse content and characters. He concentrated on how African American characters are depicted in series written by European Americans that have dominated the fiction market for young readers from grades 2 through 6 for generations. These are books "which involve the same major characters . . . in a successive series of actions, scenes, and situations" (p. 153), such as the Nancy Drew, Hardy Boys, Bobbsey Twins, Woodland Gang, and Sweet Valley Twins series. Deane concluded that most of the blatantly derogatory depictions of African Americans have vanished from these books, but so have many African American characters. A closer scrutiny of this "progress" revealed that extreme stereotypical images have been eliminated and more realistic portrayals of African American characters are presented. There has also been a tendency to overcorrect for stereotypes by not assigning any differentiating characteristics to the speech and actions of the African American characters, or to eliminate African American characters from the storyline entirely.

Hopefully, improvements have occurred in the serial books Deane analyzed in the decade since the study was conducted. But no recent research is currently available to support this possibility. Teachers can help fill this research void by having students analyze the same books included in Deane's 1989 study and using his methodological procedures or some variations on them. With sufficient training, middle and high school students should be able to critique trade books written for their age groups to determine how well they portray ethnically diverse characters, issues, and cultures. Even though their analyses will not be as sophisticated as Deane's, undoubtedly students will provide perspectives that he did not. Student participation in the construction of their own knowledge (as critiques of trade books would be) is a critical element of culturally responsive pedagogy.

J. Garcia, Hadaway, and Beal (1988) examined 33 trade books (16 fiction and 17 nonfiction) to determine if the ethnic topics, themes, and personalities treated were "typical" or "new." "Typical" referred to topics, issues, and individuals who gained prominence in the civil rights movement and cultural/ethnic revolutions of the 1960s. "New" trade books were those that emphasized issues, themes, topics, and ideas that were identifiable in multicultural literature in the 1970s and early 1980s (such as cultural affirmation, unique ethnic identities, and political activism) but not necessarily included in works designed for children. The books were competitors for the 1986 Carter G. Woodson Award, sponsored by the National Council for the Social Studies. Since 1973 this award has been given to outstanding nonfiction trade books for their sensitive and accurate treatment of a topic related to ethnic minorities and race relations. J. Garcia and associates (1988) concluded:

> While stereotypic portrayals of ethnic and minority groups in children's tradebooks are no longer prevalent, contemporary writers continue to treat overused themes, topics, and personalities that, while providing some perspectives on ethnic and minority life, do little to expand into areas that would provide young learners with more creative interpretations of America's cultural diversity. (p. 71)

In a relatively rare research occurrence, Harada (1994) analyzed adolescent fiction books about Asian Americans and found characteristics that paralleled those found by Garcia and associates. Twenty-four books published between 1988 and 1993, and targeted for 11- to 17-year-olds, were examined to determine how Asian characters from 11 countries of origin were treated. The countries were China, Japan, Taiwan, Korea, Laos, Cambodia, Burma, India, Thailand, Vietnam, and the Philippines. The books were analyzed for character portrayals, story development, language usage, historical authenticity, and cultural accuracy. Only 6 of the 11 Asian American groups were represented in the books. The largest numbers were Chinese Americans (32 percent), followed sequentially by Japanese Americans (20 percent), Korean and Vietnamese Americans (16 percent each), and Cambodian and Taiwanese Americans (8 percent each).

Biases and stereotypes were found in each of the five categories of analyses for 23 of the 24 books. Samples of these included presenting Asian Americans as being mysterious, inscrutable foreigners; all Asian ethnic groups as having the same physical traits; and both males and females as being exotic, alluring sex objects. In addition, Asians were presented as desiring and striving to be like Whites; as model minorities; and as dependent on Whites for the resolution of conflicts. Speech behavior was parodied; token or superficial historical references that had little to do with the development of character or plot were included; and there was inaccurate or restricted mention of cultural details. These results caused Harada (1994) to suggest that the potential of fiction as a "powerful and natural vehicle for providing a thoughtful reflection of the values and beliefs of a culture" (p. 55) is not being realized in adolescent literature about Asian Americans. If this is to happen, authors must stop "recycling the super achiever and China doll images" (p. 55) and become much more responsible about "weaving authentic details and accurate cultural information into quality works for all young readers" (p. 56). Harada's admonishments and advice can be easily extended to all types of instructional materials and curriculum designs about all ethnic groups and for all levels of learners.

How Mexican American girls and women are portrayed in realistic fiction books for K–3 students was the focus of analysis in studies conducted by Rocha and Dowd (1993) and by Ramírez and Dowd (1997). In the first study, two sets of realistic fiction books featuring female characters were examined. Nine of these were published between 1950 and 1969, and 20 between 1970 and 1990. Those in the Ramírez and Dowd study (a total of 21) were published between 1990 and 1997. Seven criteria were used to analyze the content of these books: characterization, plot, theme, point of view, setting, style of writing, and special features.

The findings of both studies are similar to those of research on the portrayal of other ethnic groups. Improvements are occurring across time in how Mexican American females are portrayed in books for young children. There are fewer stereotypes, a greater variety of roles, settings, and activities, and more modernity in profiling Mexican American people and culture. Yet the major story themes of the 1990–1997 books are similar to those of the 1970–1990 period, with heavy emphasis on acculturation, satisfaction with self, Mexican heritage, privacy, goals and dreams, and the resolution of dilemmas. The recent books include more generic themes, such as relationships, individualism, and family. Ramírez and Dowd (1997) consider this an asset because universal experiences can make these books more readily understood by readers from other ethnic and cultural backgrounds. Increasingly, recent publications also are including special features that indicate the authors' cultural knowledge, Spanish-language skills, and affiliation with Mexican American culture.

Despite these improvements, realistic fiction books about Mexican American females for young children are not as good as they need to be. The authors of both studies found that some significant stereotyping and traditional ethnic "typecasting" remain. Mexican American females are too frequently depicted in traditional hairstyles and clothing and too often engaged in music, dancing, fiestas, and other celebrations. The characters were rarely shown participating in school activities or employment outside of the home. The story settings are more rural than urban (a reversal from books published in the 1970–1990 period); located away from permanent residence, such as vacation sites; depict old-fashion dwellings more than modern, contemporary ones; and never use an upper-class milieu (Ramírez & Dowd, 1997; Rocha & Dowd, 1993).

What accounts for these seemingly mixed results of how ethnic groups are portrayed in literary sources and textbooks? Ramírez and Dowd (1997) think they are a normal result of the developmental process of creating a rich body of multiethnic literature:

> With a proliferation of books comes more diversity in the literature as a whole. No one book has to present all of a culture—nor should it. For example, when so many books about Mexican Americans present facets of religion and religious practice, a book that seems to focus on what many see as superstition does not carry the negative weight it would if it were one of only two or three. In fact, its existence may very well enrich our understanding of diverse religious practices when read alongside other books. (p. 54)

Implicit in this explanation is some important advice for teachers. It is quite unlikely that any one author, book, or other reference is ever capable of providing a complete profile of ethnic groups and their cultures, contributions, and experiences. Therefore, teachers should routinely use a combination of resources to teach about ethnic and cultural diversity.

Some Improvements Are Evident

Other authors also have found positive results in how literary resources written for school-age students portray cultural diversity. Two of these are Heller (1997) and Hafen (1997). Heller reviewed more than 50 children's picture books to determine how African American fathers were portrayed. Several themes emerged that conveyed positive characterizations. These include the role of the father in nurturing and child-rearing; recreational activities with children; discipline; household maintenance and management; occupational and economic activities; and visits with children after absences caused by some crisis. Males in the extended family and community were also depicted in positive fathering roles and relationships. These findings are particularly noteworthy because of popular conceptions about the absence of fathers from African American families and the potential negative effects this can have on children's identity, self-concept, and various aspects of school achievement. Resources like the books on Heller's list can be used in classroom instruction to dispel myths and compensate for voids in Black father–child relationships.

The books cited in a study conducted by Hafen (1997) on popular images of Native Americans in contemporary literature were published between 1985 and 1996. The authors were successful in combining traditional tribal heritages with mainstream and contemporary cultures. They demonstrate how Native Americans are engaged in the reinterpretation and self-creation of a contemporary identity without forsaking traditional cultural values. These books also show how ethnic-minority literature can be simultaneously particular and universal. Their positive portrayals are a welcome relief to the way Native Americans are too often presented in textbooks—as one-dimensional, exotic figures frozen in historical times, invisible in contemporary society, or restricted to statistical listings in the demographics of social problems such as crime, poverty, and unemployment. Resources such as these and the information they present are invaluable to culturally responsive teaching. They should be particularly comforting and helpful to teachers who are concerned about whether teaching multicultural education will create irresolvable tensions between unity and diversity, similarities and differences among the people of the United States.

However, Mihesuah (1996) warns against being overly optimistic about how Native Americans are portrayed in media readily accessible to children and youth, especially those produced from outside the ethnic communities. She suggests that distortions of Native Americans and their cultural identities can still be found "in every possible medium—from scholarly publications and textbooks, movies, TV shows, literature, cartoons, commercials, comic books, and fanciful paintings, to the gamut of commercial logos, insignia and imagery that pervade tourist locales throughout the Southwest and elsewhere" (p. 9). High school and college mascots can be added to this list of media that perpetuate stereotypes of Native Americans (Pewewardy, 1991, 1998). The stereotypes transmitted vary in range and intensity "from the extremely pejorative to the artificially idealistic, from historic depictions of Indians as uncivilized primal men and winsome women belonging to a savage culture, to present day ... mystical environmentalists, or uneducated, alcoholic bingo-players confined to reservations" (Mihesuah, 1996, p. 9).

The quantity and variety of culturally validating books, written in authentic voices and providing insider perspectives, are numerous for African Americans, Latinos, and Japanese Americans. Those for other groups of color are also increasing rapidly. The *Multicultural Review* is a useful resource for some of these. It regularly publishes lists of recommended books, films, videotapes, and microfilm collections on a wide variety of ethnic groups, such as Hmongs, Thais, Laotians, Cambodians, Vietnamese, and Filipinos, as well as Native Americans, Puerto Ricans, African Americans, Mexican Americans, Chinese Americans, Japanese Americans, Jewish Americans, Romanian Americans, and Caribbean Americans. The topics examined vary widely, too. Among them are male and female characters and concerns; historical and contemporary issues, events, and perspectives; biographies, autobiographies and picture books; short stories; fiction and nonfiction; myths and folklore; rhymes and poetry; literary critiques and scholarly treatises. Valuable complements to textbooks, they have the potential to profoundly enrich student learning about the culture, history, and life experiences of ethnically diverse groups.

MASS MEDIA AS CULTURALLY RELEVANT CURRICULUM CONTENT

Mass media are powerful sources of curriculum content about ethnic and cultural diversity. Frequently the images and information they convey are contradictory to what is desirable and need to be corrected or countered by classroom instruction. Occasionally the reverse is true; some media presentations of ethnic peoples and experiences are positive and even complementary to school instruction. Either way, the images are too easily accessible and their influence too powerful for teachers to ignore how ethnic groups and issues are presented in television programming, films, newspapers, magazines, and music videos. Students bring this information and its effects to the classroom with them. Therefore, ethnic diversity in mass media should be part of the curriculum content of culturally responsive teaching.

The role that television alone plays is very extensive, with millions of viewers tuning in several hours each day. Because of its pervasiveness, Perkins (1996) calls television "omnipresent." This omnipresence is both quantitative and qualitative. The quantitative impact is indicated by the sheer number of hours children spend watching television daily. Common estimates are that they spend on the average of 20–25 hours per week watching television. The programs they view include a wide range of cartoons, movies, music videos, news reports, documentaries, prime-time series, syndicated "family classics," and an avalanche of advertisements. At this rate, by the time students graduate from high school they will have spent more time viewing television than in formal classrooms (Perkins, 1996). Qualitatively, television programming is always involved in constructing knowledge, creating images, cultivating consumer markets, shaping opinions, and manipulating values about ethnic and cultural diversity.

Uneven Progress in Treatment of Ethnic Diversity

For the most part, the numerical and qualitative presentation of groups of color in the mass media follows trends in textbooks and literary materials. Portrayals of ethnic and cultural diversity are more numerous, positive, and varied now than in the past, but not without some remaining problems. Disparities exist among ethnic groups in favor of African Americans, and groups of color appear most frequently in programs with specific ethnic themes. Surfing national network, local, and syndicated television channels at any time of any day of the week produces many African Americans. In some cases, the entire cast and the setting of the programs are Black; in others, they have recurrent supporting roles. African Americans also are highly visible in news programs—as reporters and subjects—on national networks and local affiliates. There is a growing presence of African Americans in the movie industry, both in front of and behind the cameras—as stars and in supporting roles; as writers, producers, directors, and technicians; in both all-Black and predominantly White productions.

The kind of treatment that African Americans are receiving in the mass media does not exist to the same extent for Latinos, Native Americans, and Asian Americans. Individuals from these ethnic groups appear only occasionally as guest performers in entertainment television programs and movies dealing with specific ethnic-related topics. Asian American and Latino newscasters are more commonly found on local rather than national newscasts. Thus, Mexican Americans are familiar faces on local news programs in the Southwest, and Japanese and Chinese Americans (especially females) are visible in such states as California, Hawaii, and Washington. Puerto Ricans may frequently be on the air in New York, but not elsewhere. In comparison to African Americans, the numerical representation of these ethnic groups is minuscule. Except for the exceptional individual actor here and there, selective historical documentaries, and special events, Native Americans are virtually invisible in these media.

Changes Are Not Always Improvements

Numerical ethnic representations in media do not ensure content quality. Ethnic groups may appear to be validated while simultaneously being subtly stereotyped. This can be done in many ways, including topic, focus, dialogue, personal image, and characterization. The recurrent plot of situation comedies in which the female character inevitably is the voice of resolution in family conflicts perpetuates traditional views of women as emotional anchors, peacekeepers, nurturers, and moral monitors in families. Slapstick comedy, gangs, crime fighting, and in-vogue urban young adult and teen life are the themes of most television programs and movies in which African Americans are prominent. Violent crimes, more than any other single category, is what makes African Americans and Latinos subjects of the news. Some daytime talk shows are notorious for enticing African American, Latino, and European American teens and young adults to be guests on programs dealing with gangs, violence, and emotionally abusive, unstable male–female intimate relationships.

Even when mass media are used to offset negative stereotypes of ethnic groups, the results can be counterproductive, perpetuating that which they claim to dispel. A case in point is the 1995 Disney animated production of *Pocahontas*. In an instructive critique, Pewewardy (1996/ 1997) explains how this movie perpetuates some longstanding stereotypes about Native Americans. Pocahontas is portrayed as maidenly, demure, and so deeply committed to a White man that she violates the cultural rules of her own ethnic community. According to Pewewardy, this image of a young Native American woman was created to serve the purposes of European American mythology. For example, he suggests that the concept of "celestial princess" was probably an English, not a Native American, creation. Other stereotypes and racism in *Pocahontas* are transmitted through the language used to refer to Native peoples (e.g., "savages," "heathens," "devils," "pagans," "primitive") and the lyrics of the movie's song "Savages, Savages." Pewewardy (1996/1997) proposes that instead of countering a stereotype, Disney created "a marketable 'New Age' Pocahontas to embody our millennial dreams for wholeness and harmony, while banishing our nightmares of savagery and emptiness" (p. 22). Like textbooks, this movie avoids dealing with the uglier side of the English encounter with the indigenous people, such as their greed, dishonesty, and hegemony. The stereotypes embedded in *Pocahontas* are not overt or blatant. They can be undetected by people who do not thoroughly understand Native American cultures or their historical experiences with mainstream European American society.

Another example of attempts to compensate for damages inflicted by stereotyping Native Americans is the decision to place Sacagawea on a new $2 coin to be minted in 2000 (Figlar, 1998). U. S. Mint director Philip Diehl sees this selection as bestowing honor specifically on Sacagawea, a Shoshone teenager, for her physical courage, generosity, hospitality, and interpreter skills in assisting Lewis and Clark in 1804 on their explorations of the western frontier, and more generally on Native Americans. Some Native Americans will undoubtedly agree with this assessment and be pleased with the choice, while others may consider it an act of tokenism and misplaced significance. Negative sentiments may be prompted by questions about the merits of giving this "distinction" to a teenager (Sacagawea was thought to be 16 years old at the time she traveled with Lewis and Clark) and someone whose claim to fame is based on her service to European Americans, not contributions to her own ethnic community. Even her physical characteristics are unknown and cannot be described with certainty, thereby making her visibility "opaque." Diehl initially thought this uncertainty could be countered by having the coin carry a design of "Liberty" as a Native American woman to represent Sacagawea (Figlar, 1998). The final image was selected from designs created by New Mexico sculptor Glenna Goodacre, who used a Shoshone college student as a model (Axtman, 1999).

These factors may cause still others to question the reality of Sacagawea's significance (and by whose standards) and to wonder if the only way Native Americans can gain recognition is by *serving* mainstream European American individuals, culture, society, and ideology. What progress toward accomplishing cultural equity is there in honoring the contributions of ambiguous individuals and limiting significance to servitude? This scenario and the questions it brings to mind about "dubious distinctions" also apply to other groups of color. One example is the ironic and conflicting messages conveyed by the Academy Award nomination of Morgan Freeman (an African American male) as best supporting actor for his performance in *Driving Miss Daisy*. In this role he played the chauffeur for a European American matriarch.

Ethnic Diversity in the News

News reporting is another powerful media source of curriculum content about people of color. Unfortunately, much of the information and many of the images it transmits are negative and stereotypical. Research conducted by C. Campbell (1995) provides specific illustrations of this general trend. He did textual analyses of 39 hours of local newscasts from 29 cities to determine the symbolic and connotative cultural meanings they transmitted about racially and ethnically related issues. Campbell concluded that television journalism perpetuates invisibility, marginality, erroneous conceptions, and a "myth of assimilation" for people of color. These practices are reminiscent of the tendencies of textbooks to avoid contentious aspects of ethnic, racial, and cultural diversity and to inflate the level of racial harmony. In television news this is done by overembellishing the success of a few prominent individuals as proof that racial inequalities, social injustices, and power differentials no longer exist in U.S. society or can be easily overcome by personal initiative.

Campbell (1995) suggests ethnic stereotyping is common enough across television news organizations to represent "a hegemonic consensus about race and class that sustains myths about life outside of white 'mainstream' America" (p. 132). The consequences can be profound:

> When the local news ignores life outside of middle-American/dominant culture parameters, it contributes to an understanding of minority cultures as less significant, as marginal. When journalists attempt to cover life in minority communities but neglect and dismiss the attitudes and perceptions of people of color, they compound that sense of marginality. When the news sustains stereotypical notions about nonwhite Americans as less-than-human, as immature, as savages, as derelicts, it feeds an understanding of minorities as different, as "other," as dangerous. (p. 132)

Creating Images and Constructing Knowledge About Ethnic Diversity

The images mass media convey about ethnic groups and issues often are not accurate, intentional, or overt, but they are always powerful. A compelling example of these effects are the results of a study entitled "A Different World: Children's Perceptions of Race and Class in the Media." This survey was conducted by Lake Sosin Snell Perry and Associates, and involved 1,200 children between 10 and 17 years old, with equal representation of European, Asian, Latino, and African Americans. The important general findings indicated that children in all four ethnic groups (1) are not always encouraged by the ethnic images they see on television; (2) perceive that Latinos and African Americans are depicted more negatively than European and Asian Americans; (3) are aware of media stereotypes at an early age; and (4) understand the power of television to shape opinions. As one African American child stated, "People are inspired by what they see on television. If they do not see themselves on TV, they want to be someone else" (J. Allen, 1998, p. A8). The Roper Organization (1993) found that most people in the United States depend on television for their news and consider it more credible than newspapers reporting. The portrayals TV presents about individuals easily become *uncontested* truth that is generalized to entire groups.

How the mass media "cast" different ethnic individuals, issues, and experiences can deeply affect the attitudes of viewers about their own as well as other ethnic groups. This influence can be cognitive, affective, positive, negative, baffling, and insightful. According to Cortés (1995):

> The issue of media as multicultural information source goes well beyond the question of accuracy. In news, the constant reiteration of certain themes, even when each story is accurate in and of itself, may unjustifiably emphasize limited information about an ethnic group. . . . Similarly, the repetition of ethnic images by the entertainment media add to viewer's pools of "knowledge," particularly if news and entertainment coincide and mutually reinforce each other in theme, approach, content, perspective, and frequency. (p. 172)

These actions of entertainment and news mass media constitute a kind of *ideological management* (Spring, 1992). This is the deliberate exclusion or addition of information to create certain images, to shield consumers from particular ideas and information, and to teach specific moral, political, and social values. Two examples demonstrate the workings of ideological management in media. The first is the Public Broadcasting Station (PBS) production of *Ethnic Notions* (Biggs, 1987). It presents a poignant historical analysis of how stereotypical characterizations of African Americans were created and institutionalized by television and movies. The second example is *Killing Us Softly* (Lazarus, 1979) and its sequel, *Still Killing Us Softly* (Lazarus, 1987), produced by Cambridge Documentary Films. They demonstrate how sexist and exploitative images, as well as suggested violence against European American women, are portrayed, cultivated, and disseminated through televised and print advertising. These are wrenching exposés, even though women of color are excluded from the analyses, except for one passing reference to African Americans. Hopefully, some major changes have occurred since 1987 in how women of all ethnic groups are portrayed. But this hope remains to be proven by careful research and analysis.

Perkins (1996) provides another illustration of how television constructs knowledge that is important to culturally responsive teaching. She reviewed research on the influence of television on African American females' perceptions of their physical attractiveness. The conception of beauty presented in the mass media is based on Eurocentric standards—albeit idealized, sexist, and unrealistic ones. The ideal beauty is a tall, slim, lithe, debonair blue-eyed blonde with flawless hair, teeth, and skin, who radiates confidence, sexuality, and desirability on all fronts—intimately, socially, economically. The immutable racial characteristics (e.g., skin color, hair texture, bone structure, body type) of African American females make it impossible for them ever to achieve these ideals. Too frequently they are presented as large, nonsexual, overbearing, assertive, bold, and argumentative. These portrayals help to shape public opinion about what constitutes beauty and can negatively affect the social self-esteem of those deemed unattractive (Dates & Barlow, 1990).

Ideological management is not restricted to the mass media and popular culture. Educational media, including textbooks, films, and videos, do this, too. Their tone, topic, text, setting, format, and character development create a "viewing experience" that invites audiences to engage in particular kinds of social, political, and ideological involvements as the story, action, and discourse unfold (Ellsworth, 1990). Research in media studies over the last 25 years or so presents compelling evidence that educational film, video, and photographic representations are not neutral carriers of content. Instead, content reflects particular cultural, social, and political meanings (Ellsworth & Whatley, 1990).

Some media programs are genuine advancements in making society more ethnically inclusive and egalitarian, as is evident in the increasing numbers of women and ethnic groups involved in more aspects of media programming—writing, producing, directing, and performing. Other programs are ambiguous and convey conflicting information about ethnic diversity. For example, why can Japanese, Chinese, and Filipino Americans participate in local and national news broadcasting but be virtually invisible in prime-time entertainment programs? Why can Native Americans be present in documentaries dealing with conflicts among ecology, traditional ethnic economies (such as fishing rights), and industrial development but otherwise be excluded from mainstream news and entertainment programs?

Subtle racial stereotypes transmitted through films, television, videotapes, and other popular media can leave deep emotional and psychological scars on children of the targeted ethnic groups, and on others as well (Pewewardy, 1996/1997). Mihesuah (1996) offers some alternative explanations and helpful advice for counterbalancing 24 commonly held stereotypes about Native Americans that are transmitted through mass media. Among them are that all Native Americans are alike; they were conquered because they were inferior; they were warlike and treacherous; they get a free ride from the government; they are stoic and have no sense of humor; and they contribute nothing of worth to U.S. society and culture.

Debunking these kinds of myths and other ethnic biases in the mass media should be a central feature of culturally responsive teaching. It is also important for students and teachers to understand that curriculum content is not just the information taught in schools. The experiences students have outside of school, such as those provided by all forms of mass media, are also powerful influences on learning. These are often overlooked in schools because they do not have the official designation of "curriculum." Yet the only contact many students have with ethnically diverse people is through the mass media. For others, media images are important gauges for how society views and values their ethnic groups. Either way, the "societal curriculum" (Cortés, 1991) comes to school with students, and teachers must contend with it as they struggle to make education more culturally responsive for diverse ethnic groups.

CULTURALLY DIVERSE CURRICULUM CONTENT EFFECTS

Discussion of the effects of multicultural curriculum content on the performance of underachieving students of color is limited here to reading, writing, math, and science. These subjects and skills are selected for emphasis for five reasons. First, it is both politically expedient and pedagogically valid for the implementation and effects of culturally responsive teaching to be located in areas of school curricula generally considered most significant. Second, math, science, reading, and writing constitute the academic core in most educational settings and are usually used to assess student achievement. Third, reading abilities strongly influence performance in other academic tasks and subjects. Fourth, math and science (especially advanced-level courses) have high stakes and high status attached to them. They are considered the "gateways" to academic development and career opportunities beyond K–12 schooling for those students who have access to and high levels of performance in them. Fifth, more research and practice guidelines are available on multicultural curriculum content for reading and writing than for other school subjects, and more curriculum reforms have been undertaken to increase the participation of students of color (particularly Latinos and African Americans) and females in math and science than in other school subjects. As explained in Chapter 1, achievement is conceived broadly to include academics, standardized test scores, course grades, and other performance indicators and measures. Among these are increased enrollment in advanced-level, high-status courses; the quantity and quality of participation in instructional discourse; improved interest in and motivation for learning; feelings of efficacy among students; and meeting the criteria and expectations of specific programs of study.

Reading and Writing Achievement

Most multicultural curriculum effects on student achievement in reading and writing derive more from "experimental" and "special" projects than from regularly taught content, topics, skills, and courses. They also tend to combine reading and writing with some kind of ethnic literature. Although the number of programs on which information is available is rather small, their results are consistently supportive of the theoretical claims about the pedagogical power of culturally responsive teaching. A few of these are discussed here to illustrate their effects on achievement.

One of these "special projects" that used culturally pluralistic content to teach reading and writing is the Multicultural Literacy Program (MLP) (Diamond & Moore, 1995). It was implemented in the Ann Arbor, Inkster, and Ypsilanti, Michigan, school districts over a four-year period, with a multiethnic student population in grades K–8. The program included multiethnic literature, with whole-language approaches, and a socioculturally sensitive learning environment. The literature highlighted contributions of Asian Americans, Latinos, Native Americans, African Americans, and Native Hawaiians in a variety of traditional folktales, song lyrics, poems, fiction, essays, biographies, and autobiographies.

The program designers decided to use multicultural literature to teach reading and writing because it resonates with students' creative ways of thinking and illuminates common human connections among ethnically different people. Literature also is a powerful medium through which students can confront social injustices, visualize racial inequities, find solutions to personal and political problems, and vicariously experience the issues, emotions, thoughts, and lives of people otherwise inaccessible to them. These literary encounters help students "become critical readers, who learn to view the world from multiple perspectives as they construct their versions of the truth, . . . [and] make informed and rational decisions about the most effective ways to correct injustices in their community" (Diamond & Moore, 1995, p. 14).

No quantifiable data (such as increased standardized test scores and grade point averages) are available on how the MLP affected student achievement, but other powerful indicators of its success do exist. Its creators and facilitators cite classroom observations and analysis of samples of student works to indicate that the program has positive effects. On these measures of achievement students exhibited:

- More interest and enjoyment in reading multicultural books
- More positive attitudes toward reading and writing in general
- Increased knowledge about various forms, structures, functions, and uses of written language
- Expanded vocabularies, sentence patterns, and decoding abilities
- Better reading comprehension and writing performance
- Longer written stories that reflect more clarity and cohesiveness
- Enhanced reading rate and fluency
- Improved self-confidence and self-esteem
- Greater appreciation of their own and others' cultures (Diamond & Moore, 1995)

These achievements were evident across groups of students who differed by ethnicity, cultural background, and intellectual ability. The results are consistent with the findings of other researchers, such as Mason and Au (1991), Bishop (1992), and Norton (1992). They, too, found that exposing children to literature that includes characters, settings, and events similar to their lived experiences produces positive academic, personal, and social results virtually identical to those generated by the Multicultural Literacy Program.

Another literature-based literacy program that produced many different kinds of academic improvements for the students involved is the Webster Groves Writing Project (WGWP). It included several different components of culturally responsive pedagogy, but only its curriculum content is examined here. This project was located in a small, suburban, economically diverse school district of approximately 4,400 students (three-fourths European Americans and one-fourth African Americans) that included five municipalities in Missouri: Webster Groves, Rock Hill, Warson Woods, Glendale, and parts of Shrewsbury (Krater et al., 1994). At its peak, 14 English teachers and 293 students in grades 6–12 were involved. Initially African Americans were targeted, but after the first 2 years the project was extended to all students in the participating teachers' classes who were performing below grade level.

The WGWP was organized around eight key principles and strategies that combined African American cultural characteristics and contributions with process and literature approaches to writing. The principles were building on students' strengths; individualizing and personalizing instruction; encouraging cooperative learning; increasing control of language; using computers; enhancing personal involvement with reading and writing; building cultural bridges; and expanding personal horizons. Among the specific elements of African American culture woven into the curriculum content were short stories and personal narratives written in conversational styles; oral language interpretations; storytelling, script reading, and play writing; memorizing poetry, proverbs, and quotations; call–response and dramatic performance; language variation as demonstrated by a variety of literary forms; and factual information about African American history. Samples of literature produced by such distinguished authors as Langston Hughes, Virginia Hamilton, Alice Walker, Richard Wright, Paul Lawrence Dunbar, Gwendolyn Brooks, Toni Morrison, Sterling Brown, and Nikki Giovanni were used to teach these cultural features.

Effects of the WGWP on student achievement were determined by performance on standardized tests, analysis of student writing samples, and teacher observations of student behaviors. Significant improvements occurred on all these measures. At the end of its first year, the scores of the participating students on the district's writing assessment increased by an average of 2.0 points compared to a mean increase of 1.6 for all students. The scores for the African American students in the project increased by 2.3 points in middle schools and 1.7 points in high schools. Past writing assessments in the district had shown increases of 1.0 point from grade to grade over an academic year.

In the subsequent years of the project, all the participating students continued to make greater improvements in their writing skills than their counterparts. The performance of African Americans was comparable to that of other project students. Increases in their scores on the writing assessments ranged from 0.7 to 4.0 points across the first 4 years of the project. This achievement was equal to the improvement of other participating students, but slightly lower than the average growth for all students in the district, which ranged from 1.0 to 4.6 points. There was one deviation from these improvement trends. This occurred for grades 9 and 10 in the second year of the project, when the achievement of all targeted and African American students declined. Despite these improvements, the total writing scores of the African American students continued to be significantly lower than those of other students in the entire district (Krater et al., 1994).

During the fifth year of its existence, the Webster Groves Writing Project shifted from local district measures to the Missouri state writing test to assess student performance. Again, the results were positive. Sixty-seven percent of the eighth-graders (215) in the project scored above the state mean, and 14 percent (45) scored below the mean. Only 6% of all students taking the Missouri writing test scored 5 or 5.5 out of a possible score of 6 points; 20 percent of them were participants in the Webster Groves Writing Project (Krater et al., 1994). In addition to these test scores, there were other indicators of the positive effects of this project on student achievement. The writing samples demonstrated improvements in the development and organization of ideas, specific word choices, introductions and endings, and focused thinking and clarity of expression. The students themselves expressed greater confidence in and satisfaction with their writing. This was particularly true of the African Americans. The overall success of the Webster Groves Writing Project led the school district to adapt its principles and methods to K–9 mathematics and two other districts to adopt the model for their writing programs.

Additional evidence of the successful use of ethnic literature to improve the literacy achievement of students is provided by Grice and Vaughn (1992). They studied the responses of African and European American third-graders to African American culturally conscious literature; that is, picture books, novels, biographies, and poetry with African American topics, storylines, characters, and settings. These resources were selected to stimulate pride in cultural heritage; celebrate the triumphs of notable African Americans; develop commitment to community; value family life; and empower young readers by enhancing their self-confidence and decision-making skills. Four *qualitative* indicators were used to assess the effects of this curriculum on student achievement. They were (1) *comprehension* (did the students understand what the books were about?); (2) *authenticity* (did the students think the story and characters could be real?); (3) *identity* and *involvement* (could the students personally relate to and see themselves in the story?); and (4) *evaluation* (did the students like or dislike the books, and why?).

Twenty-one of the twenty-four books used in the project were categorized as "culturally conscious" and three were "melting pot" (the characters were middle-class and no explicit references were made to their racial identity). Of these, twenty were picture books, two were juvenile biographies, and four were realistic fiction works with characters close in age to third-graders. They were varied across situation, textual focus, and genre to include African American heritage, biography, community, family ties, friendship, poetic verse, and male and female characters. The students who were selected to participate in the program read 2 years below grade level and had scored below the 25th percentile on the MAT-6 achievement test. Before the research began, they had demonstrated the ability to follow storylines, form opinions about the realism of characters and story plots, project themselves into stories, and explain their evaluation of books comparable in difficulty to the ones used in the study.

Regardless of ethnicity and gender, the students preferred books about family, community, and friends. The level of acceptance and identification was higher for African Americans (especially females) than European Americans. Both European and African Americans found the books about African heritage and those in poetic verse more difficult to understand and accept, but they were somewhat less problematic for the African American students. The contextual knowledge, prior experiences, and cultural background of students either facilitated or interfered with their ability to receive the messages from the books (Grice & Vaughn, 1992).

These findings support some general claims frequently made about culturally responsive pedagogy. Students from one ethnic group can learn and appreciate the cultures and contributions of other groups, and teaching students' their own cultural heritages is personally enriching. Without adequate background knowledge and contextual orientations, multicultural content can have negative effects. This was apparent in the reactions of the students in the Grice and Vaughn study to the books about African heritage. Both the European Americans and the African Americans rejected the stories about Africa because they did not have sufficient background knowledge to understand or appreciate them (Grice & Vaughn, 1992). Reactions such as these support Crawford's (1993) assertion that a mismatch between the intellectual, cultural, and experiential schemata of students and those represented in topics and texts of instructional materials impedes comprehension. Conversely, when academic and experiential schemata match, students find reading materials easier to understand and more useful in increasing mastery of other literacy skills.

Since 1987, the Rough Rook Demonstration School on the Navajo Reservation in Arizona has used cultural content to increase the academic achievement of its students. The program designed for this purpose is the Rough Rock English–Navajo Language Arts Program (RRENLAP). This is a bilingual/bicultural initiative to improve students' language, literacy, and biliteracy skills (Dick, Estell, & McCarty, 1994). The program began in 1987 as an experiment with kindergartners and first-graders, eventually expanding to include grades K–6. Its mission was to modify "cutting-edge" pedagogies, such as whole-language approaches, cooperative learning, and literature-based literacy instruction, to fit the linguistic and cultural contexts of students at the Rough Rock Community School. An example of this adaptation was a third-grade unit on wind that included the study of local and regional climatology, Navajo directional symbols and oral narratives, and journal writing in Navajo and English. Over time, less reliance was placed on commercially published reading and language arts materials, and more on ones written by the students and teachers themselves that reflected local community culture (Dick et al., 1994).

The RRENLAP produced significant improvements in student achievement. On locally developed criterion-referenced measures of reading comprehension, the K–3 students showed a gain of 12 percentage points, and their median percentile rank scores on the CTBS reading vocabulary test doubled, although they still remained below the national average. The first group of students who spent four years in the program made an average gain of 60 percentage points in their Navajo and English listening comprehension scores over three years. Teachers' qualitative assessments indicated consistent improvement and control of vocabulary, grammar, social uses of writing, and content area knowledge for the RRENLAP students (Dick et al., 1994; Lipka & McCarty, 1994). This project illustrated another important principle of culturally responsive teaching. That is, *sustained collaboration* among school staff with different capabilities, and between schools and community members, is a useful way to develop relevant curriculum content and instructional programs for ethnically diverse students.

The Kickapoo Nation in Kansas has tried to make the education available to children and youth of its tribal community more academically successful by instituting a reform plan called the "Circle of Learning" (Dupuis & Walker, 1988). Begun in 1985, it was designed to incorporate Kickapoo cultural characteristics into the educational process. Specific goals of the program included improving academic achievement; developing positive self-images; teaching competitive skills tempered with cooperation and sharing of resources; facilitating cultural maintenance and adaptation; and increasing participation of Kickapoo families and community in the educational process. Students learned their cultural values, native languages, histories, and contributions along with academic subject-matter content and skills. Some of the values taught included respect for the wisdom and dignity of elders, fortitude, community allegiance, bravery, caring and mutual assistance, generosity, and self-determination. In fact, "Kickapoo culture is woven into the total fabric of the curriculum" (Dupuis & Walker, 1988, p. 31). The only evidence of the effects of the Circle of Learning on student achievement comes from an attitude survey administered to the students 2 years after the program began. All the respondents felt that it had increased their interest and participation in school, self-confidence, feeling of efficacy in dealing with the non-Indian world, understanding the importance of honoring their own cultural values, and pride in their ethnic identity (Dupuis & Walker, 1988).

Math and Science Achievement

The existence and effects of culturally pluralistic curriculum content are less evident in math and science than in reading and writing. While many math and science programs earmarked for ethnically diverse students of color exist, most have little or no specific cultural content. These programs tend to be specifically funded supplements to the regular curriculum designed to improve the participation of students of color in advanced-level math and science courses and career preparation. Their culturally pluralistic content is limited largely to identifying ethnic individuals and contributions to the fields of interest and involving ethnic professionals as mentors for students.

Curriculum initiatives to improve the participation and achievement of "at-risk" students of color in math, science, and engineering courses have existed since the mid-1970s. They range from relatively small single-district to extensive regional and national programs; from early interventions for elementary and middle school students to enrichments and academic outreach initiatives for high schoolers; and from privately funded to state and federally financed projects. All these initiatives have similar curriculum goals, content, structures, and effects on student achievement. In addition to increasing course enrollments and math and science test scores, the goals include raising the self-esteem and career aspirations of low-achieving students; developing understanding and appreciation of the economic utility of math and science; providing at-risk students with more motivational and meaningful contexts for learning; modeling active, practical, and integrative approaches to learning; exposing students to leaders in the fields; and teaching "creative sciencing" skills, such as reasoning, problem solving, and higher-order thinking. Most of the programs operate after school, on Saturdays, and during the summers. They also use a variety of measures and indicators to assess student performance. Among these are standardized test scores, advanced-level course enrollments, observations of involvement levels, self-reports of interest and motivation, and the frequency and quality of participation in science fairs.

An example of school district programs is the Teaching Excellence for Minority Student Achievement in the Sciences (TEMSAS) project. It is designed for preadolescents and operates in 10 schools in Los Angeles. In 1995 approximately 87% of the participating students were African American and 13% were Latino. Of these, 64% were males and 36% were females (Adenika-Morrow, 1995). The Urban Schools Science and Mathematics Program (USSAMP) and the Qualitative Understanding and Amplifying Student Achievement and Reasoning project (QUASAR) are representative of regional efforts to increase ethnic and gender diversity in high-status math and science courses for middle school Latino and African American students. In 1993 USSAMP was implemented in the Atlanta, Cleveland, and Detroit public schools (Archer, 1993). It is one of the few of these programs that is explicit in including information about the contributions and careers of Africans and African Americans in math, science, and technology. QUASAR, which operates in six school districts, includes some European American students as well African Americans and Latinos (Lane, 1993; Silver, 1995; Silver & Stein, 1996).

The most extensive national effort to date to improve the math achievement of ethnically diverse students is EQUITY 2000. Sponsored by the College Board, this project began in 1990 with six pilot sites (Fort Worth, Texas; Milwaukee, Wisconsin; Nashville, Tennessee; Prince George's County, Maryland; Providence, Rhode Island: and San Jose, California). By the 1995–1996 school year, it had expanded to include more than 500,000 students in 700 schools in 14 school districts (Everson & Dunham, 1995, 1996). In late 1996 the College Board decided to extend the project to 10 to 15 additional school districts each year for the next 5 years. In 1997 the Fort Wayne, Indiana, and Memphis, Tennessee, public school systems adopted EQUITY 2000, the regular project was introduced into nine school districts, and customized versions were developed for three others.

EQUITY 2000 has produced improved performance for all ethnic groups involved (Latinos, Asian American, African Americans, European Americans). This improvement includes increased enrollments in and percentage of students passing high school algebra and geometry; more advanced-placement programs and testing participation (especially for Latinos and African Americans); higher passing rates in courses and grade point averages; higher rates of PSAT, NMSQT, SAT, and ACT test-taking among African Americans and Latinos; and increases in the number of students who self-declare their intentions to take more advanced math classes, attend college, and major in math or math-related fields of study (Everson & Dunham, 1995, 1996; *AP at all Equity 2000 Sites*, n.d.; *Equity 2000*, n.d.). For example, from 1991 to 1997 enrollment in tenth-grade geometry or some higher math (e.g., calculus) increased from 35% to 69% for African Americans, from 21% to 49% for Latinos, from 59% to 77% for Asian Americans; and from 49% to 72% for European Americans (www.collegeboard.org).

Project IMPACT is both similar to and different from other math and science programs. Its targeted students are much younger and more ethnically diverse than those involved in most other math improvement projects. They are in grades K–3 and include African Americans, Haitians, Cambodians, Vietnamese, Korean Americans, Middle Easterners, and Central and South American Latinos. To accommodate this diversity, the criterion-referenced measures used to assess student achievement are administered in six languages (English, Spanish, French, Portuguese, Vietnamese, and Khmer [a Cambodian dialect]) (P. Campbell, 1996).

The American Indian Science and Engineering Society (AISES) is a nonprofit national organization (www.aises.org). It was created in 1977 by Native American scientists, engineers, and educators to improve the academic achievement of Native American students in the science, math, and engineering fields. Through a wide variety of programs AISES offers financial, academic, and cultural support to American Indians and Alaskan Natives from middle through graduate school; provides professional development activities to enable teachers to work better with Native American students; develops culturally appropriate curricula and instructional materials for; and builds partnerships with tribal communities, schools, corporations, foundations, governmental agencies, and organizations to accomplish its goals. In 1999 AISES's membership included 2315 members, 48 affiliated high schools, 132 science and engineering professional, 1162 college student members, 507 pre-college members, and 514 Sequoyah Fellows (individuals who contribute $1000).

Two major pre-college curriculum projects are sponsored by AISES. One is the Comprehensive Enrichment Program. It conducts intensive summer math and science study camps that serve as many as 350 students per year. The other project is the annual National Science Fair which involves more than 1000 elementary and secondary school students. Participation in the programs increases high school graduation and college attendance rates. Ninety percent of the students who attend regular AISES summer programs graduate from high school compared to the 52% national average. Over 50% of those who participate in the summer programs, science fairs, and mathematics competitions for 2 years or more enroll in college compared to 17% of Native American students nationally.

Other math and science projects for students of color offer additional evidence of success in improving achievement. Over a 2-year period, the number of students in the QUASAR project who performed at the highest levels of mathematical reasoning, problem solving, and communication on a project-designed cognitive assessment instrument increased from 18% to 40%. The students also did better than their counterparts on the eighth-grade National Assessment of Educational Progress (NAEP) mathematics test and had higher enrollment and passing rates for ninth-grade algebra (Lane, Silver, & Wang, 1995; Silver & Lane, 1995; Silver & Stein, 1996). Project IMPACT students (grades K–3) performed better than nonparticipants on problem solving and reasoning as well as mastery of whole-number concepts, place values, and fraction meaning (P. Campbell, 1996). Teachers observed increased pleasure, involvement, and competence in science and math investigations and experiments among the students who participated in TEMSAS (Adenika-Morrow, 1995).

USSAMP for grades 6–8 and the Detroit Area Pre-College Engineering

Program (DAPCEP) for grades 7–12 used participation in science fairs, as well as course enrollments and mastery of content, as indicators of student achievement. In 1992, all of the 71 science fair entries from one Detroit USSAMP school (for students in grades 6–8) won a prize, including 36 gold awards (grand, first, second, and third places). One class of 35 won 18 prizes, 10 of which were gold (Archer, 1993). The number of DAPCEP entries in the annual Detroit Metropolitan Science Fair increased from 26 (11%) in 1977 to 1,326 (62%) in 1990. Winning entries increased from 2 to 118 (Hill, 1990).

Two projects are reported in the professional literature that include explicit cultural content about ethnically diverse native groups. One deals with Native Alaskans and the other with multiple Native American tribal groups. Local teachers worked closely with Yup'ik community elders to create cultural affirmation in schools so that students could have a better chance to succeed academically. The curricular content these culturally responsive educators produced met the standards of the National Council of Teachers of Mathematics, while simultaneously teaching Yup'ik culture. Yup'ik songs, dance, and drumming were used to teach numerical systems, place values, measurement, symmetry, and pattern. Traditional ways of knowing also were incorporated into the teaching of science. For example, Yup'ik elders taught teachers how to observe and interpret sunrises, sunsets, and moon stages to predict weather patterns (Lipka & McCarty, 1994). Unfortunately, no information is available on this project's effects on achievement, even though interest in learning tasks did increase and the students reacted positively to the inclusion of their culture in the curriculum.

Matthews and Smith (1991) studied the effects of culturally relevant instructional materials on the interests, attitudes, and performance of Native American students in science and language arts. The participants in the study were 203 fourth- through eighth-graders, 10 teachers, and 17 classes in 10 schools from eight Bureau of Indian Affairs (BIA) agencies. The students were distributed among 11 tribal affiliations: Navajo, Sioux, Tohono Odham (Pagago), Hopi, Kiowa, Cheyenne/Arapaho, Yakima, Comanche, Wichita, Caddo, and Ponca. The project covered a 10-week period during which teachers of the experimental group used Native American cultural content to teach 25 hours of science and 25 hours of language arts. Teachers in the control group taught the same number of hours and skills, but without the specifically designed materials. The culturally relevant content included biographical profiles of Native Americans in different careers who use science in their daily lives; math- and science-related activities developed by the Math and Science Teachers for Reservation Schools (MASTERS) Project, which was supported by the National Science Foundation (NSF); science activities from the Career Oriented Materials to Explore Topics in Science (COMETS) and the Outside World Science Projects (OWSP); and 12 sketches from the American Indian Science and Engineering Society (AISES) publications.

Achievement data were collected, using a pretest–posttest design, on students' attitudes toward Native Americans in science-related fields (measured by an Attitude Toward Indians in Science scale) and knowledge of science concepts (assessed by the Science Concept Questionnaire). The results indicated that students taught with Native American cultural materials had more positive attitudes and higher levels of achievement than those who were taught similar skills without the culturally relevant inclusions. No differences were apparent in these effects by the gender of students. More than two-thirds of the students said they learned more about science and that their teachers made science interesting to learn. There also was a positive, but low, correlation between attitude toward and achievement in science. The effects of the culturally relevant materials varied by ethnic groups, with non-Navajo students having higher achievement than the Navajos but no significant differences in attitudes. These results prompted Matthews and Smith (1991) to suggest that curriculum content on Native Americans should deal explicitly with the cultural characteristics and contributions of specific tribal groups.

In general, mathematics and science programs targeted to students of color have improved achievement (especially in the form of advanced-level course enrollments, grade point averages, and participation in science fairs) without the benefit of using significant amounts of multicultural content. Some skeptics may see this as evidence that culturally diverse content in school curricula is not needed to increase academic achievement. But before conceding to this point, some other interpretations should be considered. First, culturally responsive pedagogy includes more than curriculum content. Math and science programs may be tapping into some of these other components, such as using instructional delivery strategies that are congruent with the learning styles of students. Second, these programs include those features of culturally responsive pedagogy that emphasize high achievement expectations for students and use instructional initiatives that are deliberately targeted to specific ethnic groups. Much implicit cultural content can be conveyed through these expectations and emphases, especially if the teachers and directors of the projects are culturally sensitive in other ways. Third, even higher levels of achievement might result if math and science curricula included more explicit culturally diverse curriculum content.

IMPROVING CULTURALLY DIVERSE CURRICULUM CONTENT

Much more cultural content is needed in all school curricula about all ethnic groups of color. The need is especially apparent in math and science and for ethnic groups other than African Americans. This is true for those subjects in which some initiatives are already underway as well as those which have not changed at all. This means designing more multicultural literacy programs in secondary schools and more math and science programs at all grade levels; teaching explicit information about gender contributions, issues, experiences, and achievement effects *within ethnic groups*; and pursuing more sustained efforts to incorporate content about ethnic and cultural diversity in regular school subjects and skills taught on a routine basis.

Educators should be diligent in ensuring that curriculum content about ethnically diverse groups is accurate, authentic, and comprehensive. This goal can be accomplished by working in collaboration with ethnic scholars, community leaders, and "cultural brokers," as well as combining information from many disciplines to generate culturally relevant curriculum content for diverse ethnic groups. Culturally responsive curriculum content also should deal simultaneously with concepts, principles, and ideas (such as oppression, identity, powerlessness and privilege, culture, and struggle) generalizable across ethnic groups and knowledge about the particular lives, experiences, and contributions of specific groups (Banks, 1991; Gay, 1975, 1988, 1995). For example, students need to learn about Asian Americans in general and the many different ethnic groups usually included in this category, such as Chinese, Vietnamese, Filipino, Cambodian, Korean, Japanese, and East Indian Americans.

Several other important implications for culturally responsive pedagogical practices are embedded in the nature and effects of culturally diverse curriculum content examined thus far. One is the need to *regularly* provide students with more accurate cultural information about groups of color in order to fill knowledge voids and correct existing distortions. This information needs to be capable of facilitating many different kinds of learning—cognitive, affective, social, political, personal, and moral. It should be multiethnic, cover a wide range of perspectives and experiences, and encompass both tangible (artifacts) and intangible (values, beliefs) aspects of culture (Banks & Banks, 1997; Hilliard, 1991/1992; Nieto, 1999; J. King, 1994). No single content source is capable of doing all of this alone. Therefore, curriculum designers should always use a variety of content sources from different genres and disciplines, including textbooks, literature, mass media, music, personal experiences, and social science research. Information derived from new and emerging ethnic-centered and feminist literary and social science scholarship should also be included.

Students should learn how to conduct ideological and content analyses of various sources of curriculum content about ethnic and cultural diversity. These learning experiences involve revealing implicit values and biases, modifying attitudes and perceptions, developing different evaluation criteria, and acting deliberately to first deconstruct and then reconstruct common ethnic and gender typecastings. Students can begin by compiling background information on the ethnicity, gender, expertise, experience, and motivation of textbook authors and media programmers. Then, they might search for evidence of how these "positionality factors" affect the presentations writers and directors make about ethnic issues and groups. Phrases and words in dialogues of characters in TV programs and movies, themes, topics and scenarios depicted, and stories in textbooks that are age-, gender-, and ethnic group–specific can be analyzed in search of this evidence. The students can compare different versions and interpretations of the same issues, such as African, Chinese, Latino, and Filipino American approaches to women's liberation.

These learning activities make manifest what is meant by knowledge being a social and situated construction, not a universal and absolute reality, and the influence of *contextuality* in meaning-making. They will also be useful in counteracting the negative emotional and academic effects of the racism and sexism that continue to be embedded in both formal and informal curriculum content. The skills that students apply in these analyses, such as inquiry, critical thinking, collecting data, verifying evidence, perspective taking, and comprehending and communicating information, represent significant academic achievement in and of themselves.

Teachers and students should conduct their own research on how textbooks, the mass media, trade books, and other curriculum content sources affect knowledge, attitudes, and behaviors toward ethnic and cultural diversity and mastery of various academic skills. Many assertions exist about what these effects are, but too little actual data are available to substantiate them. Operating in the traditions of participatory observations and collaborative action research, students and teachers should study themselves in their own classrooms on a routine basis. They might examine such issues as: What issues about ethnic groups and aspects of cultural diversity are most palpable, stress-provoking, difficult, and easy to master? How are receptivity and resistance to cultural diversity manifested by students, and how these are mediated? How are these reactions distributed by gender within ethnic groups and among different ethnic groups? What kinds of instructional materials work best for which students? What constitutes mastery of multicultural curriculum content and its associated evidence?

Shor and Freire (1987) speak convincingly about the educational values of these kinds of learning experiences. They see them as foundations for high-quality, liberatory teaching. The critical reflection, uncertainty, curiosity, demanding inquiry, and action they demand and cultivate are indispensable to effective learning. This "research-teaching" also has practical value for improving student achievement. It helps teachers to develop curriculum content that is intrinsically motivating; places students and teachers in closer interaction with each other and facilitates better collaboration between them; and produces grassroots knowledge and perspectives that challenge the official ideologies marketed by schools (Shor & Freire, 1987, pp. 8–10).

Finally, students and teachers should become scholars of ethnic and cultural diversity, and generate their own curriculum content. They can do library research; conduct interviews and oral histories; participate in shadow studies; organize cultural exchanges; do site observations of ethnic communities and institutions; and collect personal stories covering a wide spectrum of individuals according to ethnicity, gender, age, generation, educational level, career, country of origin, and residential location. The information these inquiries produce can be used to contest, correct, supplement, and/or replace existing textbook and mass media content.

CONCLUSION

Students are exposed to a wide variety and quality of content about ethnic and cultural diversity. This exposure is both formal and informal, direct and tacit; it encompasses what is officially delivered in schools as well as what is offered through "societal curricula," especially as conveyed through the mass media and tradebooks. Whether the images of ethnic diversity these content sources convey are positive or negative, they have powerful influences on students, including self-perceptions, attitudes toward others, what is considered "truth" and knowledge worth knowing, and how they respond to classroom instruction. Students who see their ethnic groups portrayed negatively in literary and trade books, television programs, movies, newspapers, and advertising may not value themselves or trust that schools will do anything differently. Unfortunately, their suspicions have been too often confirmed by racially biased instructional materials. Ethnically diverse students who feel invalidated in society and school are not likely to perform as well as they might on academic tasks, if for no other reason than that these prejudices interfere with their motivation to learn, time-on-task, and persistence in learning engagements. Consequently, all sources of curriculum content, both within and outside of schools, should be revised to be more accurate and inclusive in their representations of cultural diversity. Good information is a necessary element of culturally responsive teaching and the improvement in student achievement.

Some notable progress has been made over the last few decades in how the histories, lives, cultures, and contributions of African, Asian, Native, Latino, and European Americans are portrayed in textbooks, literary books, and the mass media. The most blatant stereotypical characterizations have been eliminated. Yet these frequently used sources of curriculum content are not as good as they should be. Their flaws demand continuous improvements from all sectors of society and the educational profession. Teachers and students can and should be active participants in improving the quality of these instructional materials. Being directly involved in the construction of knowledge about ethnic and cultural diversity is an important way to practice culturally responsive pedagogy.

Curriculum sources and content that provide accurate presentations of ethnic and cultural diversity offer several other benefits for improving student achievement. First, they provide those who have never had close personal contact with members of ethnic groups other than their own with opportunities to communication and engage with diverse people as well as to confront themselves. This experience alone will calm some fears, dispel some myths, and produce some learning that cannot be obtained from books and other media sources. Removing the threat and intimidation from new knowledge enhances receptivity toward and mastery of it. Second, students are actively involved in their own learning. Participatory engagement tends to have positive effects on achievement. Third, students have real power to help structure their own learning. They thus have some real control over their own academic destinies. Surely students will learn better that which is of their own creation.

Theory about the potential of multicultural curriculum content for improving the achievement of ethnically diverse students is rich and extensive, but supportive research is rather sparse. Much more empirical and practice documentation is needed to support these theoretical claims. In compiling this evidence, emphasis should be on specifying curriculum content effects on different types of achievements, such as grade point averages, test scores, participation in classroom discourse, and students' self-esteem and feelings of efficacy; how these effects are distributed within and across ethnic groups; and achievement effects derived from the incorporation of multicultural content into the curricula of all subjects and skills taught in school. Beyond the early elementary grades (K–2) students, along with their teachers, can contribute to the development of this fund of knowledge by "telling their own stories" about how exposure to multicultural curriculum content has affected them personally. Student commentaries are powerful evidence for determining the effectiveness of educational reforms, but they are too often overlooked. Culturally responsive teaching corrects this oversight by including the needs, knowledge, and participation of students in all aspects of the educational enterprise, including the selection, design, and analysis of curriculum content and the determination of its effects on achievement.

Several important messages for the future implementation of culturally responsive teaching can be derived from the curricular programs, practices, and research discussed in this chapter. To begin with, even curricula with minimum cultural content improve student achievement, according to a variety of indicators, across ethnic groups, grade levels, and subject or skill areas. The multiple achievement effects include higher scores on standardized tests, higher grade point averages, improved student self-concepts and self-confidence, and greater varieties and levels of student engagement with subject matter. The range of these effects is very encouraging, and it indicates that there are many ways in which teachers can design culturally responsive curricula for African, Asian, Native, and Latino American students. However, more evidence is needed to document the effects of multicultural content on student achievement in all subjects taught in schools, at all grade levels, and for all ethnic groups.

CHAPTER 6

Cultural Congruity in Teaching and Learning

If teachers are to do effective culturally responsive teaching, they need to understand how ethnically diverse students learn. This is necessary because the processes of learning—not the intellectual capability to do so—used by students from different ethnic groups are influenced by their cultural socialization. Indeed,

> the sociocultural system of the child's home and community is influential in producing culturally unique preferred modes of relating to others . . . culturally unique incentive preferences, . . . as well as a preferred mode of thinking, perceiving, remembering, and problem solving. All of these characteristics . . . must be incorporated as the principal bases upon which programs for instituting changes in the school must be developed. (Ramírez & Castañeda, 1974, p. 32)

The mere mention of ethnically specific learning styles causes contention and resistance from many. The opponents are quick to point out that "not everyone within a ethnic group learns like that." And right they are. There are exceptions to any cultural descriptions. Every individual in an ethnic group does not have to exhibit cultural characteristics as described for those characteristics to be valid. Characteristics of learning styles are pedagogically promising to the extent that they illuminate patterns of cultural values and behaviors that influence how children learn, and they provide functional directions for modifying instructional techniques to better meet the academic needs of ethnically diverse students (Bennett, 1995a). Therefore, learning styles should be seen not only as categories for labeling students but also as tools improving the school achievement of Latino, Native, Asian, and African American students by creating more *cultural congruity* in teaching–learning processes. In examining learning styles, it is important to remember that how, or whether, they are expressed by individual members of ethnic groups is influenced by other variables. Critical among these are level of ethnic affiliation, social class, education, and degree of traditionalism. As explained in Chapter 1, cultural characteristics are likely to be more "pure" and come closer to approximating conceptual profiles among group members who have high levels of ethnic identification and affiliation, are poor, have low levels of education, and are rather traditional in their cultural expressions.

INTRODUCTION

Whereas Chapters 3–5 dealt with important and necessary components of culturally responsive teaching, this one focuses on the most fundamental aspect; that is, the process of instruction. The ethic of caring (Chapter 3) constitutes the *ideological grounding*, cultural communication (Chapter 4) is the *tool*, curriculum content about ethnic and cultural diversity (Chapter 5) is the *resource*, and instruction is the actual *praxis* of culturally responsive teaching. Instruction combines all the other components into coherent configurations and puts them into action to expedite learning. It is the *engagement*, the *interaction*, the *dialectic discourse* of students and teachers in the *processes* of teaching and learning. Interactional processes are absolutely imperative to the implementation of culturally responsive teaching. They can nullify, enrich, counteract, or complement other components of teaching.

Interactions between students and teachers may vary widely in form, function, and effect, but there is no question about their existence. Irvine and York (1995, p. 494) explain that "teaching is an act of social interaction, and the resultant classroom climate is related directly to the interpersonal relationship between student and teacher" (p. 494). Whether direct or indirect, intellectual or emotional, physical or social, didactic or communal, literal or symbolic, verbal or nonverbal, interactions are the ultimate sites where teaching and learning happen—or do not happen.

Instructional effectiveness is often minimized by inconsistencies in the rules and protocols governing interactions in different cultural systems. In fact, mastering the substantive content of instruction may be jeopardized by violating the procedural protocols about how learning processes are supposed to unfold (Holliday, 1985). Therefore, establishing congruity between different aspects of the learning processes of ethnically diverse students and the strategies of instruction used by classroom teachers is essential to improving their academic achievement. This continuity requires that teachers contextualize the instruction of students of color in their various cultural forms, behaviors, and experiences (Irvine & York, 1995).

Culturally diverse instructional bridging and contextualizing—or scaffolding—exemplify several generally accepted principles of learning. These are summarized by Howe (1984) and Ormrod (1995). Among them are the following:

- Students' existing knowledge is the best starting point for the introduction of new knowledge (principle of similarity).
- Prior success breeds subsequent effort and success (principle of efficacy).
- New knowledge is learned more easily and retained longer when it is connected to prior knowledge, frames of reference, or cognitive schematas (principle of congruity).
- Reducing the "strangeness" of new knowledge and the concomitant "threat of the unfamiliar" increases students' engagement with and mastery of learning tasks (principle of familiarity).
- Organizational and structural factors surrounding how one goes about learning have more powerful effects on the mastery of new knowledge than the amount of prior knowledge one possesses, per se (principle of transactionalism).
- Understanding how students' knowledge is organized and interrelated—their cognitive structures—is essential to maximizing their classroom learning (principle of cognitive mapping).

These principles suggest that it is not enough for teachers to know "what the learner knows about individual facts and concepts" (Howe, 1984, p. 68). They also need to understand how students come to know or to learn so that they can convey new knowledge to them through their own learning systems. The goal of this chapter is to explain these "connections" and demonstrate the positive effects they have on student achievement. The discussion is organized into five sections. The first presents a brief summary of general aspects of ethnic learning styles. The emphasis is not on the debate about the validity of ethnic learning styles but on the constellation of components that comprise them.

Each of the four remaining parts of the chapter is devoted to discussions of instructional practices and research studies that amplify components of different learning styles. The second section deals with descriptions and effects of comprehensive instructional interventions. These are programs that encompass several different aspects of learning styles. Since they were designed as composites, to discuss their features separately would compromise the integrity of the programs. The third part of the chapter focuses on teaching techniques with different groups of color that are grounded in cooperative and collaborative learning, and the effects of these on student achievement. Instructional practices and research emphasizing active and affective engagement are discussed in the fourth section. The last part of the chapter examines the effects of ethnic-centered programs, such as African American and Native American schools and classes. Culturally responsive teaching does not advocate the physical separation of students by ethnic groups for instructional purposes. But to the extent that these arrangements employ culturally situated teaching and learning, they can be seen as a variation of culturally responsive teaching.

LEARNING STYLES BASELINE

By the time children begin their formal school career at 5 years of age, they already have internalized rules and procedures for acquiring knowledge and demonstrating their skills. These cognitive processing protocols are learned from their cultural socialization. They may be refined and elaborated over time, even superseded on occasion for the performance of certain tasks. But the core of these culturally influenced rules and procedures continues to *anchor* how individuals process intellectual challenges for the rest of their lives.

A learning style is the process one habitually uses for cognitive problem solving and for showing what one knows and is capable of doing (More, 1989; Shade, 1989). Guild and Garger (1985) add that the essence of learning styles can be attained from analyzing what people routinely do when they interact with new ideas, people, situations, and information. This involves (1) cognition (ways of knowing); (2) conceptualizing (formulating ideas and thoughts); (3) affective reacting (feeling and valuing); and (4) acting (exhibiting some kind of behavior). Bennett (1995a) agrees that learning styles are the cognitive, affective, and behavioral ways that individuals perceive, interact with, and respond to learning situations. According to Shade and New (1993), learning styles have perceptual and thinking dimensions. The perceptual deals with preference for sensory stimulation (e.g., sight, sound, touch, motion, etc.), and thinking patterns have to do with how information is processed, such as organizing, analyzing, inferring, appraising, and transforming. Many conceptualizations of learning styles describe them in terms of bipolarity. One end of the continuum is represented by analytical, reflective, abstract, field-independent, detail-specific, and deductive approaches to learning; the other by relational, impulsive, concrete, field-dependent, general, holistic, and inductive processes (Barbe & Swassing, 1979; Dunn, Dunn, & Price, 1979; Hollins et al., 1994; Irvine & York, 1995; Morris, Sather, & Scull, 1978; Ramírez & Castañeda, 1974; Shade, 1989).

Overall characterizations of learning styles suggest that they are not monolithic, situationally idiosyncratic, or static traits. Instead, they are multidimensional, habituated processes that are the "central tendencies" of how students from different ethnic groups engage with learning encounters. They encompass eight key dimensions. No ranking of importance is intended by the order in which these learning style dimensions are presented. Conceptually, they should be considered as an interactive composite. Operationally, their separate identities provide different opportunities for designing culturally compatible instruction for ethnically diverse students.

- *Procedural*—the preferred ways of approaching and working through learning tasks. These include pacing rates; distribution of time; variety versus similarity; novelty or predictability; passivity or activity; task-directed or sociality; structured order or freedom; and preference for direct teaching or inquiry and discovery learning.
- *Communicative*—how thoughts are organized, sequenced, and conveyed in spoken and written forms, whether as elaborated narrative storytelling or precise responses to explicit questions; as topic-specific or topic-chaining discourse techniques; as passionate advocacy of ideas or dispassionate recorders and reporters; whether the purpose is to achieve descriptive and factual accuracy or to capture persuasive power and convey literary aestheticism.
- *Substantive*—preferred content, such as descriptive details or general pattern, concepts and principles or factual information, statistics or personal and social scenarios; preferred subjects, such as math, science, social studies, fine or language arts; technical, interpretative, and evaluative tasks; preferred intellectualizing tasks, such as memorizing, describing, analyzing, classifying, or criticizing.
- *Environmental*—Preferred physical, social, and interpersonal settings for learning, including sound or silence; room lighting and temperature; presence or absence of others; ambiance of struggle or playfulness, of fun and joy, or of pain and somberness.
- *Organizational*—preferred structural arrangements for work and study space, including the amount of personal space; the fullness or emptiness of learning space; rigidity or flexibility in use of and claims made to space; carefully organized or cluttered learning resources and space locations; individually claimed or group-shared space; rigidity or flexibility of the habitation of space.
- *Perceptual*—preferred sensory stimulation for receiving, processing, and transmitting information, including visual, tactile, auditory, kinetic, oral, or multiple sensory modalities.

• *Relational*—Preferred interpersonal and social interaction modes in learning situations, including formality or informality, individual competition or group cooperation, independence or interdependence, peer–peer or child–adult, authoritarian or egalitarian, internal or external locus of control; conquest or community.
• *Motivational*—Preferred incentives or stimulations that evoke learning, including individual accomplishment or group well-being, competition or cooperation, conquest or harmony, expediency or propriety, image or integrity, external rewards or internal desires.

Some ethnic-group members exhibit "purer" learning style characteristics than others. The degree of purity is affected by such variables as levels of in-group ethnic identification and affiliation, education, social class, and gender. For instance, highly ethnically affiliated African Americans will exhibit strong preferences for "group-ness" across procedural, motivational, relational, and substantive dimensions of learning because of the values their culture places on communalism, working collaboratively to accomplish tasks, affective emotionalism, and informal social interactions. Independence and self-initiation will permeate the various learning style dimensions for middle-class European Americans, since their culture values competition, individualism, and upward mobility. Culturally traditional Japanese and Chinese American students may be more bi-stylistic. Because of the emphases their cultures place on familial obligations and harmonious relationships (Fox, 1994; Tong, 1978), their motivation and preparation for academic performance tends to be communal and group-focused, but they are quite individualistic and deductive in actual performance delivery. They also tend to perform well on mechanistic, technical, and detail-specific learning tasks instead of the more humanistic, socially-oriented, and holistic emphases that are usually preferred by communal learners (B. Kim, 1978; Leung, 1998; Nakanishi, 1994).

Additional assistance in recognizing the learning styles of students of color and designing compatible instructional strategies can be gained from theory, research, and practice on teaching through sensory modalities (Barbe & Swassing, 1979), multiple intelligences (Armstrong, 1994; L. Campbell, Campbell, & Dickinson, 1996; H. Gardner, 1983; Lazear, 1991, 1994) and brain lateralization (Springer & Deutsch, 1998). Although these models were not created specifically with people of color in mind, there is a great deal of parallelism between them and ethnic learning styles. They can be easily overlaid on each other as well as on various models for enhancing teaching effectiveness. For example, Armstrong (1994) illustrates connections among Gardner's seven intelligences (logical, verbal, visual, kinesthetic, musical, interpersonal, intrapersonal) and the taxonomy of cognitive objectives (knowledge, comprehension, application, analysis, synthesis, evaluation) of Bloom (1956). He demonstrates how multicultural curriculum content can be taught by organizing ethnic individuals and their contributions by type of intelligence. Lazear (1994) is quite comprehensive in his suggestions for how students' knowledge and skills can be assessed for each of the seven kinds of intelligences.

MULTIDIMENSIONAL CULTURALLY CONGRUENT INSTRUCTION

Three highly successful programs are discussed here to illustrate the effects of instructional interventions that incorporate multiple elements of cultural compatibility on the achievement of students of color. Their achievement effects are also multiple and varied. These programs are the Kamehameha Early Education Program (KEEP), the Multicultural Literacy Program (MLP), and the Webster Groves Writing Project (WGWP).

Kamehameha Early Education Program

KEEP began in 1972 (and lasted for 24 years) as a multidisciplinary educational research and development effort to create a language arts program that would improve the reading performance of underachieving Native Hawaiian children in grades K–3 (Jordan, 1985). In addition to improving academic performance, KEEP intended to increase these students' ownership, investment, pride, and engagement in the educational enterprise (Jordan, Tharp, & Baird-Vogt, 1992). Since its beginning, several researchers (Au, 1993; Au & Kawakami, 1994; Boggs et al., 1985; Cazden et al., 1985; Tharp & Gallimore, 1988; Wong Fillmore & Meyer, 1992) have been investigating the achievement effects of matching teaching styles to the Polynesian-based discourse, activity, participation, performance structures, values, beliefs, and behaviors of Native Hawaiian students.

Among the key instructional features of KEEP are small cooperative learning groups, highly interactive discussion processes using an E–T–R sequence (experience–text–relationship), and student engagement in "talk-story" or "co-narration" to construct and communicate meaning in the classroom. The classroom is arranged in activity centers that provide many opportunities for students to participate in collaborative efforts and instructional conversations with the teacher and one another. In these centers, kindergartners engage in peer interactions 50% of the time and first-graders as much as 70% of the time (Tharp & Gallimore, 1988). KEEP also uses a natural-context approach to language development that is strongly shaped by how discourse skills are acquired and applied in Native Hawaiian homes, communities, and culture. While the greatest emphasis in reading instruction is on comprehension, regular attention is given to developing vocabulary, sight phonetics, and decoding skills.

The achievement effects of KEEP are profound. For several years the program has consistently met its primary goal of achieving mean scores near or at the 50th percentile on standardized tests of reading achievement. After the program had been in existence for 15 years, the percentile mean of reading achievement of the first-graders was 55.7 compared to 31.7 for students in non-KEEP classes. The performance of participating and nonparticipating second-graders was 52.5 and 28.8, and for third graders it was 47.8 and 25.5, respectively. These levels of achievement represent major improvements from the 13th percentile average when the program first began. Two other achievement effects are noteworthy. First, KEEP teachers give significantly more praise and less criticism to students than other teachers. Of the three types of praise feedback used most often in the classrooms—*management* for deportment behaviors, *academic* for learning-task related behaviors, and *verbal negatives* (scolds and desists) for unacceptable behavior—the means for KEEP teachers are 21.80 for management, 13.87 for academics, and 2.07 for verbal. The comparative means of other teachers on these types of feedback are 6.03, .65, and 6.01, respectively. Second, KEEP students have an average of 85% engaged time on academic tasks, which is 20 percentage points higher than the means of comparison classrooms (Tharp & Gallimore, 1988).

Multicultural Literacy Program

The Multicultural Literacy Program (MLP) has many of the same purposes and features as KEEP, but for different student populations, and its content is more multiethnic. The project uses different types of literature genres by and about Asian, Native, Latino, African, and Native Hawaiian Americans to teach reading and writing. The student participants are mostly African Americans, Latinos, and European Americans. Since the curricular components and their effects on student achievement were discussed earlier in Chapter 5, the focus here is on its socioculturally sensitive learning environment features.

This component of the MLP involves recontextualizing learning, using alternative social structures and methods of instruction, and with teachers acting as cultural mediators. Classroom learning is connected to the real-life situations and cultural heritages of African, Latino, European, Native, and Asian Americans. Students' own conceptual understandings, knowledge, experiences, attitudes, and values are used to engage them with reading materials. Teachers demonstrate how learning is a social process and affected by the entire community (Diamond & Moore, 1995). The intent of these techniques is to increase the interest in and appeal of instructional tasks and to empower students through better achievement in reading and writing.

The MLP offers a variety of group arrangements and social settings for learning. Among them are learning centers, peer interactions, multiple reality-based reading opportunities, different types of cooperative learning groups, and emotionally and academically supportive communities of learners. More specific teaching strategies include multicultural story features (setting, character development, problems, actions and events, resolutions, etc.) in read- and think-alouds, sustained silent reading (SSR), directed reading–listening–thinking activity (DRLTA), readers' theater, choral reading and reading aloud, personal response to literature, and dramatic interpretation. These strategies stem from the idea that since learning is influenced by students' social and cultural background, it can be best facilitated in socioculturally compatible school contexts and communities (Diamond & Moore, 1995).

Teachers in the Multicultural Literacy Program perform three major functions in creating socioculturally sensitive learning environments for their diverse students. They act as:

> (1) cultural organizers who facilitate strategic ways of accomplishing tasks so that the learning process involves varied ways of knowing, experiencing, thinking, and behaving; (2) cultural mediators who create opportunities for critical dialogue and expression among all students as they pursue knowledge and understanding; and (3) orchestrators of social contexts who provide several learning configurations that include interpersonal *and* intrapersonal opportunities for seeking, accessing, and evaluating knowledge. (Diamond & Moore, 1995, p. 35, emphasis in original)

Webster Grove Writing Project

The culturally responsive instructional dimensions of the Webster Groves Writing Project (WGWP) fall within four of its eight principles and strategies—building on students' strengths, individualizing and personalizing instruction, encouraging cooperative learning, and building bridges and expanding horizons. The teachers in this project translated cues derived from African American cultural values, communication and social interaction patterns, and performance styles into compatible instructional techniques to improve students' writing skills. A set of more specific strategies emerged that applied across the general categories, including:

- Affirming the strong personal voice in African American informal interactions and formal writing
- Building on oral discourse habits and interpretation
- Incorporating performance and role-playing as regular features of teaching and learning
- Validating African American dialect and expressive modes as a functional communication system and assisting students in analyzing and
  appreciating them
- Valuing and using African American culture habitually, rather than
  just on special occasions
- Developing a sense of trust, community, and mutual responsibility for
  learning among students and with teachers
- Consistently combining individual and group efforts and accountability
  for task performance
- Creating classroom climates and opportunities for collaborative com-
  posing, revising, and editing writing tasks
- Using a system of peer response, tutoring, and study buddies
- Affirming personal responses to reading (Krater et al., 1994)

While the existing frames of reference of students are always the
starting points or anchors, instruction does not end there. The WGWP
teachers use the confidence that affirmation of these orientations generated to entice and obligate students to "expand their horizons." These
expansions take the form of "code-shifting" to learn the writing and
speaking conventions of mainstream society and schools. This is accomplished by helping students connect their oral creative strengths to the
demands of reading and writing in school as well as by using their skills
in storytelling, oral interpretation, role-playing, improvisation, script
reading, and call–response. Hanley (1998) used similar techniques with
middle school African Americans to examine their knowledge construction within the context of drama production and performance.

Other reading and writing skills are also contextualized within African American cultural, performance, and learning styles. The expressive
verbal technique of "rapping" (for an explanation, see Kochman, 1972;
Smitherman, 1977; Baber, 1987) is used for book talks, character development, and advertisements. Sermonizing motifs of speaking and class-
response discourse patterns are frequently employed by students to demonstrate their understanding of the cultural techniques and embedded
conventional literary skills (e.g., topic selection, purpose, clarity of development, point of view, and audience appropriateness). They learn by
doing "in the familiar" before broaching the unfamiliar, or alternative,
communicative modes. Consequently, speech and performance precede
writing narratives and reading texts since these are the cultural strengths

and the "expressive anchors" of African American culture. Instead of using a static grammatical structure, language variations are learned by performing aloud and fine-tuning the voice (dialogue within a narrative) and discourse features (Krater et al., 1994). The WGWP teachers hasten to explain that European American students respond positively as well to the dramatic, performance, expressive, participatory, and collegial ambiance of these teaching styles.

Students in the WGWP work together in cooperative arrangements to complete assigned tasks. These arrangements include several major components. First, all group members assume separate but interrelated functions needed to successfully complete tasks. Rewards for group success are given to all members or to none. Second, individual accountability within the group context is expected. Each student assumes responsibility for his or her own tasks, as well as the effective functioning of the group. Third, face-to-face interactions and interpersonal skills are practiced, since genuine cooperative learning requires students to have physical and intellectual access to each other as resources, process monitors, and facilitators. They are taught how to work together; how to praise, criticize, and support each other; how to care about each other; and how to create minicommunities. Fourth, students are given time for debriefing and self-reflection. These processes involve the study groups' assessing the quality of their functioning and the processes they use to accomplish assigned tasks (Krater et al., 1994).

In addition to the improvement in test scores and writing skills discussed in Chapter 5, the Webster Groves Writing Project produced some noteworthy results in personal and social achievement. The thinking of the students was more focused, as evidenced in writing samples that had more details and clearer explanations. Students expressed more confidence in their ability to write and more enjoyment of writing. These reactions were particularly apparent in self-selected writing topics, a finding consistent with those of Chapman (1994). More African Americans than European Americans (two-thirds compared to one-half) were satisfied and surprised with the skills and self-disclosures their writings revealed. These results confirmed the project staff's assertions that:

> Some of the joys of writing are clarifying what you already think, discovering feelings you didn't know you had, surprising yourself with a well-turned phrase, and unearthing a relationship between ideas. Self-satisfaction during the process is the immediate reward; communicating clearly to others is a delayed fulfillment. (Krater et al., 1994, p. 398)

The WGWP also had significant effects on the participating teachers in ways that are important for culturally responsive teaching. They learned (and modified their thinking and instructional behaviors accordingly) that effective teaching and learning really are *informed, dialectic, and dynamic processes* in which roles are fluid and even reversible—where, frequently, teachers become students and students become teachers. Indeed, culturally different students are often the best teachers about themselves if teachers learn how to recognize and receive the knowledge they have to give. By the end of the project, attitudes of the WGWP teachers had changed significantly. They no longer believed specific teaching methods made the most difference in improving the writing achievement of underachieving African American students. Instead, they mused:

> Our interactions with, our concern for, and our immersion with our students as *persons* are the key. . . . We began as teachers who wanted to learn how to help our students write better. Now we want to learn what our students have to teach us. We are still teachers of writing, but first we are teachers of students. (Krater et al., 1994, p. 415, emphasis in original)

COOPERATIVE LEARNING

Cooperation, collaboration, and community are prominent themes, techniques, and goals in educating marginalized Latino, Native, African, and Asian American students. Two major reasons help to explain these pedagogical trends. First, underlying values of human connectedness and collaborative problem solving are high priorities in the cultures of most groups of color in the United States. Second, cooperation plays a central role in these groups' learning styles, especially the communicative, procedural, motivational, and relational dimensions. Therefore, they should be key pillars of culturally responsive teaching. Several research projects and instructional programs have demonstrated the feasibility of community, collaboration, and cooperation for improving the achievement of students of color. Some focus on the processes of cooperative learning in general, and others emphasize cooperative learning in specific subject or skill areas.

General Cooperative Processes and Achievement Effects

Findings of the eight research studies reviewed by Losey (1997) provide support for the pedagogical power of cooperative learning for Latino students. These studies demonstrated that the academic achievement of Mexican Americans improved when they helped design their own assignments, discussed assigned tasks, worked collaboratively with each other in small groups, had "informal, almost familial" relationships with teachers (p. 310), perceived they belonged to a classroom community, and felt that their cultural experiences and the use of both Spanish and English were validated. These kinds of learning environments and techniques led to greater reasoning and clarity of expression in writing and reading as well as higher scores on school district writing proficiency tests.

Slavin (1987, 1992, 1995) and Stevens and Slavin (1995) provide additional evidence of the pedagogical power of cooperative learning. They report that, for the most part, this instructional technique has similar positive effects for students across ethnic, gender, and ability groupings, achievement measures, and intervention scale (classroom or school, short- or long-term). These include more interethnic group social interactions and friendships, increased academic achievement in a variety of subjects, improved academic self-concepts, and higher levels of confidence and efficacy for students of color. Results from Stevens and Slavin's 2-year study of five cooperative elementary schools in suburban Maryland, involving 1,012 students in grades 2–6, indicate that cooperative learning works as well at the school level as in individual classrooms. Students in these schools performed better than their peers in traditional schools on reading vocabulary and comprehension, language expression, and mathematics computation as measured by subscales of the California Achievement Test (CAT), Form C. The findings in this study are not disaggregated by ethnic groups, so we do not know who is accounting for what kind of performance.

For several years Cohen and her colleagues (Cohen, 1984; Cohen, Kepner, & Swanson, 1995; Cohen & Lotan, 1995) at Stanford University have been studying the effects of status differences in the interactional dynamics of heterogeneous cooperative learning groups and the effects of equalizing status on the achievement of individual group members. This research is significant because students of color are often assigned lower status with respect to achievement expectations, and most of the participating students are Latinos, low-income European Americans, and Southeast Asian immigrants. As part of the Program for Complex Instruction at Stanford University, Cohen and associates have developed several ways to modify academic status differences and change patterns of classroom participation. Among these are students' using each other as resources in mixed-gender cooperative learning groups; the use of multiple-ability, higher-order thinking and problem-solving tasks that require a wide range of intellectual abilities and skills; publicly assigning competence in *valued abilities* to low-status students; and validation, with practice opportunities, of multidimensional intelligence and academic ability.

In one of the studies involving 13 classrooms in grades 2–6, the students used Finding Out/Descubrimiento (FO/D), which is an English–Spanish math and science curriculum. Completion of the learning tasks require reading, writing, and computing; the use of manipulatives; reasoning, hypothesizing, visual and spatial thinking; careful observation; and interpersonal skills (Cohen & Lotan, 1995). Cohen and associates (1995) explain the value of these teaching techniques in noting that, "Multiple-ability tasks enable a much wider range of students to make important contributions; they set the stage for challenging the assumption that there is only one way to be smart" (p. 23). As this lesson is learned and status attitudes shift accordingly, the level of participation in learning experiences of low-status students increases, which, in turn, leads to higher academic achievement.

Cooperative Mathematics Learning and Achievement

The work of Treisman (1985; Fullilove & Treisman, 1990) with Latino and African American students at the University of California at Berkeley demonstrates how collaborative learning can improve the achievement of students in higher education. This is a very significant study because college students are not included very often in discussions about culturally responsive teaching. Treisman created the Mathematics Workshop Program (MWP) to improve the achievement of African American and Latino students in a first-semester calculus course (Mathematics 1A) for science and engineering majors. The intervention was modeled after the successful communal study habits of Chinese Americans. Since its inception, the MWP has been implemented at the University of California campuses at Los Angeles, San Francisco, and San Diego, California Polytechnic at Pomona, and several high schools throughout the United States.

Treisman spent 3 years informally observing how African American and Chinese American undergraduates prepared homework assignments and studied for quizzes and exams, and interviewing them about their study habits. He noted that the African Americans studied for shorter periods of time and alone, separated social activities from academic study, and had a very high rate of failure. By comparison, the Chinese American students studied for longer periods of time, combined social and study time, had a high passing rate, and received high grades in the calculus course. Their study habits involved exchanging mathematical knowledge, checking and correcting each other's work, and sharing insights about how they arrived at solutions and proofs for problems. Treisman concluded that this type of dialogue was a major reason for the Chinese American students' high success rate in calculus (Fullilove & Treisman, 1990). Like the African Americans in Albury's (1992) "communal learning contexts," these students had no motivation for ensuring that all members of the group succeeded other than that derived from their own sense of ethnic kindredness and cultural connectedness.

The MWP is promoted as an honors program whose goal is for every participant to earn an *A* grade in first semester calculus. This is a conscious effort to attract high achievers and students willing to work to accomplish academic success. In the fall before the academic year begins the prospective participants are invited to an orientation, where they are introduced to the "success ethos" of the program. Once enrolled in the MWP, the students are organized into study groups of five to seven individuals. They work together for approximately 2 hours twice a week on carefully constructed and unusually difficult problems. During these study sessions, the students help each other find solutions, understand the principles and ideas on which the problems are based, and share strategies for finding solutions and determining proofs. Graduate students work with each study group to monitor discussions, assess how well the students have mastered key principles, and provide assistance in working through difficulties encountered with problem solutions (Fullilove & Treisman, 1990). This "practice-with-feedback" process parallels how students are expected to demonstrate their skill mastery on quizzes and examinations.

Achievement data on 646 students who participated in the MWP over 9 years indicate that the program is tremendously successful. Two to three times as many of them earned grades higher than their non-MWP peers. Improvement in students' course grades, collected at two different times, support this conclusion. Only 3 percent of the students in 1978–1982 and 7 percent in 1983–1984 received grades of D+ or less. The percentage attaining a B– or above was 54 in 1978–1982 and 58 in 1983–1984 (Fullilove & Treisman, 1990; Treisman, 1985). Three other important achievement effects resulted from the MWP intervention. First, even those MWP individuals assumed to be at high risk for academic failure (Equal Opportunity Program participants and special admits) performed better than non-MWP students with stronger academic backgrounds and potential for college success. Second, the proportion of MWP participants from the lowest performance triad of the SAT-M (scores of 200–460) who earned grades of B– or above in Mathematics 1A was comparable to that of non-MWP students who scored in the highest triad (scores of 560–800). Third, the university persistence and graduation rates of MWP African American students was 65 percent, compared to 41 percent for their non-MWP peers. The persistence rates of MWP students with the lowest SAT-M scores was greater than those of non-MWP African Americans with scores in the top triad (Fullilove & Treisman, 1990; Treisman, 1985). Unfortunately, achievement data on Latino students are not available.

Jamie Escalante did for high school Latino students what Treisman did for African Americans college students. He reversed their achievement patterns in calculus by incorporating elements of their cultural values, work habits, learning styles, and background experiences into teaching. All the participants in the Escalante Math Program (Escalante & Dirmann, 1990; Mathews, 1988) were considered highly "at risk" for academic failure, and most teachers felt they were incapable of succeeding in advanced-placement (AP) courses. In 1979 at Garfield High School in East Los Angeles where Escalante taught, no Latinos were enrolled in calculus or took the AP tests. The school staffed only 6 Algebra I and 10 Geometry and/or Algebra II classes. Ten years later, more than 500 students had successfully taken the AP calculus tests, and the school was staffing 25 Algebra I and 30 Geometry and/or Algebra II classes, as well as offering AP physics, chemistry, and biology. In 1978, 10 AP tests were given in the school and one Latino student took the calculus exam. In 1989, Garfield High School administered more than 450 AP tests in 16 different subjects. Of all Latinos nationally who took the AP calculus exam, 25–30 percent of them had taken Escalante's program.

In 1987 alone, Garfield High School produced 27 percent of all Mexican Americans in the U. S. who scored 3 (average) in advanced-placement Calculus AB and 22 percent in Geometry BC. Thirteen other calculus students scored 5 (highest possible) and 19 scored 4. More than 87 percent of all Garfield's test-takers in 1987 were Latinos, and the remainder were Asian Americans. No other inner-city school had ever produced so many students who had taken so many advanced-placement tests or scored so well on them. In fact, of 15 public schools with the greatest numbers of students taking AP Calculus tests in May 1987, Garfield ranked fourth and was the only one with predominately lower-class Latino students (Escalante & Dirmann, 1990; Mathews, 1988).

Escalante's success, which was popularized in the feature film *Stand and Deliver* (Menendez, 1988), resulted from the teacher's personal convictions, commitment, and influence, combined with cooperation, camaraderie, caring, hard work, and ethnic pride among the students (Mathews, 1988). Escalante and his students worked together in small teams in a climate that cultivated intellectual champions, and where mutual assistance, fun, humor, serious intellectual work, accountability, and cultural sensitivity were always present. He explains why creating this kind of instructional ethos and community of caring was imperative to student success:

> I am trying to give my students two things: "roots" and "wings." I feel a great responsibility to teach my students respect for values that will sustain

their families, their school, their community, their race, their culture, and their country; to a large extent, students discover their cultural heritage in the classroom. . . . I do not merely teach math, I teach respect for American democratic values and institutions. . . . We owe it to our succeeding generations to ensure that our students learn these aspects and become full participatory citizens in our country. With these roots firmly in place, they are more likely to develop wings to fly to success, even greatness. (Escalante & Dirmann, 1990, p. 419)

Cooperative Literacy Learning and Achievement

Sheets (1995a, 1996) achieved success in AP Spanish language and literature with Latino students reminiscent of what Escalante did in calculus. Over a 3-year period (between 1989 and 1992) in the Seattle, Washington, public schools, 20 of the 29 "at-risk" students who participated in a class designed to prepare them to take the AP Spanish Language and Literature tests passed with scores high enough (3 or above) to receive college credit. The students involved were high school sophomores, juniors, and seniors who were considered "at risk" for academic failure. They were native Spanish speakers but had no formal skills in reading or writing the language. Sheets credited the students' achievement to the combination of instructional strategies she used. They included

> the use of the Spanish language as the medium of instruction, affirmation and validation of ethnic identity, development of self-esteem, curricular content emphasis on the students' cultural heritage, history, and literature, and implementation of learning strategies that matched their preferred learning styles (e.g., oral language, cooperative learning, peer support, and family involvement). (1995a, p. 189)

In addition to remarkable academic improvement, other high-level achievement resulted from Sheets's efforts. For example, a strong and effective support system of peer mentoring evolved, in which students bartered other services in exchange for the academic assistance they received from each other. Out of this reciprocity emerged strong "feelings of togetherness, unity, community, and family. The class was never an individual effort! . . . Cooperation was actualized and internalized" (Sheets, 1995a, pp. 192, 191). Confidence in and efficacy of individual skills also increased, as did cultural knowledge, Spanish-language competence, pride in cultural heritage, and school attendance and behavioral records.

Another cooperative learning program designed to make entry to and success in high-status literacy courses more accessible to poor, urban students of color is Advancement Via Individual Determination (AVID)

(*AVID*, n.d.; Mehan, Hubbard, Lintz, & Villanueva, 1994; Mehan et al., 1996; Swanson, Mehan, & Hubbard, 1995). It grew out of one English teacher's concerns (at Clairemont High School in San Diego) for the academic plight of Latino and African American urban students bused to her school. They were not assigned to the kinds of courses, or achieving at levels, that would gain them entry into California's leading colleges and universities. This teacher persuaded 30 of these students, with GPAs of 1.5 to 2.5, to enroll in academically rigorous courses for which they had no prior preparation. The intent was to teach the students academic coping skills, improve their achievement levels through advanced-placement course enrollments, have them achieve higher grade point averages, and increase college attendance. These continue to be AVID's primary goals. Opportunities to participate in the program have been extended to include European Americans, Asians/Pacific Islanders, and Native Americans.

Pedagogically, AVID practices "untracking" by placing low-income, low-achieving students in college preparatory biology, algebra, English, and foreign-language courses with middle-class, high-achieving European Americans (Mehan et al., 1994; Mehan et al., 1996). The participants also enroll in an elective college readiness class that meets daily throughout the school year. Peer and college tutors work with them in study groups and individually to reach levels of academic achievement that meet college expectations. Trained teachers instruct the students in lessons from the Maximum Competency Materials developed specifically for AVID. College instructors of first-year survey courses teach minilessons to acclimate them to college-level academic work. The participants also receive lessons in note-taking, study skills, test-taking, time management, preparation for college entrance/ placement and SAT exams, effective textbook reading, library skills, and preparing college admission and financial applications. They are expected and taught how to work collaboratively, build on each other's strengths, engage in inquiry methods of academic problem solving, and develop an ethos of success. Cooperative learning is used to teach students to take responsibility for their own and each other's academic success and to improve their listening, thinking, speaking, and writing skills. In these learning situations, teachers act as coaches and facilitators (*AVID*, n.d.; Mehan et. al., 1996; Swanson et al., 1995).

The AVID staff and coordinators contend that student placements and academic instruction alone are not sufficient to realize the project's achievement goals. A network of personal supports, or what Mehan and associates (1996) call "social scaffolding," has been developed to complement the instructional interventions. These supports are reduced gradually as the students become more personally competent and academically self-sufficient. Specific aspects of this scaffolding are training in thinking critically and talking analytically about learning problems; developing a sense of camaraderie and community; teaching the social knowledge and skills needed to operate effectively in school culture; and encouraging students to display identifying markers that link them to the AVID program, such as spending time in a specially designated classroom, using notebooks decorated with an AVID logo, and wearing badges of distinction. The staff act as academic, social, and personal advocates for the participating students while they are in high school and serve as mediators or liaisons for them between high school and college. In other words, this program explicitly teaches low-income, linguistically and ethnically different students the *cultural capital* that leads to school success that middle- and upper-class students learn implicitly at home (Mehan et al., 1994; Mehan et al., 1996; Swanson et al., 1995).

The success of AVID can be seen in the magnitude of its dissemination, and the impact it has had on student achievement. As of May 1995, the program was being implemented in 400 middle and high schools in California, Arizona, Colorado, Missouri, Kentucky, and Virginia; seven countries in Asia and Europe; and 10 U. S. Department of Defense Dependent Schools. In San Diego County alone, AVID graduated 800 seniors in 1995. More than 1,500 administrators, teachers, counselors, and tutors participated in AVID staff development in the 1993–1994 school year, and 1,200 more took part in the 1994 summer institutes. In 1995, six institutes were held in California, Kentucky, Virginia, and Germany (Mehan et al., 1996).

AVID has produced some impressive improvements in the academic achievement of the participants. Since 1990 in San Diego alone, 3,333 students have graduated from the program, and 98% of them were admitted to 2- and 4-year colleges and universities. Between 1990 and 1994, 92.8% of AVID graduates enrolled in college. This rate is 75% higher than the overall averages for the state of California, and well above the national averages. For African Americans it was two and a half times higher, for Latinos three times, for European Americans two times, and for Pan-Asians one and a half times. And these students are staying in college at a much higher rate. The latest evaluation report of the project indicates that 89% of AVID students who enroll in college are still there 2 years later. The longer students stay in the program, the better their college enrollment and persistence records. More than half (58%) of AVID students enroll in GATE (gifted and talented education), honors, and advanced classes in high school. Their course grades also improve significantly. Eighty-four percent of the students are earning GPAs of 2.0 or above in academic classes, and 44 percent have GPAs of 3.0 or better.

This is true regardless of the students' socioeconomic background and ethnic-group identity (Mehan et al., 1994; Mehan et al., 1996; Swanson et al., 1995).

Mehan and associates (1996) highlight yet another important achievement of AVID students. Latinos and African Americans are developing the kind of linguistic styles, academic skills, and social behaviors needed to achieve in mainstream high schools and colleges *without sacrificing their cultural and ethnic identities*. They become effective "cultural border crossers" (p. 187) by engaging in academic pursuits with their AVID peers at school and recreational and social activities with their neighborhood friends after school. Because AVID uses students' own cultures and experiences as instructional resources, in conjunction with the professional expertise of different types of teachers, participants can better accomplish the "two interrelated goals [AVID has] found to be important in their academic achievement: maintaining their street identity while developing their academic identity" (Mehan et al., 1996, p. 209). This accomplishment is especially noteworthy because of observations such as those made by Fordham and Ogbu (1986) and Fordham (1993, 1996) that some students of color sabotage their own academic achievement to avoid compromising their friendships with low-achieving peers or being accused of "acting White."

The effects on African Americans of learning in communal contexts and cooperative groups was investigated by Albury (1992). Low-income African and European Americans from the same neighborhoods were asked to match 25 words with definitions. After a baseline score was established, the students were organized into three-member, same-race teams and assigned to one of four performance arrangements. Those in the "individual criteria" option were advised to study alone, and they would receive a reward if they got 15 of the 25 definitions correct. In the "interpersonal competitive" structure, students were told to study alone, and only the team who got the highest score would be rewarded. Students in the "group competition" setting were informed that their group was competing with others, and if they got the highest score of all groups they would be rewarded. The "communal" learning team members were not offered any rewards but were reminded of their shared community backgrounds and told that they needed to work together, share responsibility, and help each other so that their group could receive a better score. After studying the word list, the students were given a posttest. The European American students who studied under the "individual criteria" had the highest performance, followed by those in the "interpersonal competitive" learning context. African Americans in the "communal" study option performed best, followed by those in the "group competition" learning context (Albury, 1992; Boykin, 1994).

Doing Cooperative Learning

A very important message for culturally responsive teaching derives from these cooperative learning instructional programs and research projects. Cooperative learning works well for underachieving students of color on multiple levels. However, participation of all individual members of cooperative learning groups cannot be assumed to be of comparable quality, even when the groups are organized along ethnic lines and by free choice. Deliberate efforts are needed to ensure that this happens. Some teachers may try to accomplish this by unilaterally assigning students to groups and tasks and roles to individuals within groups. This will not work for an obvious reason: If teachers make all the decisions in the groups, then these are neither student nor cooperative groups; they are the teacher's groups.

A more constructive course of action is for teachers and students to work together to develop criteria for selection of group members, performance accountability, and monitoring of the groups' process dynamics. Then students should be allowed maximum choice within these parameters. *This is structured rather than total free choice.* Concerted efforts should be undertaken to build ethnic, racial, gender, social, and ability diversity into the organization and task assignments of groups. Heterogeneous groups work best and are consistent with the underlying values and explicit goals of multicultural education. However, in some settings and for some learning tasks, groups of the same ethnicity and gender may be desirable—or unavoidable, given the demographics of some schools and classrooms.

This similarity can be compensated for somewhat by ensuring ability diversity within each group. Cohen's (1984; Cohen & Lotan, 1995) work offers some guidance for how this can be accomplished. She recommends making certain that the learning tasks are sufficiently complex to require multiple abilities for their successful completion. Group members can then complement each other's strengths and compensate for each others' weaknesses. H. Gardner's (1983) multiple intelligences, Barbe and Swassing's (1979) sensory modality strengths, and various ethnic learning style characteristics (Shade, 1989) are helpful guides for selecting members so that "multiple intellectual ability" is as much a feature of group membership as it is of the tasks to be learned. Another way to compensate somewhat for minimum diversity on variables important in forming cooperative groups is to change the composition of the groups often. Then, even groups of the same ethnicity can experience different ability configurations.

Although the pedagogical potential of cooperative learning is powerful, it can be aborted or distorted if students and teachers do not know how to work in groups. Teachers should not assume that students (or themselves) automatically know how to do cooperative learning. Many have not had any prior experiences with it, or their experiences have been negative. Working in groups is a skill that has to be learned by both students and teachers. Initially, some students may resist it; others may use it as an excuse to avoid working and assuming their fair share of the learning responsibilities. Others may be threatened about the possibility of not receiving due recognition and "credit" for their individual efforts. Some teachers may see this learning arrangement as threatening their authority and classroom control, consuming too much time, and being pedagogically inefficient because the students undoubtedly will not analyze topics exactly as the teachers would.

These issues can be negotiated and managed as students and teachers become more skilled in group dynamics. Some effective ways to diminish the doubts about cooperative learning (especially for students and teachers who prefer to learn in individual arrangements) are to (1) create a climate and ethos of valuing cooperation and community in the classroom that operates at all times, not just when cooperative tasks are performed; (2) start small and phase cooperative learning into instruction gradually on the levels of both frequency and magnitude; (3) allow time and provide opportunities for students and teachers to become comfortable with and skilled at cooperative learning; (4) initially use a combination of individual, small-group, and whole-class learning activities; and (5) use multitiered task assignments and be very clear in explaining these to students. The last strategy allows students to attach themselves to specific tasks within a group context, thereby satisfying their need for individual task responsibility and recognition.

ACTIVE AND AFFECTIVE ENGAGEMENT

Emotionality, variability, novelty, and active participation are important aspects of the learning styles of some ethnic groups and the ways in which they demonstrate what they know. For them, teaching and learning are more than cognitive and technical tasks; they are also active and emotional processes. Consequently, all these are critical features of culturally responsive teaching.

Boykin and his colleagues at Howard University have conducted a series of studies (see B. Allen & Boykin, 1992; Boykin, 1994) that demonstrate the effect of teaching strategies that include these features on the achievement of African American students. Together they address several elements of traditional African American culture as well. The pertinent ones for this discussion have been summarized by Boykin (1983, 1986, 1994; B. Allen & Boykin, 1992) as a vivacious rather than a mechanistic approach to living; behavioral expressiveness that integrates movement, rhythm, music, and dance; verve, or high levels of energy and sensory stimulation; emphasis on emotions and feelings; communal and social connectedness that transcends individual privileges; cultivation of individual expressiveness in personality traits and an inclination for spontaneity in behavior; preference for oral and aural communication modalities; and social time orientations.

Varied Formats and Multiple Sensory Stimulation in Teaching

Boykin (1978, 1982), Tuck (1985), and Tuck and Boykin (1989) examined the effects of varied and intense sensory stimulation (verve) on the academic task performance of African American students. Their studies are grounded in the findings of previous researchers, such as Guttentag (1972), Guttentag and Ross (1972), Morgan (1990), and Shade (1994), which show that many African American students prefer learning situations that are active, participatory, emotionally engaging, and filled with visual and physical stimulation. For example, Guttentag and Ross found that when spontaneous and directed physical performances, or "acting out ideas," were used in teaching preschool African Americans, they learned basic concepts such as big–small, over–under, above–below quickly, easily, and thoroughly.

More recently, Howard (1998) examined how culturally relevant pedagogical principles are manifested in the actual behaviors of elementary teachers of African American students during reading instruction. "Dramatic performance" was a prominent feature of their teaching repertoires. One participant was especially adept at and consistent in dramatizing her teaching. Howard (1998) described her talents and techniques as follows:

> Louise used pedagogical practices filled with emotion and passion, and connected students to the learning process through her theatrical performances. . . . It was not unusual for [her] . . . to go into five-to-ten minute performances that included hopping around the classroom, raising her voice several octaves, acting out various characters, and becoming completely immersed in a scene, character, or story. (p. 133)

Howard concluded that this dramatic performance style of teaching had positive effects on the learning motivation, interest, efforts, and achievement outcomes of students. His perceptions were confirmed by the reactions and comments of students. Many followed Louise's example and encouragement to read with feeling, emotion, and conviction, and their recitations became "performances" as they acted out meanings of words and comprehension of reading passages. These performances provoked rich intellectual discourse as students asked numerous questions about the passages read and engaged in analyses of story plots, events, and role characterizations. Many of the students found Louise's teaching style funny, exciting, and engaging; it also made understanding and remembering what was taught much easier (Howard, 1998).

In their studies, Tuck and Boykin (1989) used experimental designs in which third, fourth, and sixth-graders were exposed to problem-solving tasks presented in unvaried and varied formats. In the unvaried format, all tasks of one type were presented before any tasks of a different type were introduced. In the varied format, tasks were presented in random order with no more than two of the same kind occurring sequentially. These studies also compared how students from home environments with different levels of sensory stimulation reacted to variations in learning task formats. The results indicated that (1) African American students perform significantly better in learning contexts and tasks with high variability; (2) children from home environments with high levels of sensory stimulation perform better in high-variability contexts, while children from homes with low levels of sensory stimulation perform the same across varied and unvaried task presentations; (3) European American students performed better than African Americans on constant-format tasks; (4) European and African Americans perform better on varied-format tasks, but the amount of improvement was substantially greater for African Americans; (5) the preference of African Americans for varied task formats was not a function of academic ability, since it was the same for both high and low achievers; and (6) African American students engage in more off-task and nonpersistence behaviors in unvaried learning formats than European Americans.

Using Music and Movement in Learning

Another teaching technique for improving the academic performance of African Americans is to incorporate rhythmic music and movement in learning activities. This has been demonstrated by B. Allen (1987), Boykin and Allen (1988), B. Allen and Boykin (1991, 1992), and B. Allen and Butler (1996) in two experimental studies. Allen and Allen and Boykin examined the effects of music and movement on a picture-pairing task performed by low-income European and African Americans in first and second grade. In one experimental condition, the learning task was accompanied by music, physical actions, and handclapping, and music was played while the students were tested on these skills. In the other no music was present. Allen and Boykin replicated these experimental conditions with third- and fourth-graders. They were interested in the effects of music and movement on the analogical reasoning abilities of low-class African American and middle-class European American students.

The results of the two studies were virtually identical. The African American students performed the learning tasks much better to the accompaniment of music and movement, while the European Americans did much better without. Informal classroom observations provided additional support for these findings. B. Allen and Boykin (1992) noticed that the African American students exhibited signs of restlessness and boredom during the learning sessions devoid of music and movement. Their eyes frequently wandered away from the task, and they attended to their hands and feet more so than to the learning materials and tasks. These results led the researchers to conclude that African American students can "attain levels of academic achievement equal to their more educationally successful peers if certain factors derived from their cultural experiences are incorporated into task contexts" (Allen & Boykin, 1992, p. 325).

Further support of the positive effects of using rhythm, motion, and movement in teaching African American students comes from the experiences of teachers in actual classrooms. Two examples illustrate these strategies. One is of an urban middle school language arts teacher in Long Beach, California. She tells about the unsuccessful struggle of trying to teach grammar to academically "at-risk" African American students using traditional methods. To overcome these obstacles, she created a "rap" about the parts of speech, shared it with the students, and asked them for their input to improve the quality. Together, she and the students created a modified version. Using the rap, all the students learned the parts of speech with 100 percent accuracy with little effort, and they significantly improved their ability to use them correctly in both academic and social writing and speaking.

The other example is of a middle school math teacher in a school district near St. Louis, Missouri. Although the location is suburban, it is a rather poor community, and almost all the students in the school are African American. The situation involved teaching fractions to an eighth-grade class made up entirely of African Americans. The teacher had been involved in a long sequence of unsuccessful efforts to get a particular female student to understand fractions based on eighths (e. g., 1/8, 4/8, 7/8, etc.). Apparently acting spontaneously and without forethought, he asked eight students, including the targeted one, to come to the front of the room and form a circle. He then demonstrated the various fractions, in relationship to the whole, by moving the students in and out of different configurations. The students were shifted around (actually moving about) several times to form 1/8, 2/8, 3/8, and so forth, with the student who was having difficulty understanding the concept being a part of all of the changing configurations. The teacher then pointed out what the formation was and its relation to the remainder of the whole. Thus, the targeted student could *see* that when she alone was moved from the circle, she was 1/8 (one of eight), while those remaining in the circle symbolized 7/8 (seven of eight).

Within a matter of minutes, and by physically acting out the ideas, the student had mastered the concept that had totally baffled her only a short time earlier. The other students who actively participated in the "performance," as well as the rest of the class, were captivated by the experience and were learning along with her. Once the targeted student's understanding because obvious, the teacher commented, "Now, you see what I mean." The student responded rather nonchalantly, "Of course! Why didn't you say it this way earlier." Embedded in this situation is instructional compatibility with multiple aspects of African American culture and learning styles—movement, performance, dramatic flair, co-operative learning, group context, personalization, rhythm, emotionality, and holistic engagement.

ETHNIC-CENTERED CLASSES AND SCHOOLS

In some cases, special classes and entire schools have been created specifically to center their curriculum and instruction in the cultural heritages of particular ethnic groups. African American academies, American Indian heritage schools and colleges, historically Black colleges and universities (HBCUs), and Chicano, Japanese American, and other ethnic studies programs are examples of these educational initiatives. These "ethnic-centered" programs are closely akin to culturally responsive teaching. The mission of both is to teach diverse students academic skills through their cultural frames of reference and to teach them their cultural heritages. However, the scale of action and constituency are different. Ethnic-centered instructional programs are particular expressions of the more general ideas of culturally responsive teaching. They deal exclusively with one ethnic group (e.g., African American), while culturally responsive teaching attends to many ethnic groups.

To date, no Asian-centric public elementary, middle, or high schools exist, and no information could be located on the few experiments with Latino-centric schools. Some of the language and literacy classes created for limited-English-speaking students from these ethnic groups may include features of culturally responsive teaching. But they come under the auspices of bilingualism and therefore fall outside the boundaries of this book. Tribal-controlled Native American schools on reservations can be considered ethnic-centric if their instructional practices are framed within tribal cultures. But, again, there is little readily accessible information on the specific pedagogical practices of these schools; many vague references exist instead. The exception is the Rough Rock Navajo Demonstration School, which was introduced in Chapter 5. By far the most information available on the theoretical conceptions, advocacy, implementation, and effects of ethnic-centered pedagogy deal with African Americans. The presentation here reflects this reality. Brief discussions are devoted to Native American initiatives and more extensive ones to African American–centric schools and classes.

Native American–Centric Pedagogy and Achievement Effects

Kleinfeld and Nelson (1988) reviewed studies conducted in the 1970s that examined whether adapting instruction to the learning styles of Native Americans would increase learning. The specific learning style features analyzed were visual abilities, low verbal skills, and learning by observation. They found very few studies that had tested these claims empirically, and these provided only meager support. Kleinfeld and Nelson conclude their reviews with skepticism about the wisdom of pursuing research and practice in adapting teaching strategies to presumed Native American learning styles. However, they tempered this skepticism somewhat by cautioning against "efforts to adapt instruction to narrowly defined ability patterns" (p. 98).

This raises the possibility that learning styles, conceptualized in these studies as "cognitive ability patterns," were misconstrued. Kleinfeld and Nelson conceded that effective teachers adapt to the contexts in which they teach, including the cultures of students—their background knowledge, experiences, values, communication patterns, and interests. These features are more compatible with current conceptions of learning styles (as described earlier in this chapter). Another problem with Kleinfeld and Nelson's analyses is the very small number of studies (which they readily acknowledge) and the fact that all the studies reviewed were conducted in the early to mid-1970s. Conceptualizations of learning styles have improved significantly since then (see for example, Shade, 1989), but research on actual (not speculative) school achievement effects of matching teaching strategies to Native American cultural orientations continue to be sparse.

Some empirical support for cultural compatibility's improving the academic performance of Native Americans students is provided by Coggins, Williams, and Radin (1997) in their work with the Ojibwa community in northern Michigan. Their study of 19 families revealed that the identification of mothers with the traditional Native American values of sharing, other-centeredness, harmony with nature, non-interference, and focus on extended family has positive effects on their children's academic and social functioning in school. Elementary school students from these family backgrounds performed well in reading, language arts, science, and math. Other studies have shown positive relationships between the retention of traditional Native American values and the academic success of Sioux college students (Huffman, Sill, & Brokenleg, 1986) as well as high school completion and academic achievement among Northern Cheyenne girls (Ward, 1994). Because of these results Coggins and associates recommended that cultural revitalization programs for different Native American groups be integrated into their routine educational experiences. Knowledge of traditional cultural values and heritages can be an important anchor for Native American students as they navigate their community and school cultures, expectations, responsibilities, and performances. Thus, being bicultural can facilitate academic achievement. These suggestions fit well within the purview of culturally responsive pedagogy.

Another study providing evidence about the power of Native American–centric pedagogy to improve student achievement was conducted by Deyhle (1995). She studied Navajo students in two high schools over 10 years—one was a reservation school and one was not. Contrary to the claims of some that performance will be lower in "racially isolated" schools populated by students of color, Deyhle observed the opposite. Students at the reservation school performed much better than those at the nonreservation school, as indicated by lower dropout rates, greater satisfaction with school, and stronger feelings of support from school personnel. Similar patterns were also apparent for the reservation students who attended the nonreservation school, compared to the ones who lived in the town. Deyhle (1995) attributes these differences to the degree of cultural affiliation students had with their ethnic community and the amount of cultural integrity present in school programs and practices:

> The more academically successful Navajo students are more likely to be those who are firmly rooted in their Navajo community . . . are not alienated from their cultural values and who do not perceive themselves as inferior to the dominant group. . . . In contrast, those who are not academically successful are both estranged from the reservation community, and bitterly resent the racially polarized school context they face daily. (pp. 419–420)

African American–Centric Pedagogy and Achievement Effects

Supporters of African American–centric programs suggest they are needed because conventional education does little if anything to teach African Americans their history and culture. This void causes students to be culturally dislocated or disaffiliated, which can interfere with academic achievement and psychoemotional well-being. Molefi Asante (1991/1992), a leading Afrocentrist, asserts that students "may learn, but, without cultural grounding, the learning will have destroyed their sense of place" and personal integrity (p. 30). Asa Hilliard (1991/1992), another well-known proponent of Afrocentricism, proposes that "schools must . . . accept the fact that some racial and ethnic groups have endured hundreds of years of systematic defamation that has distorted, denied, and deformed the truth of their cultural and historical reality" (p. 14). Conversely, when students are centered in their own cultural heritages and performance styles, they are more motivated to learn, perform better academically, and are better disciplined (Asante, 1991/1992).

African American–centered schools and/or classes designed to accomplish these goals exist in several school districts throughout the United States, including Milwaukee, Detroit, Philadelphia, Baltimore, Atlanta, San Diego, Seattle, Miami, Washington, DC, and New York City (Watson & Smitherman, 1996). Most of the schools serve students in grades K–8, but some of the classes do operate in the grades 9–12. Almost all African American–centered programs are part of public school systems and enroll both males and females. Officially, students from all ethnic groups can enroll in them, but virtually all of those who actually attend are African Americans.

Common Pedagogical Characteristics. Regardless of geographic location, school level (elementary or middle), type (entire school or classes within schools), or targeted population (male, female, or coeducational), African American–centered programs have a three-part instructional agenda. They aim to improve the academic achievement in basic literacy (reading, writing, math) and intellectual (critical thinking, problem solving) skills; contribute to the cultural socialization of students by teaching African and African American history, heritage, and culture; and facilitate individual development through improved self-concepts, self-expression, self-reliance, and self-confidence (Abella, 1995; J. Foster, 1994; Lipman, 1995; Watson & Smitherman, 1996). A climate for learning is created in which students are validated, held in high esteem, expected to achieve high performance, and supported in meeting expectations. The principal of the Robert W. Coleman School in Baltimore called this ambiance a "conspiracy of caring" (Lipman, 1995). Collin Williams spoke similarly about the African American Academy in Seattle, which he described as a "a place of success, where students are not put down, and there is no blame or shame at being African American" (personal interview).

Another common feature of African American–centric programs is teaching the seven principles (Nguzo Saba) of Kwanzaa (Riley, 1995). They are used as guidelines for designing and implementing instructional programs, as standards of personal conduct, and as criteria for creating a community climate in the entire school. The African American Academy in Seattle, Washington, demonstrates how these social and political principles for unifying and mobilizing African American people in general can be applied to education. Its translated versions of Nguzo Saba for students are:

- *Umoja (unity)*—Having school spirit and good things to say about my school
- *Kujichagulia (self-determination)*—Making good choices and being responsible for my own behavior
- *Ujima (cooperative work and responsibility)*—working and playing together in a friendly way with other children at school
- *Ujamaa (cooperative economics)*—Contributing with other children to my school projects and programs
- *Nia (purpose)*—Coming to school to learn, and working hard at it
- *Kuumba (creativity)*—Thinking of ways to make my classroom and school better and more pleasant places to learn
- *Imani (faith)*—Having confidence in myself, and remembering that when I do my best, I make myself and my school succeed (*Parent Handbook*, n.d.)

These principles and related learning activities usually unfold within a milieu of collaborative efforts signaled by students working together for collective betterment, ceremonies and rituals of bonding, celebrations of success, and community service within and outside of school (Abella, 1995; J. Foster, 1994; Lipman, 1995; Watson & Smitherman, 1996). For example, at the Songhai Empire at Leeds Middle School in Philadelphia, ujima and kuumba are developed through a series of student-managed groups and activities. Among them are the eighth grade Imperial Guard, who help with hall conduct management, act as ambassadors of the "Empire," and serve as role models for sixth- and seventh-graders. Another organization is Imhotep, a group of students who provide tutorial support for others in the Songhai Empire. Both the Paul Robeson Academy in Detroit and the African American Academy in Seattle have regularly scheduled harambees. These are "community gatherings," or all-school assemblies where students and staffs reaffirm commitments, refocus attentions, and celebrate accomplishments. Harambee at the African American Academy is also the time when students who have been selected for their academic achievement and community services (called "scholars") are honored and visitors, guests, and parents are recognized.

Almost all African American–centered programs have some kind of pledge, motto, school song, and identification signals through which students are taught community values, codes of conduct, and institutional allegiance. The Seattle African American Academy uses several inspirational songs, one of which is "Too Legit to Quit." Its motto is, "The future belongs to the prepared child." The school creed, which is recited as part of the students' daily routines, is:

> I am a winner of excellence in every way.
> What I can think, I can write, I can read, and I can say.
> I will always say "YES" to right. I will say "NO" to wrong
> With all others, I will try to get along
> Respect I'll give—respect I'll earn
> I know that I came to the Academy to learn.
> There are some things no one can take from me;
> My pride, my self-discipline, my awesome dignity.
> And so I will do my best to excel in every way, for
> I am a winner of excellence today . . . and always! (*Parent Handbook*, n.d.)

Achievement Effects. Although data on the effects of African American–centered programs on achievement are still emerging, the preliminary results are very encouraging. On all measures of achievement, these schools report improvements, and student performance levels tend to be higher than those of African Americans in other schools. Academic achievement indicators are most often grades assigned by teachers and scores on standardized tests, such as the Iowa Test of Basic Skills, Comprehensive Test of Basic Skills, Stanford Achievement Test, and California Achievement Test.

In the 1997–1998 school year, scores on the Iowa Test of Basic Skills for second-graders at the Seattle Academy were 4 points higher in reading, 1 point lower in language arts, and the same in math as those of their ethnic peers in other schools. Compared to the previous year at the Academy, the reading scores increased by 4 points, while math and language arts remained the same. Performance in language arts for students in grades 6–8 increased by 2 points between 1997 and 1998 but declined in both math and reading by 3 points. This achievement was better than that of their ethnic peers in the district as a whole—by 4 points in reading, 6 in language arts, and 3 in math. On the eighth-grade writing assessment, 93.8 percent of the Academy students performed at or above the accepted standard, compared to 71.6 percent of other African American students in the district. Academic performance in the lower grades is not quite as good. Only 48.8 percent of the Academy third-graders and 56.3 percent of fifth-graders performed at or above standard in writing, compared to 65.8 percent and 76.1 percent, respectively, for African American students in other schools (C. Williams, 1998).

Other African American–centered programs and schools also report improvements in academic achievement for their students. The Songhai Empire students achieved the greatest improvements in math and science, determined by the percentage of A's and B's received. They also did better than their ethnic peers in other schools, as did participants in the Afrocentric Enhancement, Self-Esteem Opportunity Program (AESOP) in Miami (Abella, 1995) and the Malcolm X Academy in Detroit. In 1995 Malcolm X students in grades 1–6 performed better than the district average in reading and math as indicated by higher scores on the California Achievement Test. The seventh-graders achieved likewise on the Michigan Assessment of Educational Progress (Watson & Smitherman, 1996).

Discipline and attendance are also generally better in African American–centered academicies and classes. Disciplinary infractions (e.g., suspensions, offensive language, physical assaults) declined 80 percent during the first year of the Songhai Empire and 100% the second year, when no serious disciplinary infractions of any kind occurred (*Songhai Empire*, n.d.). No students were given long-term suspensions or expulsions at the African American Academy during the 1997–1998 school year. Since 1992, disciplinary code violations at Malcolm X Academy have been consistently less than 5 percent of all cases for their respective grades (Watson & Smitherman, 1996). Average daily attendance at the Seattle Academy is 95.8 percent for grades 1–5 and 95.9 percent for grades 6–8, compared to 94.3 percent and 90.8 percent, respectively, for African Americans attending other schools (C. Williams, 1998). Another important testament to these schools' success with attendance is the observation made by the principal of the Seattle Academy. He noted that his students "can't wait for school to start and they don't want to leave at the end of the day. Many are here long before the doors open in the morning and I have to make them go home when I leave several hours after school is supposed to be over for them" (C. Williams, personal interview).

The fact that students do not want to leave the Seattle Academy at the end of the school day may be symptomatic of yet another kind of success that African American–centric schools are achieving, one that is a critical component of culturally responsive pedagogy. This is the psychoemotional well-being of students. It is an achievement that is difficult to quantify and is overlooked in many analyses of the needs and accomplishments of underachieving students of color. Yet it is crucial. A long history of educational theory, many research findings, and frequent personal stories of students and teachers indicate that academic achievement and psychoemotional well-being are complementary, if not causally related.

Most African American–centered programs also report improvements in the self-concepts of students and in their feelings of confidence and capability. AESOP documented this with the higher self-esteem scores the participating students received on the McDaniel-Piers Young Children's Self-Concept Scale (Abella, 1995). The staff of the Songhai Empire asked students and parents to share their perceptions about how being a part of the program affected them. The following comments are representative of the responses they received:

Student 1: "I feel different and better about myself now than I did before. I feel good about myself and I have more faith in myself. It helped me to learn to talk and treat people the way I would want them to treat me."

Student 2: "It has encouraged me to get up in the morning and to be proud of who I am. It also changed the way I look and think about others."

Student 3: "It has helped me find my true inner self. I thought for all these years I knew who I was—come to be I was just fooling myself."

A parent of one of the students wrote to the principal of Leeds Middle School, where the Songhai Empire is located:

The last two years have been very rewarding . . . for my son. When he first entered your school in the 7th grade he had a low self esteem. In the two years he has been at Leeds I've seen a big change in him. He is more confident in himself, and happier. This is due to the dedicated teachers you have at your school, who take an interest in our children, and are good role models for them. . . . I think it's good when a child comes home and willingly shares his experience of the day with his parents.

Research conducted by Hudley (1995) supports the positive effects of African American–centered instruction on the self-concept of students and their feelings of efficacy. He studied a group of sixth- to eighth-grade

African American males in southern California who participated in one of these self-contained learning environment. Half of the students were taught using African American culturally relevant instruction and half were not. During one entire school year, information about African American history, culture, contributions, and sociopolitical issues was incorporated into the students' social studies, science, math, and language arts classes. The students read literature by African American, African, and Afro-Caribbean authors in language arts and used statistics about African Americans' income, life cycles, and population distributions to practice mathematical problem solving and calculations. These learning tasks were complemented with teaching techniques that emphasized cooperative learning, higher-order thinking, and critical analysis.

Two instruments were used to measure student achievement. The Self-Perception Profile of Learning Disabled scale assessed student perceptions of personal competency and self-worth. This scale provides information on 10 different competencies—general intellectual ability, global self-worth, reading, spelling, math, writing, athletics, social acceptance, physical appearance, and behavioral conduct. The Social Support Scale for Children measured perceptions of the support received from parents, teachers, classmates, and close friends. Students in the African American–centered class performed better than their peers on all indicators of achievement, including higher grade point averages; positive perceptions of teachers as fair, caring, helpful, and supportive, and classmates as friendly, attentive, and accepting; and greater confidence in social and intellectual abilities. Hudley (1995) concluded that these improvements occurred because the program "created a cadre of academically confident young men who supported one another's achievement strivings" (p. 53). The success achieved by AVID, Sheets, Escalante, and Treisman are similarly accredited.

These examples demonstrate that specific ethnic-centered programs and practices have some positive effects on student achievement, including academic performance, self-esteem, school attendance, and discipline. The longer students participate in these programs, the better their performance. Yet the overall level of their academic achievement often continues to be lower than national averages. This tendency suggests the need for further instructional reforms, social changes, and sustained efforts to maximize the school performance of African Americans and other underachieving students of color. Ethnically centered programs also illustrate that more academic achievement occurs when other types of learning are facilitated at the same time. This explains why teachers and administrators involved in these educational settings speak with as much conviction about reaffiliating students with their cultural heritages, creating feelings of community and reciprocity, and developing self-respect and self-esteem as they do about increasing academic performance. Nurturing the total human condition is their mission, their methodology, and the ultimate indicator of their success.

CONCLUSION

Several important general lessons emerge from the specific culturally responsive instructional programs and practices discussed in this chapter. The praxis of culturally responsive pedagogy confirms the theory. When instructional processes are consistent with the cultural orientations, experiences, and learning styles of marginalized African, Latino, Native, and Asian American students, their school achievement improves significantly. This success is most evident in learning "spaces" where culturally relevant content, teacher attitudes and expectations, and instructional actions converge.

Students of color come to school having already mastered many cultural skills and ways of knowing. To the extent that teaching builds on these capabilities, academic success will result. In other words, *the successful succeed*. This principle suggests the need for educators to redirect their orientation to teaching students of color who are not doing well in school away from the "don't have, can't do" orientation toward a "do have, can do" mindset. Translating this mindset into instructional action begins with accepting the cultural knowledge and skills of ethnically diverse students as valuable teaching–learning resources and using them as scaffolds or bridges to academic achievement. This has been done effectively by the Kamehameha Early Elementary Program for Native Hawaiians, the Webster Groves Writing Project and the Math Workshop Program for African Americans, and the Escalante Math Program for Latinos. Other instructional interventions should follow suit.

A single area of achievement (such as academic performance) is maximized when multiple areas of learning (e.g., academic, cultural, personal) are facilitated at once and different teaching techniques are used, all within the cultural contexts of various ethnic groups. This applies to skills within subjects, different subjects across school curricula, and domains of human functioning. The comprehension of factual information, problem identification, and critical and moral reflection complement each other. Reading improves when writing skills are taught at the same time. Mathematical calculations make more sense when they are embedded in problem-solving exercises about issues relevant to the life experiences of different ethnic groups. Mastery of academic skills is easier when social, emotional, and psychological learning is considered as well. Thus, multiplicity and diversity are the mainstays of culturally responsive teaching and the venues for enhanced academic achievement for students of color.

Culturally responsive practices unveil some solutions to the seemingly unsolveable mystery of the perpetual underachievement of marginalized students of color. They are not being taught in school as they learn in their cultural communities. This discontinuity interrupts their mental schemata and makes academic learning harder to achieve. Filtering teaching through the cultural lens of Native, Latino, African, and Asian American students can lead to much greater school success. These students deserve nothing less. The programs and practices discussed in this chapter point to some instructional techniques that work and provide directions for others to follow. It remains for more teachers to heed the clarion call and go forth with diligence and devotion.

CHAPTER 7

Culturally Responsive Pedagogical Praxis: A Personal Case

Thus far I have functioned primarily as an "off-stage" narrator for the story of culturally responsive teaching that was constructed in Chapters 1–6. I shift roles for this chapter. I will now step onto center stage to share some personal experiences. They are about some of the characteristics of my own teaching beliefs and practices that I think exemplify culturally responsive praxis. The story these experiences convey is incomplete in that it illustrates some but not all principles of culturally responsive teaching, and the information provided is not exhaustive. Despite these limitations, hopefully my story will further crystallize how the theory of culturally responsive pedagogy can be translated into practice.

INTRODUCTION

Invariably, teaching is a personal endeavor, and what it looks and feels like in actual practice is best conveyed through personal stories. These stories transmit an affective ambiance and level of clarity that defy even the best of abstract or conceptual descriptions. They inform, enforce, and encourage with a potency that is impossible in reporting research, explaining theory, and summarizing collective practices. Personal stories of practice move understanding of concepts and principles beyond cognition to embrace the psychoemotional energy, the exuberance, and the ethical convictions that are embedded in all good teaching. The power of the personal story, then, provides the reasons for this chapter. While other discussions have provided a wealth of varied information about culturally responsive teaching, they have looked at it largely from the outside. This discussion provides some glimpses of it from the inside out. In other words, it takes the reader into the *dynamics of teaching*, where the heart of cultural responsive pedagogy lies.

My students are predominately European Americans, especially those in teacher education. However, my graduate students include a wide variety of ethnic groups, both nationally and internationally. They are Taiwanese, Chinese and Chinese Americans, Japanese and Japanese Americans, African Americans, Filipino Americans, Latino Americans, Cambodian Americans, biracial Americans, and European Americans. The students also are in various stages of their professional education. Some are enrolled in teacher certification programs. Others are experienced teachers who are returning to school for master's and doctoral degrees. Of these, some will remain in classroom teaching, some will assume administrative positions in K–12 education, and others will become college professors. Many of my students are interested in cultural diversity and social justice issues. They are also concerned about how they can teach differently to improve the learning outcomes for students from a variety of ethnic, cultural, social, and linguistic backgrounds. Consequently, culturally responsive teaching is an important item on their professional agendas.

BEING SUPPORTIVE AND FACILITATIVE

Whether in formal classroom settings, advising situations, or informal contacts on and off campus, I try to be supportive and facilitative of students' intellectual, personal, social, ethnic, and cultural development. Students working on assignments often want to know, "What exactly do you want us to do?" When I respond, "I don't know other than for you to put forth genuine effort, do your best, and address all aspects of the assigned tasks within the context our class goals, readings, and discussions," they are puzzled. My assignments never deal with merely reproducing factual information; they focus on application, analysis, interpretation, and transfer of knowledge. For instance, my students are not asked to learn about stages of ethnic identity development among Latinos and African Americans as an end in itself. They are to derive from this knowledge implications for improving the quality of teaching and learning. While I do not have a single specific end product in mind that everyone is to accomplish, I do provide the students with parameters in which they are expected to perform. For example, I might specify several questions to guide their analyses, such as the number and types of learning activities they need to develop in creating simulated lesson plans. Or I will identify the categories of information (e.g., person, event, place, image, etc.) to be included in an observation log on "cultural diversity in our daily lives" and the kind of information that should accompany each entry (such as multiethnic samples, description, cultural traits the observations illustrate, and how the observations can be used to teach that).

Even my doctoral students initially want me to tell them what to do for their research. They often ask, "What should I do?" My response is, "This is your degree and/or dissertation, so the question is not for me to tell you what to do, but to help you do what you want to do to the best of your ability." This response is not meant to be insensitive, but to let students know from the outset that I want to help them find their own focus and develop their own skills, rather than imposing my professional priorities onto them. Unlike some professors who expect their graduate advisees to conduct research that is a continuation of their own, I discourage this. Nor do I try to direct students toward one methodological approach over another. But whatever their choices are relative to research topics and procedures, I do insist on high-quality performance. In the dissertation-writing process, I am notorious among my advisees for demanding "do-overs." I give generously of my time, support, and other resources to ensure that my students achieve highly. In many instances, this means going the extra mile with them and mobilizing professional networks to access expertise that is beyond my personal abilities. For me, this is within the normal duties of an adviser, if he or she is genuinely an advocate for students.

I think graduate school is the time for students to begin developing their own professional interests and independence. I work with them toward these ends. As we work together, I try to be simultaneously friend, mentor, model, critic, teacher, and confidante. This does not mean that I aim to be a "buddy" and neglect my teaching responsibilities. Rather, I try to model the importance of students and teachers interacting with each other in multiple ways and on many different levels. This, to me, is essential to effective teaching and learning since both encompass more than academic skill development. In performing these diverse roles, I hope to help students grow in similar directions and act accordingly in their own careers.

I think living and learning should be filled with significance, enjoyment, inquiry, and action. And I believe all of these are best achieved when personal struggles for academic betterment and the joys of achievement are shared with others. In trying to facilitate these accomplishments for myself and my students, I am driven more by the need to abide by my own professional ethics and personal morality than any policies and practices recommended by external sources. Personally, these criteria are being genuine and authentic in all that I do. Professionally, they mean making my classes and other "teaching" situations intellectually stimulating and exciting. These criteria also mean empowering students by teaching them how to improve their own decision-making, cognitive-processing, problem-solving, and self-reflecting skills.

RITUALS AND ROUTINES

Some common rituals exist across my classes that are symbolic of my values and pedagogical priorities about preparing teachers to work well with ethnically and culturally diverse students (especially African, Latino, Asian, and Native Americans) who are marginalized and underachieving. One of them is building a sense of community among students and creating a classroom ambiance characterized by inquiry, discourse, personal involvement, and novelty. I begin doing this on the first day of classes with some mind-boggling and very unorthodox "ice-breaking" conversations and experiences. On one occasion I asked the students to form pairs and to look at each other closely enough to identify subtle physical features. This excluded things like hair and eye color, height, race, and gender. After a short period of time, the pairs took turns describing each other to the rest of the class. On the surface, this sounds like a simple task to do; in fact, it is very difficult and unnerving. Many people in the United States do not look closely enough at each other to discern individual traits. This is especially so cross-racially. The exercise was intended to convey the idea that teachers really do have to look closely to see *individual differences within ethnic and cultural groups* and to teach this lesson through experience.

In another first-day exercise, I asked several randomly selected students to publicly declare their ethnic identities and give us "personal evidence" of their claims of ethnic ownership. If they said, "I am Italian American, or Korean–African American," then they had to provide some examples of values, beliefs, and behaviors that signal these ethnic identities. Each student was probed in depth about his or her ethnicity before the next one was asked anything. The first student asked to share was someone who had had another class with me. She was familiar with my routines, and I knew she would handle the exercise very well. She served as a model for the other students who followed. Her modeling was not so much about the content of what she shared as a signal to the other students that they would live through the "inquisition." After all the students shared, I asked the rest of the class what they thought was going on, if other people's revealing of their ethnicity prompted them to do likewise, and if there were any messages in this exercise for teaching K–12 students about ethnic and cultural diversity.

Therefore, on the very first day of class students are introduced to some key elements of my pedagogical style. They learn from the outset that every teaching exchange involves describing, documenting, and analyzing experiences or events; sharing individually and communally; engaging in personal and professional reflections; learning by doing; and constantly seeking to improve classroom instruction for the benefit of underachieving students of color. This is my advocacy in all of my teaching and is it always made evident. These "ice-breaking" activities also are intended to (1) let students know that my classes are going to be conducted in a manner that is very different from what they are accustomed to in most of their other college learning experiences; (2) provide a demonstrated example of how I engage with issues and relate to students, and how I expect students to interact with me and each other; (3) and begin creating a sense of camaraderie, an esprit de corps, a climate of caring, and a community of learning where we assist each other in the struggle to know and share in the celebration of our success.

LEARNING COOPERATIVELY AND SUCCESSFULLY

I do not believe in competitive learning or punitive grading. Rather than encouraging students to compete with each other for grades and using grades as controlling devices, I design my classes for all students to be maximally successful. I try to provide opportunities for every student to achieve the highest grade possible (although I would prefer not to give grades at all). I do this by designing learning experiences and projects to demonstrate learning that has several different components at multiple levels of complexity. None are about merely regurgitating factual information. I am more interested in students' understanding what they read, analyzing critical issues, and applying the knowledge they acquire to teaching situations. When we examine principles of multicultural curriculum design, students are expected to understand them conceptually, and then create some examples of how these can be translated to actual practice in classroom instruction. Embedded in class projects are some aspects that every student should be able to accomplish with relative ease. Therefore, even novices should never complete a task without getting some portion of it correct. Conversely, there are other parts of the assignments that all students should find intellectually challenging—but not the same ones for everyone.

I believe very strongly in the power of cooperative learning, learning by doing, and prospective teachers' learning in ways similar to how they should teach their own students. Consequently, these are distinguishing features of my classroom dynamics. My students and I share teaching tasks and trade student–teacher roles. As small groups take on the responsibility to "teach" different topics to the class, I become an ex officio student/teacher member of each to assist in getting the task done. We learn about cooperative learning by engaging in it as we learn. Using this format also increases the chances for students to be more actively involved in classroom dynamics, at different levels and in different ways.

Another way that I try to guarantee success for all students is to have them design a self-growth project which represents their commitment to the causes we are pursuing and in which they make a contract with themselves and me to do something for their own individual development. For example, in one case, when we were studying "prejudice reduction," a student made a personal contract with herself to stop being a tacit supporter (through silence and nonresistance) of her father's habitual use of racial slurs when referring to Latino, Japanese, Chinese, and African Americans. All the students have to do in order to receive maximum credit for the self-growth contracts is fulfill the terms they themselves have specified, document the fulfillment of the terms, provide a reflection on how this experience affected them, and explain how this activity or some facsimile can be used in teaching K–12 students.

CHOICE AND AUTHENTICITY ARE ESSENTIAL TO LEARNING

When I give tasks to students that require mastery of key concepts we have explored in class, there are always opportunities for them to choose from a variety of options. One of these options is for them to propose a task of their own. The only stipulation is that whatever they propose to do be similar in magnitude, focus, and intent as the options I have provided. Thus, variety of tasks and personal participation in the decision-making process about how to demonstrate mastery are hallmark features of the "partnership in learning" principle that informs my teaching.

In one class that was studying multicultural curriculum and instruction, the students were given an assignment to apply the principles we had examined by developing a micro-multicultural curriculum on a selected issue. The list of issues included ones that they were likely to encounter in actual school and societal situations. Among them were "the changing images of ethnic diversity in mass media," "cultural conflicts in social interactions," "mainstream consumption of cultural diversity," "quality of public transportation for different ethnic groups and communities," and "ethnically diverse pattern of consumerism." To complete these projects, the students were to simulate the steps that are commonly involved in curriculum development. They began by forming small design committees and collecting data about these issues prior to designing their curricula. For example, the students working on the transportation topic collected information on bus routes and schedules, took bus rides through different communities, made observations about the advertisements, decorations and cleanliness of the buses, noted the demeanor of the bus drivers, and talked with some of the regular passengers. The group working on mass media decided to focus on billboards. They scanned billboards in several different communities before beginning to create their curriculum. The decision to go on these "scouting" expeditions was the students'. I only advised them that their curricula needed to be "realistic." The results of these preliminary analyses informed the curriculum decisions and made their final projects more authentic with respect to what was designed for hypothetical K–12 students.

In creating the micro-curricula, my students had to complete several different tasks. These involved:

- Choosing a targeted student audience and school context, and providing an explanation for these choices that addressed multicultural education needs. These choices created some baselines to help me determine the quality of the subsequent tasks.
- Selecting a goal for the focus of the curriculum from a list common to multicultural education, such as acquiring knowledge about ethnic and cultural diversity, reducing prejudices, and engaging in social action to promote social justice.
- Including several different content samples and learning activities (specified by number and type), such as geographic, reading, and mathematical skills, as well as cognitive, affective, and action experiences.
- Developing some creative techniques for marketing the completed micro-curricula to selected audiences. These could be commercials, slogans, logos, jingles, or public announcements.
- Anything else the students decided to use to make their micro-curricula uniquely and persuasively illustrative of the mission of multicultural education.

TEACHING TO ENABLE AND EMPOWER

Periodic "process checking" is also a regular part of my classroom discourse. I review with students the requirements of assigned tasks prior to completion to determine how well their group dynamics are going. The purposes of these "checks" are to see if what is expected is clear to them; to find out if the students are experiencing any major substantive problems with the tasks; to see how their "community-building" is coming along; to booster their confidence; and to reaffirm, through public declaration, my faith in their ability to complete the tasks successfully. To me, being very public and genuine about conveying confidence in students' ability to accomplish high-quality performance is fundamental to effective teaching and learning. This is true whether the students are in kindergarten or doctoral programs.

I do not believe I should use the power of my position as professor to threaten or intimidate students, or to keep the knowledge I am supposed to know shrouded in mystery. My task should be to make knowledge accessible to students and to diffuse the threat and anxiety that are often part of the learning process. I try to do this by teaching my students how to "read between the lines" of professional writings by learning how to locate the authors' central streams of thought; discerning assumptions and beliefs embedded in their ideas and explanations; locating cues that reveal authors' disciplinary frames of reference and preferred metaphors (these are very revealing indicators of value emphases); and, whenever possible, sharing something personal about the authors. I constantly explain the motivations behind my own actions as a scholar, theorist, researcher, and pedagogue.

What does this have to do with culturally responsive teaching? Everything. Scholars, like classroom teachers, are ethnic and cultural beings. Their attitudes and values are nested in their writings, research, and teachings. These need to be revealed and then analyzed to better understand their particular positions and points of view. Learning to discern how the "positionality" of authors affects their analyses of educational issues during their preparation programs may become a habit that teachers take into the classroom and pass on to their students. Furthermore, it is an excellent way to dispel the notion that scholars are infallible or the only ones with legitimate claims to expertise. In the process of revealing the constraints of one's positionality, the power of another's perspectives is unfolded. The intellectual give-and-take that results is a compelling illustration of the social construction of knowledge in action. This is something that I particularly want my students to understand and include in their teaching.

As part of a class I teach on "Teaching African American Students," we examine cultural characteristics that affect teaching and learning. Because many of my students have no personal interactions with African Americans, they find these descriptions to be abstractions that are difficult to visualize or to consider as anything but stereotypes. To help them break through these barriers to understanding, I try to exemplify some of the cultural features we are reading and talking about. I may intersperse bits of Ebonics (such as topic-chaining talk, storytelling, sermonizing, dramatic word play) into my regular teaching discourse without any warning of what is about to happen. After a while, I shift back to more typical academic language. I may then stop the conversation and do a reflective analysis with the students on what they have just experienced. I ask if they were aware of any differences in language usage, if they understood the information being transmitted, and how they felt about what happened. Now that they have a "living example" of a cultural behavior, we can compare the theory to the practice—and possibly achieve a better understanding of both.

At first most of my students do not know what is going on, or they are captivated by my "performances," or they are too politic to challenge or differ with the professor. But with time, practice, and knowledge they become very adept in their observations and analyses, as well as their willingness to probe me about the implications of my culturally expressive behaviors for their own teaching. They seek clarifications about whether these "performances" are authentic, whether they are generalizable across person and place, and how to translate insights derived from them into better classroom instruction. These teaching techniques are very effective in demonstrating the importance and principles of culturally responsive teaching. Teacher education students who do not understand me when I speak Ebonics to them now have a personal experience with what it feels like to be intelligent but still not know what your teacher is talking about. This experience may enable them to better empathize with ethnically diverse students in their own classrooms who are in similar situations. They also have some experience with the concept and related skills of "style shifting" from one cultural system to another. This is a key concept in teaching students from different ethnic backgrounds to function more effectively in school situations without having to forsake their cultural heritages. This skill is especially important for students of color whose cultural socialization may be very different from that which prevails in mainstream schools.

KNOWLEDGE PLUS PRACTICE IS IMPERATIVE

I often give assignments that require students to take an advocacy position on some issue directed toward a specific audience. One of these asks students in teacher education courses to select a "constituent audience" and explain the benefits of multicultural education to it. The choices might include a member of the Moral Majority; a potential advocate who is willing to promote cultural diversity but lacks sufficient knowledge; a Latina grandmother who just wants her grandchildren to learn to be good citizens of the community and society in which they live; a group of new Southeastern Asian immigrants to the United States; or an elementary or middle school European American student who declares that, "My parents say this stuff about diversity is a waste of time and will interfere with me getting a good quality education." We discuss the importance of "contextualizing" pedagogical explanations and actions. I then explain how this task illustrates my belief that a critical skill and power of effective educators is being able to communicate in different ways with different audiences. The quality of students' responses to the assignment is determined more by how well they "speak in a voice" that is appropriate for their intended audiences than by the factual information provided.

In completing this assignment, one student responded to hypothetical fifth-graders who were aggressively resisting a teacher's efforts to implement multicultural education. She began by acknowledging that the students' skepticism was not exceptional, explaining that they were already learning a lot of multicultural education, and providing examples of how principles of multiculturalism applied to their immediate lives. Her tone was informative in a nonthreatening, nonjudgmental, and nondictatorial way. Thus, she diffused some of the threat of multicultural education in a way that is very appropriate for fifth-graders. My student's advocacy statement stated, in part:

> I want you to know that you're not the first to declare that you shouldn't have to learn about different ethnic groups, and you probably won't be the last. But, let me explain why this is important.
>
> First of all, let me say that you already are learning about ethnic groups whether you realize it or not. Do you watch TV? If you see people you think might be different from you on TV, you're already forming opinions of them. Do you read newspapers and magazines? If you do, you're gathering information and developing beliefs about other ethnic and cultural groups and individuals. How do you know that the information is correct or that the opinions and beliefs you're forming are fair? You'll never know if you don't learn about other ethnic groups. . . .
>
> The question then becomes whether or not what and how you are learning is a positive or negative experience for yourself and others. Is it accurate? Is it going to help or hinder you and others? Let me give you an example that might demonstrate how not hav-

ing information could hinder or prevent you from knowing what you need to know.

You are learning to play a new game. There are ten rules to follow, but at home you decide to play by only five. You learn these five rules very well and you win a lot. Later on you go to a friend's house to play the same game. He has learned all of the rules. You lose and lose but can't figure out why. Not having all of the information prevented you from playing the game as well as you might have once you were outside of your home. It might even have caused you to argue with or distrust your friend. Once you learn the other rules of the game, you find that you win some of the time and have much more fun playing the game.

In this class, we want to look at a lot of different information around us. We want to think about the stories we read and hear. We want to look at pictures of many different experiences and peoples, and talk about them. We want to speculate about how others feel and why. We want to try different things in different ways. We want to learn in ways that will better prepare us for the "game of life." Since ethnic and cultural diversity is an important part of life now and in the future, you need to know about it to be able to play the game better. As we prepare for the "game of life," we will be learning about our own as well as others' cultural differences. . . . And, we're going to discover that learning about differences is exciting. So give it a try before you decide it is unnecessary.

I also frequently use role-playing and simulations to provide students with opportunities to translate theory into practice in relation to understanding information and being more pedagogically responsive to cultural diversity in classrooms. These instructional techniques are especially useful for students who have not had any actual teaching experiences. Two examples illustrate how the learning activities operate and the range of opportunities they provide. In the first case, I told my students that representatives from the state department of education had asked me to consult with them about improving the school performance of at-risk students, a high percentage of whom were African, Latino, and Native Americans. To respond to this request I had volunteered this group of students, who, at the time, were enrolled in a class on "Multiethnic Curriculum and Instruction." Their task was to develop a prototype curriculum on "Essential Multicultural Citizenship Skills for 'At-Risk' Students in the State of Washington." I wanted my students to be cautious about accepting simplistic explanations for complex issues involved in teaching ethnically diverse students and to understand the importance of "contextuality" in educational decision making. They had to begin the task by rethinking what it means to be "at risk" if all students in Washington were affected, determining what was the best focus and tone for a curriculum for a state department of education, and deciding what constituted a "curriculum prototype." They needed to make these preliminary decisions in order to make their curriculum prototype more audience-appropriate.

The second example of using role-playing and simulation to bring an aura of practical reality to my teaching about cultural diversity involved the students in translating knowledge from one form to another. This process is a powerful testament to the quality and depth of understanding that students have acquired. The students were asked to assume the role of producers and consumers of art and mass media while we were studying philosophical beliefs about what multicultural education means and why it is important to include in school curricula and instruction. The motif adopted for the discussion was the opening day of an art exhibition. In small groups, the students became "artists" by creating visual images of the messages they had derived from reading samples of different authors' ideas about the whats and whys of multicultural education. We then converted the classroom into an art museum, and the students hung their artworks throughout. When the exhibition opened, half the students were artists who were there to talk with the audience about their artistic renditions. After some time, the roles were reversed. Those students who had been artists became audience, and the audience became artists to explain their works.

At the close of the exhibition (which coincided with the end of the class period), the students switched to another role. They became "journalists" to report on what they had seen and experienced at the "Multicultural Philosophical Art Exhibition." Each small group chose a section common to newspapers and wrote about their experiences in its "voice." For instance, a headline story, editorial, obituary, human interest page, advertisement, classified ad, comic, horoscope, and entertainment review. After all the selected parts of the newspaper were composed, representatives from the small groups arranged themselves in the proper order and then "read themselves aloud" to the rest of the class.

One small group who chose to write about their experiences in the form of a birth announcement wrote:

> The world's most awaited child finally arrived here in Seattle with the birth of "multicultural education." Father, True Democracy, and mother, Necessity, are the proudest of parents. After nearly 300 years of racism and inequality, Multicultural Education was

conceived in the 1960s. After a long and tenuous labor, Multicultural Education was finally born on June 28, 1999 [the date of the class assignment], and made her first public appearance at the grand opening of the art museum named in her honor. Famous artists awaiting her prepared a fabulous multimedia presentation for the public to herald her arrival. The thought-provoking exhibitions and presentations captured the colorful, complex, creative, and challenging personality of Multicultural Education in all of her expressive dimensions. The artists' works also alluded to the hopes, expectations, and potentials of Multicultural Education for a millennium of cooperation and collaboration among ethnically diverse groups in schools and society. Multicultural Education's older siblings, Justice and Social Activism, also were on hand for the festivities.

Another group of students selected weather forecasting as the motif for writing about their perceptions of the multicultural education philosophical art exhibition. Their creative rendition stated:

Upon entering the Museum of Multicultural Education this past Monday, June 28th, one could not help but notice the dramatic change in the *weather*. The *cloudy skies* outside were apparently no match for the *warm front* of high hopes and expectations in the gallery. Participants in the exhibition found success in clarifying the *foggy* misconceptions that have long nourished the *storms* of controversy surrounding multicultural education. Their presentations included a *downpour* of information unearthing *sunny* prognoses for the future of education grounded in culturally relevant approaches to teaching and learning. These cleansing *deluges* were followed by brilliant *sunshine* of insights and a dazzling *rainbow* of pedagogical possibilities.

In order to correct the *climate* characterized by a barrage of misunderstandings and misapprehensions, the artists for multicultural education produced a *flood* of positive anecdotal and research-based data that are sure to *precipitate* great changes in the minds of the public. With the *cold front* of misinformation in check, it looks like nothing but *clear skies* ahead.

The ten-year forecast includes a period of continued scattered *clouds* of controversy early on that will eventually develop into greater *visibility* and a hopeful *air index* of multicultural education policy formation and implementation. Finally, our *satellite weather* shows the end of the decade immersed in the *sun belt* of cultural di-

versity infusion. A few *thunderstorms* of doubt and back-peddling
might pop up occasionally on the national *radar screens* as we work
out the glitches. But, overall it looks like calm *seas*, warm *tempera-
tures*, and only moderate rainfall ahead. No *natural catastrophes*,
such as *earthquakes, hurricanes, droughts*, or *tornadoes* are expected.
So make your plans now to celebrate the increasing success of
multicultural education.

These are beautiful examples of the creativity and high-quality performance of students. They attest to the incredible capability of students for
imagination and mastery if teachers create opportunities, convey high
expectations, and provide facilitative assistance. Although these performances were produced by college students, elementary and high school
students also have the ability to be highly creative in learning activities
if they are provided ample opportunities. In addition to tapping creativity
and providing practical experiences for preservice teacher education students, simulated learning opportunities offered several other benefits that
are consistent with the theory of multicultural education and culturally
responsive pedagogy. Among them are:

- Getting students personally involved in their own learning
- Using varied formats, multiple perspectives, and novelty in teaching
- Responding to multiple learning styles
- Modeling in teaching and learning
- Using cooperation and collaboration among students to achieve com-
  mon learning outcomes.
- Learning by doing
- Incorporating different types of skill development in (e.g., intellectual,
  social, emotional, moral) in teaching and learning experiences
- Transferring knowledge from one form or context to another
- Combining knowledge, concepts, and theory with practice (i.e., engag-
  ing in praxis)
- Students reflecting critically on their knowledge, beliefs, thoughts, and
  actions.

CRITICAL ORIENTATIONS ARE IMPORTANT

The intellectual processes that students go through in my classes are
designed such that they can engage and enhance their own knowing
potential. I want them to be independent, critical, reflective, and quality
thinkers and decision makers who are consciously aware of the evolution

of their personal pedagogical positions and can monitor and assess the quality of their own behaviors. Consequently, my students are challenged to reconfigure and integrate knowledge segments from several sources to serve new purposes; to be analytical about sources of knowledge; to push the boundaries of their present knowledge frames by looking for deeper meanings and principles in descriptive texts; and to create new ways to organize and categorize information and insights. I constantly prompt them to "think about," to wonder "what if," to explain why. When I do this myself, I frequently stop the dialogue to explain how I arrived at my new categories and why I think the information should be sorted accordingly. This "explanation of processing" is intended to be an instructive model for my students to emulate in their intellectual operations with their own students.

I encourage and assist students to deconstruct conventional assumptions about and paradigms for teaching marginalized students of color and to search for more viable alternatives. In one of my classes, "Multiethnic Curriculum and Instruction," a routine activity undertaken to accomplish this task is to expose the cultural underpinnings of explanations for low academic achievement, such as lack of motivation, devaluing education, at-riskness, limited intellectuality, and parental nonparticipation. We offer alternative paradigms, such as cultural incongruity, stress and anxiety, existential distance between students and teachers, and situational competence. Each of these is examined to determine different explanations for why students are not achieving well in school and new implications for classroom instruction. In another class, on "Teaching African American Students," we consider the principles of Kwanzaa (Riley, 1995) as a pedagogical paradigm. In exploring this possibility, my students engage in activities such as translating Kwanzaa principles to the arena of teaching and learning; explaining how Kwanzaa principles exemplify African American cultural values and characteristics; and delineating how these can function as educational ideologies and classroom practices. They also develop teaching strategies and learning activities that illustrate the Kwanzaa principles in a variety of subjects, skills, grades, and school settings.

THE PERSONAL IS POWERFUL

I think interpersonal relations have a tremendous impact on the quality of teaching and learning. Students perform much better in environments where they feel comfortable and valued. Therefore, I work hard at creating a classroom climate and ambiance of warmth, support, caring, dignity, and informality. Yet these psychoemotional factors do not distract from the fact that my classes are very demanding intellectually. Students are expected to work hard and at high levels of quality. I, too, am at my best in these kind of settings. So I try to bond with my students as teacher, friend, and advocate, and to get them to accept me and each other in a similar manner. One way I do this is by legitimizing personal experiences as significant sources of knowledge. As a result, "telling our personal stories" plays a prominent part in our conversations as we struggle to capture the essence of educational ideas, theories, principles, and practices.

It is not always easy to get students (even those in graduate studies programs) to self-declare and share their personal stories. They are often reluctant to discuss their experiences, impressions, and thoughts about the issues related to the racial discrimination, ethnic inequities, and cultural hegemony encountered by many individuals and groups of color. Some are uncertain about their own ethnic and cultural identity as well as about their role in advocating for cultural diversity in teaching and learning. Their reluctance is fueled further by the fact that they are predominately European Americans and I am African American. Many of my students are initially anxious about how their comments will be received by me. I think this hesitancy is driven by a combination of intimidation by my ethnicity, fear of showing ignorance and insult, and respect for my position of dual authority (personal and professional).

To help students break out of this reluctance, during the early part of courses I talk about, critique, and even make fun of myself a lot. I share many scenarios about mistakes I have made in the past and the tentativeness and incompleteness of my early efforts to engage with the issues we are examining in class. I share successes, too, as well as experiences I am ambivalent about. My purposes in these self-disclosures are threefold: to model sharing one's own experiences and how these illustrate the pedagogical principles under study; to lead the way for my students to follow and prepare the classroom climate to make it easier for them to function in telling and analyzing their own stories; and to demonstrate that competence is not something that happens instantaneously, but rather develops over time and shifts according to contexts. In other words, I use my own stories to show how I came to be, and how I am still in the process of becoming, with respect to competence in teaching for, about, and to cultural and ethnic diversity.

As the students become more comfortable and confident about sharing their stories, I share fewer of mine and increasingly vary how this sharing is done. I may wait for the students to share their stories first before declaring my own. Or I may use the students' stories as a catalyst to prompt a memory of my own, and I tie it to their stories, as an obvious secondary narrative. On other occasions I defer the telling of stories totally to students, and I restrict my participation to extrapolating pedagogical principles from them. I also change how I react with the students' stories. Initially, I simply encourage the class members to "receive" the stories and compliment the "authors" of them for sharing. Next, I begin to invite the storyteller and other students to analyze the stories, looking for pedagogical messages within them or ways in which they illustrate specific principles of teaching. Finally, I, along with the students, "evaluate" the stories as they are told. By this I mean we make judgments about whether the stories offered are appropriate to the ongoing discourse and as illustrations of the bigger issues or ideas being developed in class. Sometimes this approach to dealing with the stories of students as pedagogical content evolves over many weeks. At other times it occurs within the duration of a single class, and may even unfold within a scenario provided by one student.

I also use a variety of techniques to dialogue with students, to capture their attention, and to engage their deep feelings and thoughts, both in and outside of the classroom. For example, when I give feedback on their papers, I share whatever thoughts or feelings their ideas prompt at the moment I read them. Sometimes it is a new insight, a question, a memory, a smile, a new thought, a gladness that they have mastered a task, or a criticism that they are performing at a level below their potential. In other words, my feedback on written assignments becomes an "interactive conversation" with my students through their papers.

CONCLUSION

The themes that run through all of my teaching and other interactions with students are "we are partners in the quest for learning" and "the better we can combine our resources, the better all of us will be. I will teach better and you will learn better."

I approach teaching as if it is an unfolding drama that is never finished. Each class session is a new episode in this drama. It has its own unique texture and function yet is a critical contribution to the construction of the larger story. I am responsible for creating the sets, props, and the rough draft of the scripts for the learning encounters that take place. But how these actually unfold is beyond my unilateral control because the students play crucial roles in my teaching. I neither dictate nor control exactly what these roles will be. I simply cast the parts, and the students construct the characters. Together, we create teaching and learning dynamics that work best for us and what we are trying to accomplish.

Consequently, completing learning tasks is simultaneously a cause for celebration and an invitation for us to return to the stage once again and add yet another segment to the continuing drama of teaching and learning. We compile our efforts, resources, experiences, and intellects to making learning ventures the best possible for everyone involved. Thus, my students and I work closely together to develop learning experiences that are simultaneously personally validating, academically enriching, socially empowering, morally uplifting, and pedagogically transforming.

CHAPTER 8

Epilogue: Moving Forth

Will culturally responsive teaching reverse the trends of school achievement for Amy and Aaron's younger siblings, their children, and the future generations of all marginalized students of color? "Yes, but ... " The equivocation of this response is prompted by considering the question from the double perspectives of theory and practice, moral courage and political power, transformation and conservation, potential and reality. The theory, morality, and transformative answer is "yes," without a doubt. Its certainty stems from the ideas that culture, teaching, and learning are interconnected and that school achievement increases to the extent to which teaching employs the cultural referents of the students to whom it is directed. The practice and political power answer is "yes," too, but somewhat qualified.

Research findings and classroom practices to date indicate that culturally responsive teaching does improve achievement. The only problem is that such classroom practices are relatively few. Whether wide-scale implementation will be forthcoming for mass numbers of students remains to be seen. Will most teachers have the courage, competence, and confidence to do what they must to make their instruction more culturally relevant? Will other dimensions of schooling that should complement classroom instruction, such as administrative, policy, staffing, and assessment reforms, be forthcoming? Will changes in society at large soon end longstanding racial discrimination and social inequities? If such changes are not made, then the achievement of students of color will not be maximized. The unfortunate precedents from existing educational practices will prevail, and yet another generation of students will experience disproportionate failure in and unpleasant memories of schools.

INTRODUCTION

The preceding chapters demonstrate how and why teachers who use culturally responsive approaches to teaching underachieving African, Latino, Asian, and Native American students improve their school performance, even in the midst of school and societal contexts that are not moving in similar directions. These experiences should encourage other teachers to do likewise. Several ideas gleaned from the discussions in Chapter 1–7 provide some important directions to follow in increasing the implementation of culturally responsive pedagogy in schools. These are discussed in this chapter.

CULTURALLY CENTERED INCREMENTAL EFFORTS MAKE A DIFFERENCE

While systemic, multidirectional attacks on educational inequities are most desirable, individuals do not have to wait for these to happen before taking action on their own. Micro-level changes, such as those that take place within classrooms, are important, too. Their effectiveness needs to be determined *within context*. Otherwise, some of their positive results may be overlooked. The descriptions, proposals, and practices of culturally responsive teaching described throughout this book are types of micro-educational reforms that have improved the achievement of many ethnically diverse students of color.

An important question is whether the progress made by micro-level changes will endure over time, especially since the initiatives that produce them may have short life spans or operate in relative isolation from other aspects of schooling. For example, curriculum and instructional reforms may produce improvement in student achievement at the classroom level that do not show up in standardized test scores. This may happen because the content of the national tests is not articulated with culturally responsive pedagogy in classrooms.

Something fundamentally different from what is currently happening must occur in how large numbers of students of color are taught if their school achievement is ever to improve significantly. This is a necessity, not a choice. The patterns of disproportionate underachievement for some segments of the African, Native, Latino, and Asian American student populations are too persistent to be chance occurrences or to respond to sporadic, cosmetic, and selective reforms. The changes need to be sustained, substantive, and comprehensive. This is another reason why classroom teachers, however dedicated and capable they may be, cannot do the job alone. Nor can schools. Concomitant changes to provide higher-quality and equitable opportunities for people of color must occur in all segments of society. Yet within their primary domain of influence, teachers can (and do) make significant contributions to student achievement through what and how they teach. Therefore, culturally responsive pedagogy is essential to improving the performance of underachieving students of color.

Some teachers are already achieving remarkable success with academically marginal Latino, Native, African, and Asian American students. They deserve to be applauded, as some were in the preceding chapters. Undoubtedly, there are many teachers who should be complimented, but their "stories" were not readily accessible for inclusion here. And there are other teachers who are not doing as well as they could in implementing culturally responsive teaching. With some cultural knowledge, pedagogical skills, encouragement, and support, they would do much better. *Culturally Responsive Teaching* is for all these individuals. For those teachers who are succeeding, it is validating. For those willing to try different approaches to teaching ethnically diverse students but are somewhat hesitant, it should be encouraging. For teachers who resist doing culturally responsive teaching with low-achieving students of color, the programs and practices presented in Chapters 1–7 represent mandates for change. The need to improve the achievement of these students is too pressing for teachers to ignore pedagogical techniques that can make a difference.

There is no big mystery about what the changes should be. Students of color should always be the center—the source, focus, and effect—of instructional programs and practices designed for them. Since they are ethnically and culturally diverse, their educational opportunities and experiences must be likewise. This culturally sensitive, pedagogical variability should become the new normative standard for accountability in teaching effectiveness.

CONFRONTING CONVENTION

To act on these ideas, teachers need to deconstruct and transform some longstanding pedagogical assumptions, beliefs, and practices. Most of them are not deliberately intended to discriminate against students of color. Instead, they are deeply embedded within the fabric of educational routines. While these assumptions and practices are "just the ways things are done" in mainstream educational processes, they can be powerful obstacles to changing teaching to make it more effective for underachieving African, Latino, Native, and Asian American students.

Tradition

One of the most recalcitrant of these obstacles is the *tenacity of tradition*. U. S. educational institutions are notoriously conservative and resistant to change. They pride themselves on being consistent over time, and the recurring appeal for the resurrection of the nostalgic past (e.g., "back to the basics") in opposition to innovations (especially after the novelty pales without leaving behind miraculous changes) is not surprising. A case in point is the current resurgence of phonics-focused, skill-and-drill reading programs, such as DISTAR, after experimentation with whole-language instruction and writing-to-read did not produce radical improvements in reading performance. The problem with these kinds of appeals is the selective memory on which they are based. That memory conveniently forgets that "the past" was not very glorious for students of color. They were not performing well then, as they are not now. Nor were the cultures and contributions of their ethnic groups honored in the curricula taught in schools. The "good times" in education—the tradition—that some wish to resurrect were the worst of times for many minority groups.

Volunteerism

Another obstacle to implementing culturally responsive teaching at the scale that is needed for it to make a real difference is the practice of *professional volunteerism*. Teacher educators, inservice staff developers, administrative and supervisory personnel, policy makers, and accrediting agencies must stop promoting or tolerating the idea that dealing with ethnic and cultural diversity in the educational process is a choice or that teachers can attend to ethnic diversity in their classrooms and professional development if they have any time left after other tasks are accomplished. Nothing is further from the truth. If the patterns of achievement among ethnic students of color are to be reversed, culturally responsive teaching preparation and practice have to be required of everyone.

Teachers are not allowed to formally teach subjects for which they have no academic preparation. Professional regulations do not even allow teachers educated in cultures very different from U. S. society to teach without additional preparation in the United States. For instance, the employment status of individuals who were high-level educational leaders in Cambodia, Nigeria, or Sri Lanka prior to immigrating does not transfer into U. S. schools. If they wish to teach at all, they have to start over by completing new preparation programs and accepting entry-level positions. The imposition of these conditions on employment for teachers is not considered harsh or unusual because of the beliefs we hold about knowledge of content and context being essential to teaching effectiveness. Since the achievement of many students of color is dependent on their ethnic and cultural differences being embraced in the classroom, teachers cannot be allowed or enticed to think that culturally responsive teaching is anything other than an obligatory and necessary part of their professional preparation and performance.

Professional Racism

Yet another obstacle to moving forward effectively with the widespread implementation of culturally responsive teaching is a subtle form of *professional racism*. It occurs in the guise of dealing with teaching ethnically different students by underscoring the need for more teachers of color. The need for more Latino, Asian, Native, and African American teachers in U.S. schools is unquestionable. But to make improving the achievement of students of color contingent upon fulfilling this need is based on a very fallacious and dangerous assumption. It presumes that membership in an ethnic group is necessary or sufficient to enable teachers to do effective culturally competent pedagogy. This is as ludicrous as assuming that one automatically knows how to teach English to others simply because one is a native speaker, or that a person has to be a time-warp traveler between modern times and antiquity to teach ancient Greek, Aztec, or Egyptian history. These assumptions also ignore the lessons learned from research that knowledge and use of the cultural heritages, experiences, and perspectives of ethnic groups in teaching are far more important to improving student achievement than shared group membership. Similar ethnicity between students and teachers may be potentially beneficial, but it is not a guarantee of pedagogical effectiveness.

In fact, some African American teachers are better at teaching European American than African American students. Some European American teachers achieve stellar success with African American, Native American, Asian American, and Latino students. Some Japanese American teachers are very effective in teaching students from a variety of Asian backgrounds (e.g., Japanese, Chinese, Filipino, Cambodian, Vietnamese, East Indian), as well as European, Native, Latino, and African Americans. Others may not be very good at teaching any of these groups. Other teachers really are best at teaching students from their own ethnic background. In all of these examples (and many others unnamed), the ability of teachers to make their instruction personally meaningful and culturally congruent for students accounts for their success, not their ethnicity identity per se. Many of the individuals introduced in Chapters 3–6 are these kind of "cultural and ethnic border-crossers" (such as Vida Hall and Lois in Chapter 3, and Treisman and the AVID project teachers in Chapter 6) in that they are members of one ethnic group and successful teachers of students from other ethnic and racial groups.

At a more insidious level is the racism and abdication of professional responsibility embedded in the assumption that only teachers from the same ethnic and racial background can be effective with of students of color. Invariably, these arguments are justified on the basis that undera-chieving students need more successful ethnic role models to identify with and emulate. On first hearing, they may sound like endorsements of an issue that many educators of color advocate. Closer scrutiny may reveal a deeper, subtle message (whether intended or not) that teachers of color can only be experts on themselves. Yet when they self-initiate support for ethnic group-specific schools or programs (such as African-centered academies and separate courses of study on various ethnic groups), the same individuals are often accused by their mainstream peers of being "separatists" or "reverse racists." What other explanation is there but racism for the empowered mainstreamers to make essentially the same proposal for teachers of color to teach students from their own ethnic groups and be applauded for it, while their peers of color are vehemently opposed. Sure, the European American arguments are more subtle, and those of the proponents of color are more overt, but the message of both is very similar—teachers of color should assume the primary responsibility (and, by extension, blame) for the achievement of students from their own ethnic groups.

The idea of students of color being taught only by teachers from their own ethnic groups is also untenable because it is undoable. Even if all teachers of color were highly competent and willing advocates of cultur-ally responsive pedagogy, there are not enough of them to take on the task by themselves and make a real difference in student achievement. Their current proportional representation in the profession, and in relation to the number of students of color in schools, is not going to increase significantly in the foreseeable future. The fact of life is that the over-whelming majority of U. S. teachers are European Americans. Even if it were wise to do so, they simply cannot be absolved or excused from the responsibility of effectively teaching students of color. Therefore, ethnic and racial identity itself cannot be used as the "scapegoat" for why either teachers or students are not performing maximally in their respective roles. All teachers, regardless of their ethnic-group membership, must be taught how to do, and held accountable for doing, culturally responsive teaching for diverse students, just as students from all ethnic and racial groups must be held accountable for high-level achievement and provided feasible means to accomplish it.

Individualism and Compartmentalization

The emphases given to individuality and compartmentalization in con-ventional schooling can also be obstacles to effective culturally responsive teaching. Many educators genuinely believe that it is only the individual, not his or her race, ethnicity, culture, or gender, that counts in the learning process. However much those who take this stand may wish it so, these variables cannot be ignored in designing and implementing pedagogical practices for improving student achievement. Individuals cannot be separated from the contexts of their lives (invariably some form of groupness) if their human integrity is to be honored and their achievement potential maximized. Culture in education does count in critical ways for both teaching and learning.

As the educational process has become increasingly complex, rampant specialization has emerged as the way to effectively manage this complexity. Thus, learning experiences, teaching responsibilities, and instructional programs are organized according to specialization of subjects or disciplines (e.g., math, science, literature) and areas within these (e.g., algebra and calculus, biology and chemistry, American and English literature). Curriculum content and instructional activities are separated according to whether they are designed to facilitate intellectual or emotional development. Some content and skills are perceived as paramount functions of the educational enterprise (intellectual development) while others are considered less so, if at all (cultural, moral, and spiritual development). Even the impassioned claim that "it's the individual that counts" is a kind of compartmentalization.

In actuality, the best potentials for and actual levels of learning achieved are holistic. They deal simultaneously with multiple aspects of the phenomena to be learned and the various dimensions of humanness. John Dewey (1902) presented a compelling argument for this fact almost a century ago. Although he was not speaking specifically about educating ethnically and culturally different students, his cogent ideas can be applied to this challenge and bear repeating. He said, in part:

> Instead of seeing the educative steadily and as a whole, we see conflicting terms. We get the case of the child vs the curriculum; of the individual nature vs the social culture. . . .
>
> The child's life is an integral, a total one. He passes quickly and readily from one topic to another, as from one spot to another, but is not conscious of translation or break. . . . The things that occupy him are held together by the unity of the personal and social interests which his life carries along. Whatever is uppermost in his mind constitutes to him, for the time being, the whole universe. That universe is fluid and fluent; its contents dissolve and re-form with amazing rapidity. But, after all, it is the child's own world. It has the unity and completeness of his own. He goes to school, and various studies divide and fractionalize the world for him. (pp. 8–10)

Educational fractionalization is exacerbated for students of color who take to school cultural heritages, experiences, needs, and capabilities that frequently are not recognized and rewarded by schools. The resulting "division of loyalties and cultural inconsistencies" provoke high levels of intrapsychic disequilibrium and intellectual/emotional stress. No wonder so many students of color are not performing as well as they could. To prevent these negative consequences, instructional programs and practices should deal simultaneously with the realities of their human wholeness, their ethnic and cultural particularities, and their individual uniqueness. These priorities are neither dichotomous nor synonymous. Instead, a symbiotic interaction exists among, as well as within, these different levels of learning. Teachers cannot claim to have attended sufficiently to all by dealing with one of them, as some are inclined to believe, as they pridefully point out that they are committed to educating *individual* students.

Cultural Hegemony

The greatest of all obstacles to culturally responsive teaching is mainstream ethnocentrism and hegemony. They effectively block the acquisition and application of new, culturally relevant pedagogical knowledge, skills, and will in teaching African, Latino, Native, and Asian American students. Some educators fail to realize that the assumptions, expectations, protocols, and practices considered normative in schools are not immutable. They are based on the standards of the cultural system of one ethnic group—European Americans—that have been imposed on all others. This cultural system is a human creation and, as such, is fallible and mutable. Its biggest fallibility is its assumed universality and "that's the right way" justifications for its beliefs, values, and behaviors. Hymes's observation (1985) that "what man has made, man can change" is instructive here for reconceptualizing the normative cultural foundations of schooling (p. xxxiii).

The imposition of Eurocentric values and orientations on everyone else is "un-American," not to mention being morally suspect and pedagogically unsound. U.S. society and culture are, in fact, comprised of a multitude of multiethnic and multivaried peoples, contributions, and influences. This obligates school programs and practices to likewise be multicultural. Furthermore, research evidence (although not as inclusive and extensive as it needs to be) consistently demonstrates that when teaching and learning are filtered through the cultural frameworks of students of color, their achievement improves dramatically. Why, then, are schools en mass not hastening to make the necessary changes? Probably because these changes require transforming prevailing paradigms of power, privilege, and normality within the educational enterprise. However discomforting this challenge may be to the guardians of pedagogical traditions, the change must occur if the performance of underachieving students is to be reversed. The failure to do so can cause irreversible damage to the intellectual development and academic achievement of some students. As the United Negro College Fund's promotional motto admonishes, "a mind is a terrible thing to waste," meaning it is too precious to be undernourished.

NEW PARADIGMS FOR PRACTICE

The legitimacy and viability of cultural diversity in teaching and learning for ethnically diverse students are far from being commonly accepted among educators. Even those who are receptive to them often do not have the depth of understanding and competence needed to guide pedagogical practices. A notion frequently expressed by teachers is the importance of "awareness, sensitivity, appreciation, and respect" for cultural diversity in racially and ethnically pluralistic classrooms. Others confess feeling guilty about the educational and societal injustices that have been imposed upon people of color. These declarations give the appearance of change, but, in fact, they are more illusionary than real. Personal awareness and empathic feelings about ethnic and cultural diversity without accompanying pedagogical actions do not lead to instructional improvements for students of color. Positive recognition of and attitudes toward ethnic and cultural diversity are necessary but not sufficient for dealing effectively with the educational needs and potentialities of ethnically diverse students. Some teachers may know very well that attitudes are not enough to accomplish sound pedagogical reforms but still focus energy and attention on them to avoid really *doing* anything.

Culturally competent instructional action is essential to achieving genuine commitment to educational equity, justice, and excellence for students of color. Teachers who truly care about students are persistent in their expectations of high performance from them and are diligent in their efforts to ensure that these expectations are realized. They know that a genuine commitment to transforming educational opportunities for their ethnically diverse students requires that they have knowledge of the cultural characteristics of different ethnic groups and of how culture affects teaching and learning, as well as pedagogical skills for translating this knowledge into new teaching–learning opportunities and experiences. They also must have the moral courage and the will to stay the course in efforts to make the educational enterprise more multiculturally responsive, even in the face of the opposition that is surely to come from somewhere. As Dillard (1997) suggests,

> Learning how to live and teach through diversity, including the inevitable struggles and contradictions, seems especially important. . . . [and] becoming a literate teacher, in relation to diversity, means doing more than writing and reading *about* culture—it means learning to *be* diverse in perspectives, skills, and knowledges. It means understanding, influencing, and participating in the lives of diverse students, schools, and the wider society. Thus, the integration and valuing of diverse and multiple literacies is [*sic*] crucial to the philosophy, pedagogy, and practice of teacher education and preparation. (p. 94, emphasis in original)

Cultivating the competence and confidence needed to implement culturally responsive teaching should begin in preservice education programs and continue in inservice professional development programs. During preservice it should include acquiring information about culture characteristics and contributions, pedagogical principles, and methods and material for ethnic and cultural diversity. This knowledge should be complemented with learning experiences for teacher education students to critically examine existing paradigms of educational thought and practice to determine whether they can be modified to accommodate ethnic and cultural diversity, or if they need to be replaced. These analyses should be supplemented with supervised practices in designing and implementing replacement models; for example, determining what "authentic assessment" means within the context of ethnic diversity and culturally responsive teaching. How might portfolio assessment be modified to better accommodate the components of the learning styles of different ethnic groups? Or what changes are needed in structured academic controversy (SAC) approaches to problem solving to make them illuminate culturally responsive teaching ideologies and methodologies?

Infrastructures also need to be created to support inservice teachers who are trying to implement culturally responsive teaching. These may need to include several different components, such as (1) staff development to acquire knowledge of ethnic diversity and culturally responsive teaching; (2) availability of necessary instructional materials; (3) systematic ways in which teachers can receive constructive feedback on their efforts and recognition for their accomplishments in implementing culturally responsive teaching; (4) activities in other aspects of the educational enterprise, such as administration, counseling, curriculum design, performance evaluation, and extracurricular activities comparable to (but jurisdictionally appropriate) culturally responsive classroom teaching; and (5) clearly defined techniques for meeting the opposition that culturally diverse people and programs may encounter in both the school and the community.

The absence of any one of these elements of cognitive, pedagogical, and political agency is likely to lead to underestimating the challenges of making education better for students of color. This possibility brings to mind preservice teachers who optimistically but naively think that their "desire to be caring and appreciative of cultural diversity" and novel multicultural curriculum designs will automatically expedite radical improvements in student learning, only to be disappointed soon after entering the classroom. This kind of hopefulness and optimism is important in teaching underachieving students of color, but it needs to be anchored in thorough preparation for and commitment to diligent struggle. The struggle requires *caring* to be complemented by content and pedagogical *competence*, personal and professional *confidence*, and moral and ethical *conviction*. How these lessons were implemented by creators of the Webster Groves Writing Project (Krater et al., 1994) is useful for others to emulate. Four years into the project, the participating teachers realized they had to change themselves if they hoped to improve the writing performance of their students. The masks and myths of cultural neutrality in teachers and cultural invisibility in students need to be deconstructed. The teachers in the project came to realize that

> we could make no headway solving our problems [improving writing achievement] until we looked carefully at ourselves, studied what we saw, changed the vision, and realized a new solution—one out of the realm of what we already knew . . . we had to move out of our comfort zone, . . . stretching ourselves to brand-new, out-of-the-ordinary solutions. We did this through self-study, kid watching, and reflection. (Krater et al., pp. 426–427)

The most compelling and instructive points in this story are that the teachers stopped blaming and trying to "fix" the students, validated the worth of the students' cultural heritages, accepted the inevitability of cultural influences on their own beliefs and behaviors, disavowed the sanctity of educational conventions, and placed the burden of change upon themselves. Additional support for the power of these contentions and orientations toward teaching students of color is evident in the research, programs, and practices discussed in Chapters 3–6. They provide powerful lessons that all teachers should learn and use to guide their instructional actions with ethnically and culturally different students.

NOW IS THE TIME

Teachers and other educators should act now, without a moment's hesitation and with deliberate speed, to revise the entire educational enterprise so that it reflects and responds to the ethnic and cultural diversity that characterizes U. S. society and its schools. The underachievement of marginalized African, Asian, Native, and Latino American students is too pervasive to do anything less. The question is not whether to act, but how soon and in what ways. Acting with deliberate speed does not mean being capricious, impulsive, or irresponsible. Nor does it mean trying to operate on good intentions alone. Instead, teachers should be trained in the knowledge and skills of culturally responsive pedagogy for ethnic diversity, systematically supported in their praxis efforts, and held accountable for quality performance within the context of cultural diversity.

Reform cannot wait until teachers and other educators are comfortable with the idea of culturally responsive pedagogy or are certain of their mastery of the skills necessary for its implementation. Change is never easy, but the consequences for not doing so should be sufficient to sustain teachers as they make the transition to new ways of teaching if they genuine care (as described in Chapter 5) about the well-being of students. If this is not adequate to motivate their pedagogical movement, then firmly applied accountability mandates should. Mastery is a developmental phenomenon that is acquired over time. And the only absolute certainty in the arena of teaching in general, and of teaching marginalized students of color in particular, is that many things done in the past must not continue in the future.

Failures and mistakes are not self-correcting; they must be deliberately transformed. Teachers can expedite this transformation for themselves and their ethnically diverse students by embracing, with diligence and enthusiasm, culturally responsive pedagogy. For a time, their training for and practice of it will probably have to occur in tandem. This notion is not unorthodox or unprecedented. There is much support in certain educational arenas for "teaching by doing," "combining theory, research, and practice," and "field-based, situated teacher education." The benefit of training for and trying out culturally responsive teaching at the same time is how knowledge and praxis can reenforce and refine each other.

PILLARS FOR PROGRESS

Teachers need guidance in their attempts to do multiculturally responsive teaching. Some general principles can be extrapolated from the specific programs and practices discussed in detail in the preceding chapters that may be inspirational and instructive for teachers. They are offered here as "pillars for progress," or assessment benchmarks by which the adequacy of efforts in implementing culturally responsive teaching can be determined. Ideally, all will occur at once, but a few are better, by far, than continuing tradition. Culturally responsive pedagogy has all of the following components:

- It is a part of all subjects and skills taught at all grade levels.
- It has multiple benefits for all students. Of all the curricular programs, instructional practices, and research projects discussed in the preceding chapters, there was no instance in which improvements occurred for some ethnic groups or area of academic functioning but not for others.
- It cannot be a happenstance, sporadic, or fragmentary occurrence. Instead, it has to be deliberate and explicit, systematic and sustained. This is not something that happens only as notations of special events; it must *characterize* children's learning opportunities and experiences at all times.
- It has multiple emphases, features, and effects. It simultaneously addresses development of academic, psychological, emotional, social, moral, political, and cultural skills; it cultivates school success without compromising or constraining students' ethnic identity and cultural affiliation. In fact, it develops competence, confidence, and efficacy in these latter areas as well.
- It uses comprehensive and integrative approaches to teaching and learning, all of which are informed by the contexts and content of the cultures and lived experiences of different groups of color.
- It cultivates an ethos of academic success as well as a sense of community, camaraderie, kindredness, and reciprocity among students who work collaboratively for their mutual personal well-being and academic achievement.
- It requires a combination of curriculum content, school and classroom learning climates, instructional strategies, and interpersonal interactions that reflect the cultures, experiences, and perspectives of different ethnic groups of color.
- It deals with the general and the particular of ethnic and cultural diversity simultaneously; that is, it encompasses concepts and principles, patterns and trends that apply to all ethnic groups and the ways in which these are uniquely manifested in the cultures and experiences of specific ethnic groups and individuals.
- It includes accurate information about the cultures and contributions of different ethnic groups, as well as moral and ethical dilemmas about

their treatment in the U. S., the redistribution of power and privilege, and the deconstruction of academic racism and hegemony.

- It teaches ethnic students of color the "cultural capital" (i.e., the informal, tacit knowledge, skills, and behaviors needed to negotiate the rules, regulations, protocols, and demand of living within educational institutions) needed to succeed in schools.

- It considers achievement to be multidimensional and uses multifocal indicators in assessing the levels of accomplishment for students. Both the acquisition and demonstration of the various dimensions of achievements are synchronized with various ethnic groups' preferred learning, performance, participation, and communication styles.

- It engages students perpetually in processes of self-knowing and self-assessment.

- It demonstrates genuine caring and concern for students of color by demanding high levels of performance and facilitates their living up to these expectations.

- It creates cultural bridges, or scaffolds, between academic learning in school and the sociocultural lives and experiences of different groups of color outside of school.

- It teaches students to imagine and develop the skills needed to construct more desirable futures and to be integral, active participants in these creations.

- It develops in students an intolerance for all kinds of oppression, discrimination, and exploitation, as well as the moral courage to act in promoting academic, social, cultural, and political justice among ethnic groups.

- It requires staff development of teachers that includes cultural knowledge and instructional skills, in concert with personal self-reflection and self-monitoring techniques for teaching to and about ethnic diversity.

- It commits institutional and personal resources, along with creative imagination, to facilitating maximum achievement for students of color.

CONCLUSION

Children are our most valuable resource and investment for the future. They are far more precious than limitless amounts of money, unchallenged fame, or the most expensive gems. They are our best investments in the future. If they do not receive a high-quality, education, the promise of a rich future will be unfulfilled. Let us act now to prevent such an unthinkable catastrophe by ensuring the best education possible for all children.

The way to do this is to implement culturally responsive teaching for students from various ethnic groups now and always.

All our children deserve to be empowered on multiple levels. Empowerment embraces competence, accomplishment, confidence, and efficacy. Their achievement needs to be academic, social, emotional, psychological, cultural, moral, and political. Children of color deserve to receive this kind of empowerment from their educational experiences so that the dream of a secure and successful future for them will no longer be deferred, minimized, or vanquished, but realized and maximized. Educators need to contribute to this realization by providing students with the best possible learning opportunities. This is a non-negotiable moral imperative and a mandatory professional responsibility. The stakes are too high and the consequences too enduring to take chances on continuing to perpetuate underachievement among students of color.

Ten years ago, the Quality Education for Minorities Project ended its policy statement, *Education That Works* (1990), with a strong reaffirmation of faith that ethnic groups of color have in the redemptive power of education. The explanations for why this is so are a fitting way to bring to a close this story of the need for, nature of, and effects of culturally responsive teaching for students of color. Speaking in a register of affiliation and kindredness with the constituent groups for whom they were advocates (Alaskan Natives, Native Americans, Mexican Americans, Puerto Ricans, and African Americans), the authors of *Education That Works* declared, "the gateway to a better life for us has always been education. . . . For us, education is freedom's foundation, and the struggle for a quality education is at the heart of our quest for liberty" (p. 1)—the ultimate achievement. Furthermore,

> The one force that has sustained and empowered *all* our people, has been the power of education. It has been our schools that have equipped individuals to take their places in the great work of transforming visions into realities. . . . Minority children, who by right and by virtue of their unlimited potential, surely deserve their own roles as visionaries and builders, are being shut out. If, indeed, education is the way we deal with the future before it arrives, then we are truly casting our future aside if we do not bend every effort to open opportunities for minority children. The door to the future for every child is first and foremost the door to the schoolhouse. (p. 89, emphasis in original)

This "doorway" is more metaphorical than literal, symbolizing access to opportunities for children to learn to the very best of their capabilities. Teachers and other educators must have as much faith in the abilities of children to learn as children have in the power of education—and act accordingly. These shared beliefs open the way to improved student performance. But they will not be realized without *culturally responsive pedagogical competence*. Teachers cannot be reasonably expected to meet these challenges if they have not been adequately prepared for them. Therefore, both preservice and inservice education agencies must include skills for culturally responsive teaching in their professional development programs for teachers. This is as crucial to improving the performance of underachieving students of color as teachers being culturally responsive in K–12 classroom instruction.

REFERENCES

AAUW report: How schools shortchange girls. (1995). The AAUW [American Association of University Women] Educational Foundation, Wellesley College Center for Research on Women.

Abella, R. (1995, August). *Evaluation of the Afrocentric Enhancement and Self-Esteem Opportunity Program* (AESOP). Miami, FL: Dade County Public Schools, Division of Program Evaluation, Office of Educational Accountability. Mimeographed.

Abrahams, R. D. (1970). *Positively Black.* Englewood Cliffs, NJ: Prentice-Hall.

Abrahams, R. D., & Troike, R. C. (Eds.). (1972). *Language and cultural diversity in American education.* Englewood Cliffs, NJ: Prentice-Hall.

Adenika-Morrow, T. J. (1995). Building self-esteem in at-risk youths through a creative approach to teaching math and science. *Equity & Excellence in Education, 28*(3), 32–37.

Albury, A. (1992). *Social orientations, learning conditions, and learning outcomes among low-income Black and White grade school children.* Unpublished doctoral dissertation, Howard University, Washington, DC.

Allen, B. A. (1987). *The differential effects of low and high movement and sensate stimulation affordance on the learning of Black and White working class children.* Unpublished doctoral dissertation, Howard University, Washington, DC.

Allen, B. A., & Boykin, A. W. (1991). The influence of contextual factors on Afro-American and Euro-American children's performance: Effects of movement opportunity and music. *International Journal of Psychology, 26*(3), 373–387.

Allen, B. A., & Boykin, A. W. (1992). African-American children and the educational process: Alleviating cultural discontinuity through prescriptive pedagogy. *School Psychology Review, 21*(4), 586–598.

Allen, B. A., & Butler, L. (1996). The effects of music and movement opportunity on the analogical reasoning performance of African American and White school children: A preliminary study. *Journal of Black Psychology, 22*(3), 316–328.

Allen, J. E. (1998, May 6). Children see minorities stereotyped on TV. *Seattle Times,* p. A8.

American Indian Science and Engineering Society (AISES). www.aises.org.

Anyon, J. (1981). Social class and school achievement. *Curriculum Inquiry, 11*(1), 3–42.

Anyon, J. (1988). Schools as agents of social legitimization. In W. F. Pinar (Ed.),

Contemporary curriculum discourses (pp. 175–200). Scottsdale, AZ: Gorsuch Scarisbrick.

Anyon, J. (1997). *Ghetto schooling: A political economy of urban educational reform.* New York: Teachers College Press.

AP at all EQUITY 2000 sites. (n.d.). New York: The College Board. Mimeographed.

Apple, M. W. (1985). The culture and commerce of the textbook. *Journal of Curriculum Studies, 17*(2), 147–162.

Aragon, J. (1973). An impediment to cultural pluralism: Culturally deficient educators attempting to teach culturally different children. In M. D. Stent, W. R. Hazard, & H. N. Rivlin (Eds.), *Cultural pluralism in education: A mandate for change* (pp. 77–84). New York: Appleton-Century-Crofts.

Archer, E. (1993). *New equations: The urban schools science and mathematics programs.* Washington, DC: Academy of Educational Development.

Arciniega, T. A. (1975). The thrust toward pluralism: What progress? *Educational Leadership, 33*(3), 163–167.

Armstrong, T. (1994). *Multiple intelligences in the classroom.* Alexandria, VA: Association for Supervision and Curriculum development.

Asante, M. K. (1991/1992). Afrocentric curriculum. *Educational Leadership, 49*(4), 28–31.

Asante, M. K. (1998). *The Afrocentric idea* (rev. and exp. ed.). Philadelphia: Temple University Press.

Ascher, M. (1992). *Ethnomathematics.* New York: Freeman.

Ashton, P. T., & Webb, R. B. (1986). *Making a difference: Teachers' sense of efficacy and student achievement.* New York: Longman.

Au, K. H. (1980a). Participation structures in a reading lesson with Hawaiian children: Analysis of a culturally appropriate instructional event. *Anthropology and Education Quarterly, 11*(2), 91–115.

Au, K. H. (1980b). *Theory and method in establishing the cultural congruence of classroom speech events.* (ERIC Document, Reproduction Service No. ED 204 465)

Au, K. H. (1993). *Literacy instruction in multicultural settings.* New York: Harcourt Brace.

Au, K. H., & Kawakami, A. J. (1985). Research currents: Talk story and learning to read. *Language Arts, 62*(4), 406–411.

Au, K. H., & Kawakami, A. J. (1991). Culture and ownership: Schooling of minority students. *Childhood Education, 67*(5), 280–284.

Au, K. H., & Kawakami, A. J. (1994). Cultural congruence in instruction. In E. R. Hollins, J. E. King, & W. C. Hayman (Eds.), *Teaching diverse populations: Formulating a knowledge base* (pp. 5–23). Albany: State University of New York Press.

Au, K. P., & Mason. J. M. (1981). Social organizational factors in learning to read: The balance of rights hypothesis. *Reading Research Quarterly, 17*(1), 115–152.

Au, K. P., & Mason, J. M. (1983). Cultural congruence in classroom participation structures: Achieving a balance of rights. *Discourse Processes, 6*(2), 145–167.

Austin, A. M. B., Salehi, M., & Leffler, A. (1987). Gender and developmental differences in children's conversations. *Sex Roles, 16*(9–10), 497–510.

AVID: Advancement Via Individual Determination. An international college preparatory program. (n.d.). Mimeographed Project Report.

Axtman, K. (1999, January 15). Native American to shine from new coin. *The Christian Science Monitor*, p. 4.

Baber, C. R. (1987). The artistry and artifice of Black communication. In G. Gay & W. L. Baber (Eds.), *Expressively Black: The cultural basis of ethnic identity* (pp. 75–108). New York: Praeger.

Baldwin, J. (1997). If Black English isn't a language, then tell me what it is. *Black Scholar, 27*(1), 5–6.

Banks, J. A. (1974). Cultural pluralism and the schools. *Educational Leadership, 32*(3), 163–166.

Banks, J. A. (1991). A curriculum for empowerment, action, and change. In C. E. Sleeter (Ed.), *Empowerment through multicultural education* (pp. 125–141). Albany: State University of New York Press.

Banks, J. A., & Banks, C. A. M. (Eds.). (1997). *Multicultural education: Issues and perspectives* (3rd ed.). Boston: Allyn & Bacon.

Barbe, W. B., & Swassing, R. H. (1979). *Teaching through modality strengths: Concepts and practice.* Columbus, OH: Zaner-Bloser.

Barber, B. R. (1992). *An aristocracy for everyone: The politics of education and the future of America.* New York: Oxford University Press.

Belenky, M. F., Clinchy, B. M., Goldberger, N. R., & Tarule, J. M. (1986). *Women's ways of knowing: The development of self, voice, and mind.* New York: Basic Books.

Bennett, C. I. (1995a). *Comprehensive multicultural education: Theory and practice* (3rd ed.). Boston: Allyn & Bacon.

Bennett, C. I. (1995b, April). *Teacher perspectives as a tool for reflection, partnerships, and professional growth.* Paper presented at the annual meeting of the American Educational Research Association, San Francisco.

Berman, L. M. (1994). What does it mean to be called to care? In M. E. Lashley, M. T. Neal, E. T. Slunt, L. M. Berman, & F. H. Hultgren (Eds.), *Being called to care* (pp. 5–16). Albany: State University of New York Press.

Bernardo, A. (1996). *Fitting in.* Houston, TX: Arte Publico.

Biggs, M. (Producer & Director). (1987). *Ethnic notions* [Video]. San Francisco: California Newsreel.

Biklen, S. K., & Pollard, D. (Eds.). (1993). *Gender and education. Ninety-second yearbook, Part 1.* Chicago: National Society for the Study of Education.

Bishop, R. (1992). Extending multicultural understanding. In B. Cullinan (Ed.), *Invitation to read: More children's literature in the reading program* (pp. 80–91). Newark, DE: International Reading Association.

Black Scholar, 27 (1). (1997).

Bloom, B. (1956). *Taxonomy of educational objectives.* New York: David Mckay.

Boggs, S. T. (1985). The meaning of questions and narratives to Hawaiian children. In C. B. Cazden, V. H. John, & D. Hymes (Eds.), *Functions of language in the classroom* (pp. 299–327). Prospect Heights, IL: Waveland.

Boggs, S. T., Watson-Gegeo, K., & McMillen, G. (1985). *Speaking, relating, and learning: A study of Hawaiian children at home and at school.* Norwood, NJ: Ablex.

Bowers, C. A., & Flinders, D. J. (1990). *Responsive teaching: An ecological approach to classroom patterns of language, culture, and thought.* New York: Teachers College Press.

Bowers, C. A., & Flinders, D. J. (1991). *Culturally responsive teaching and supervision: A handbook for staff development.* New York: Teachers College Press.

Bowie, R., & Bond, C. (1994). Influencing future teachers' attitudes toward Black English: Are we making a difference? *Journal of Teacher Education, 45*(2), 122–118.

Boyd, H. (1997). Been dere, done dat. *Black Scholar, 27*(1), 15–17.

Boykin, A. W. (1978). Psychological/behavioral verve in academic task performance: Pretheoretical considerations. *Journal of Negro Education, 47*(8), 343–354.

Boykin, A. W. (1982). Task variability and the performance of black and white schoolchildren: Vervistic explorations. *Journal of Black Studies, 12*(4), 469–485.

Boykin, A. W. (1983). The academic performance of Afro-American children. In J. Spence (Ed.), *Achievement and achievement motives* (pp. 321–371). San Francisco: W. Freeman.

Boykin, A. W. (1986). The triple quandary and the schooling of Afro-American children. In U. Neisser (Ed.), *The school achievement of minority children: New perspectives* (pp. 57–92). Hillsdale, NJ: Erlbaum.

Boykin, A. W. (1994). Afrocultural expression and its implications for schooling. In E. R. Hollins, J. E. King, & W. C. Hayman (Eds.), *Teaching diverse populations: Formulating a knowledge base* (pp. 243–256). Albany: State University of New York Press.

Boykin, A. W., & Allen, B. A. (1988). Rhythmic movement facilitated learning in working-class Afro-American children. *Journal of Genetic Psychology, 149*(3), 335–347.

Brown, A. L., Palincsar, A. S., & Purcell, L. (1986). Poor readers: Teach, don't label. In U. Neisser (Ed.), *The school achievement of minority children: New perspectives* (pp. 105–143). Hillsdale, NJ: Erlbaum.

Bruner, J. (1996). *The culture of education.* Cambridge, MA: Harvard University Press.

Burnett, C. (Director). (1998). *The Wedding* [Film]. Chicago: Harpo.

Burnett, M. N., Burlew, R., & Hudson, G. (1997). Embracing the Black English vernacular: Response to Koch and Gross. *Black Scholar, 27*(1), 233–237.

Byers, P., & Byers, H. (1985). Nonverbal communication and the education of children. In C. B. Cazden, V. P. John, & D. Hymes (Eds.), *Functions of language in the classroom* (pp. 3–31). Prospect Heights, IL: Waveland.

Campbell, C. P. (1995). *Race, myth, and the news.* Thousand Oaks, CA: Sage.

Campbell, L., Campbell, B., & Dickinson, D. (1996). *Teaching and learning through multiple intelligences.* Needham, MA: Allyn & Bacon.

Campbell, P. F. (1996). Empowering children and teachers in the elementary mathematics classrooms of urban schools. *Urban Education, 30*(4), 449–475.

Carlson, P. E. (1976). Toward a definition of local-level multicultural education. *Anthropology & Education Quarterly, 7*(4), 28–29.

Carroll, J. B. (Ed.). (1956). *Language, thought, and reality: Selected writings of Benjamin Lee Whorf.* Cambridge, MA: MIT Press.

221

Cazden, C. B. (1988). *Classroom discourse: The language of teaching and learning.* Portsmouth, NH: Heinemann.

Cazden, C. B., John, V. P., & Hymes, D. (Eds.). (1985). *Functions of language in the classroom.* Prospect Heights, IL: Waveland.

Chan, K.-N. (1981). Education for Chinese and Indochinese. *Theory Into Practice, 20*(1), 35–44.

Chan, S. (Ed.). (1991). *Asian Americans: An interpretative history.* Boston: Twayne.

Chapman, I. T. (1994). Dissin' the dialectic on discourse surface differences. *Composition Chronicle, 7*(7), 4–7.

Chun-Hoon, L. K. Y. (1973). Teaching the Asian-American experience. In J. A. Banks (Ed.). *Teaching ethnic studies: Concepts and strategies* (pp. 118–146). Washington, DC: National Council for the Social Studies.

Class divided A, [Film]. (1986). Washington, DC: PBS Video.

Coggins, K., Williams, E., & Radin, N. (1997). The traditional tribal values of Ojibwa parents and the school performance of their children: An exploratory study. *Journal of American Indian Education, 36*(3), 1–15.

Cohen, E. G. (1984). Talking and working together: Status interactions and learning. In P. Peterson, L. C. Wilkinson, and M. Hallinan (Eds.), *Instructional groups in the classroom: Organization and processes* (pp. 171–188). Orlando, FL: Academic Press.

Cohen, E. G., Kepner, D., & Swanson, P. (1995). Dismantling status hierarchies in heterogeneous classrooms. In J. Oakes & K. H. Quartz (Eds.), *Creating new educational communities* (Ninety-fourth Yearbook of the National Society for the Study of Education) (pp. 16–31). Chicago: University of Chicago Press.

Cohen, E. G., & Lotan, R. A. (1995). Producing equal-status interaction in the heterogeneous classroom. *American Educational Research Journal, 32*(1), 99–120.

Collins, M. (1992). *Ordinary children, extraordinary teachers.* Norfolk, VA: Hampton Roads.

Cortés, C. E. (1991). Empowerment through media literacy: A multicultural approach. In C. E. Sleeter (Ed.), *Empowerment through multicultural education* (pp. 143–157). Albany: State University of New York Press.

Cortés, C. E. (1995). Knowledge construction and popular culture: The media as multicultural educator. In J. A. Banks & C. A. M. Banks (Eds.), *Handbook of research on multicultural education* (pp. 169–183). New York: Macmillan.

Crawford, L. W. (1993). *Language and literacy learning in multicultural classrooms.* Boston: Allyn & Bacon.

Crawford, M. (1995). *Talking difference: On gender and language.* Thousand Oaks, CA: Sage.

Crichlow, W. C., Goodwin, S., Shakes, G., & Swartz, E. (1990). Multicultural ways of knowing: Implications for practice. *Journal of Education, 172*(2), 101–117.

Cuban, L. (1972). Ethnic content and "white" instruction. *Phi Delta Kappan, 53*(5), 270–273.

Cullen, C. (1970). Incident. In A. Murray & R. Thomas (Eds.), *The journey* (p. 93). New York: Scholastic.

Cummins, J. (1989). *Empowering minority students.* Sacramento: California Association of Bilingual Education.

Cummins, J. (1991). Interdependence of first and second language proficiency in bilingual children. In E. Bialystok (Ed.), *Language processing in bilingual children* (pp. 70–89). Cambridge, UK: Cambridge University Press.

Damico, S. B., & Scott, E. (1988). Behavior differences between Black and White females in desegregated schools. *Equity and Excellence, 23*(4), 63–66.

Dandy, E. B. (1991). *Black communications: Breaking down the barriers.* Chicago: African American Images.

Dates, J. L., & Barlow, W. (1990). *Split image: African Americans in the mass media.* Washington, DC: Howard University Press.

Davis, O. L., Jr., Ponder, G., Burlbaw, L. M., Garza-Lubeck, M., & Moss, A. (1986). *Looking at history: A review of major U. S. history textbooks.* Washington, DC: People for the American Way.

Deane, P. (1989). Black characters in children's fiction series since 1968. *Journal of Negro Education, 58*(2), 153–162.

Delain, M. T., Pearson, P. D., & Anderson, R. C. (1985). Reading comprehension and creativity in Black language use: You stand to gain by playing the sounding game. *American Educational Research Journal, 22*(2), 155–173.

Delgado-Gaitan, C., & Trueba, H. (1991). *Crossing cultural borders: Education for immigrant families in America.* New York: Falmer.

Denman, G. A. (1991). *Sit tight, and I'll swing you a tail . . . Using and writing stories with young people.* Portsmouth, NH: Heinemann.

Dewey, J. (1902). *The child and the curriculum.* Chicago: University of Chicago Press.

Deyhle, D. (1995). Navajo youth and Anglo racism: Cultural integrity and resistance. *Harvard Educational Review, 65*(3), 403–444.

Deyhle, D., & Swisher, K. (1997). Research in American Indian and Alaska native education: From assimilation to self-determination. In M. W. Apple (Ed.), *Review of research in education* (Vol. 22) (pp. 113–194). Washington, DC: American Educational Research Association.

Diamond, B. J., & Moore, M. A. (1995). *Multicultural literacy: Mirroring the reality of the classroom.* New York: Longman.

Dick, G. S., Estell, D. W., & McCarty, T. L. (1994). Saad naakih bee'enootiltji na'aikaa: Restructing the teaching of language and literacy in a Navajo community school. *Journal of American Indian Education, 33*(3), 31–46.

Digest of education statistics, 1998. (1999). Washington, DC: Department of Education, National Center of Education Statistics.

Dillard, C. B. (1997). Placing student language, literacy, and culture at the center of teacher education reform. In J. E. King, E. R. Hollins, & W. C. Hayman (Eds.), *Preparing teachers for cultural diversity* (pp. 85–96). New York: Teachers College Press.

Dilworth, M. E. (Ed.). (1992). *Diversity in teacher education: New expectations.* San Francisco: Jossey-Bass.

Doss, R. C., & Gross, A. M. (1994). The effects of Black English and code switching on interracial perceptions. *Journal of Black Psychology, 20*(3), 282–293.

Du Bois, W. E. B. (1969). *The souls of Black folk.* New York: New American Library.

Dunn, R., & Dunn, K. (1975). *Educator's self-teaching guide to individualizing instructional programs.* New York: Parker Publishing.

Dunn, R., Dunn, K., & Price, G. E. (1975). *Learning style inventory.* Lawrence, KS: Price Systems.

Dupuis, V. L., & Walker, M. W. (1988). The circle of learning at Kickapoo. *Journal of American Indian Education, 28*(1), 27–33.

Dyson, A. H., & Genishi, C. (Eds.). (1994). *The need for story: Cultural diversity in classroom and community.* Urbana, IL: National Council of Teachers of English.

Education that works: An action plan for the education of minorities (1990). Cambridge, MA: Quality Education for Minorities Project, Massachusetts Institute of Technology.

Ellsworth, E. (1990). Educational films against critical pedagogy. In E. Ellsworth & M. H. Whatley (Eds.), *The ideology of images in educational media* (pp. 10–26). New York: Teachers College.

Ellsworth, E., & Whatley, M. H. (Eds.). (1990). *The ideology of images in educational media.* New York: Teachers College.

EQUITY 2000: Creating a national equity agenda: First lessons from EQUITY 2000. (n.d.). New York: The College Board.

Erickson, F. (1987). Transformation and school success: The politics and culture of educational achievement. *Anthropology and Education Quarterly, 18*(4), 335–383.

Escalante, J., & Dirmann, J. (1990). The Jamie Escalante math program. *Journal of Negro Education, 59*(30), 407–423.

Estes, L., & Rosenfelt, S. (Producers). (1998). *Smoke signals* [Film]. New York: Miramax Films.

Everson, H. T., & Dunham, M. (1995, October). *Signs, traces, and voices: Preliminary evidence of the effectiveness of EQUITY 2000.* Mimeographed.

Everson, H. T., & Dunham, M. (1996). *Signs of success, EQUITY 2000: Preliminary evidence of the effectiveness.* New York: College Entrance Examination Board.

Eye of the storm [Video]. (1970). Washington, DC: ABC Media Concepts.

Farmer, H. S., & Sidney, J. S. (1985). Sex equity in career and vocational education. In S. Klein (Ed.), *Handbook for achieving sex equity through education* (pp. 338–359). Baltimore: Johns Hopkins University Press.

Fass, P. S. (1989). *Outside in: Minorities and the transformation of American education.* New York: Oxford University Press.

Feng, Y. (1996). *Expectations of Chinese American parents for the cultural and educational development of their children.* Unpublished doctoral dissertation, University of Washington, Seattle.

Figlar, G. (1998, June 27). Sacagawea likely choice for dollar coin. *The Denver Post,* pp. 25A, 27A.

First, J. C., & Carrera, J. W. (1988). *New voices: Immigrant students in U.S. public schools: A NCAS research and policy report.* Boston, MA: National Coalition of Advocates for Students (NCAS).

Flippo, R. F., Hetzel, C., Gribouski, D., & Armstrong, L. A. (1997). Creating a student literacy corps in a diverse community. *Phi Delta Kappan, 78*(8), 644–646.

Forbes, J. D. (1973). Teaching Native American values and cultures. In J. A. Banks (Ed.), *Teaching ethnic studies: Concepts and strategies* (43rd Yearbook) (pp. 200–225). Washington, DC: National Council for the Social Studies.

Fordham, S. (1993). "Those loud Black girls": (Black) women, silence, and gender "passing" in the academy. *Anthropology and Education Quarterly, 24*(1), 3–32.

Fordham, S. (1996). *Blacked out: Dilemmas of race, identity, and success at Capital High.* Chicago: University of Chicago Press.

Fordham, S., & Ogbu, J. U. (1986). Black students' school success: Coping with the "burden of 'acting white'." *Urban review, 18*(3), 176–206.

Foster, Jr., J. T. (1994, Spring). The Songhai Empire: An Afrocentric academy for science, math, and technology. *Sine of the Times,* pp. 26–27.

Foster, M. (1989). It's cooking now: A performance analysis of the speech events of a Black teacher in an urban community college. *Language in Society, 18*(1), 1–29.

Foster, M. (1991). Just got to find a way: Case studies of the lives and practice of exemplary Black high school teachers. M. Foster (Ed.), *Readings on equal education: Vol. 11. Qualitative investigations into schools and schooling* (pp. 273–309). New York: AMS Press.

Foster, M. (1994). Effective Black teachers: A literature review. In E. R. Hollins, J. E. King, & W. C. Hayman (Eds.), *Teaching diverse populations: Formulating a knowledge base* (pp. 225–241). Albany: State University of New York Press.

Foster, M. (1995). African American teachers and culturally relevant pedagogy. In J. A. Banks & C. A. M. Banks (Eds.), *Handbook of research on multicultural education* (pp. 570–581). New York: Macmillan.

Foster, M. (1997). *Black teachers on teaching.* New York: New Press.

Fox, H. (1994). *Listening to the world: Cultural issues in academic writing.* Urbana, IL: National Council of Teachers of English.

Freire, P. (1980). *Education for critical consciousness.* New York: Continuum Publishing Corporation.

Fullilove, R. E,. & Treisman, P. U. (1990). Mathematics achievement among African American undergraduates at the University of California, Berkeley: An evaluation of the Mathematics Workshop Program. *Journal of Negro Education, 59*(3) 463–478.

Gallimore, R., Boggs, J. W., & Jordon, C. (1974). *Culture, behavior and education: A study of Hawaiian Americans.* Beverly Hills, CA: Sage.

Garcia, E. (1999). *Student cultural diversity: Understanding and meeting the challenge* (2nd ed.). Boston: Houghton Mifflin.

Garcia, J., Hadaway, N. L., & Beal, G. (1988). Children's multicultural literature: Promoting pluralism? *Ethnic Forum, 8*(2), 62–71.

Gardner, H. (1983). *Frames of mind: The theory of multiple intelligences.* New York: Basic Books.

Gardner, J. W. (1984). *Excellence: Can we be equal and excellent too?* (Rev. ed.). New York: Norton.

Gay, G. (1975). Organizing and designing culturally pluralistic curriculum. *Educational Leadership, 33*(3), 176–183.

Gay, G. (1988). Designing relevant curricula for diverse learners. *Education and Urban Society, 2* (4), 327–340.

Gay, G. (1995). Bridging multicultural theory and practice. *Multicultural Education, 3*(1), 4–9.

Gee, J. P. (1989). What is literacy? *Journal of Education, 171*(1), 18–25.

Gentemann, K. M., & Whitehead, T. L. (1983). The cultural broker concept in bicultural education. *Journal of Negro Education, 52*(2), 118–129.

Getridge, C. (1998). Oakland superintendent responds to critics of the Ebonics policy. In T. Perry & L. Delpit (Eds.), *The real Ebonics debate: Power, language, and the education of African-American children* (pp. 156–159). Boston: Beacon.

Giamati, C., & Weiland, M. (1997). An exploration of American Indian students' perceptions of patterning, symmetry, and geometry. *Journal of American Indian Education, 36*(3), 27–48.

Gonzales, R. (1972). *I am Joaquin.* New York: Bantam.

Good, T. L., & Brophy, J. E. (1978). *Looking in classrooms* (2nd ed.). New York: Harper & Row.

Good, T. L., & Brophy, J. E. (1994). *Looking in classrooms* (6th ed.). New York: HarperCollins.

Goodlad, J. I. (1984). *A place called school: Prospects for the future.* New York: McGraw-Hill.

Goodwin, M. H. (1990). *He-said she-said: Talk as social organization among Black children.* Bloomington: Indiana University Press.

Gordon, B. M. (1993). African American cultural knowledge and liberatory education: Dilemmas, problems, and potentials in a postmodern American society. *Urban Education, 27*(4), 448–470.

Gordy, L. L., & Pritchard, A. M. (1995). Redirecting our voyage through history: A content analysis of social studies textbooks. *Urban Education, 30*(2), 195–218.

Goto, S. T. (1997). Nerds, normal people, and homeboys: Accommodation and resistance among Chinese American students. *Anthropology & Education Quarterly, 28*(1), 70–84.

Gougis, R. A. (1986). The effects of prejudice and stress on the academic performance of Black-Americans. In U. Neisser (Ed.), *The school achievement of minority children: New perspectives* (pp. 145–158). Hillsdale, NJ: Erlbaum.

Grant, L. (1984). Black females' "place" in desegregated classrooms. *Sociology of Education, 57*(2), 98–111.

Gray-Schlegel, M. A., & Gray-Schlegel, T. (1995/1996). An investigation of gender stereotypes as revealed through children's creative writing. *Reading Research and Instruction, 35*(2), 160–170.

Greenbaum, P. E. (1985). Nonverbal differences in communication style between American Indian and Anglo elementary classrooms. *American Educational Research Journal, 22*(1), 101–115.

Grice, M. O., & Vaughn, C. (1992). Third graders respond to literature for and about Afro-Americans. *The Urban Review, 24*(2), 149–164.

Grossman, H., & Grossman, S. H. (1994). *Gender issues in education.* Boston: Allyn & Bacon.

Guild, P. K., & Garger, S. (1985). *Marching to different drummers*. Alexandria, VA: Association for Supervision and Curriculum Development.

Guilmet, G. M. (1979). Instructor reaction to verbal and nonverbal-visual styles: An example of Navajo and Caucasian children. *Anthropology & Education Quarterly, 10*(4), 254–266.

Guttentag, M. (1972). Negro–White differences in children's movement. *Perceptual and Motor Skills, 35*(2), 435–436.

Guttentag, M., & Ross, S. (1972). Movement responses in simple concept learning. *American Journal of Orthopsychiatry, 42*(4), 657–665.

Hafen, P. J. (1997). "Let me take you home in my one-eyed ford:" Popular imagery in contemporary Native American fiction. *Multicultural Review, 6*(2), 38–44.

Haley, A. (1976). *Roots: The saga of an American family*. Garden City, NY: Doubleday.

Hall, W. S., Reder, S., & Cole, M. (1979). Story recall in young Black and White children. Effects of racial group membership, race of experimenter, and dialect. In A. W. Boykin, A. J. Franklin, & J. F. Yates (Eds.), *Research directions of Black psychologists* (pp. 253–265). New York: Russell Sage Foundation.

Hampton, H. (Executive Producer). (1987). *Eyes on the prize*, I–VIII [Video]. Los Angeles: PBS.

Hanley, M. S. (1998). *Learning to fly: Knowledge construction of African American adolescents through drama*. Unpublished doctoral dissertation, University of Washington, Seattle.

Harada, V. H. (1994). An analysis of stereotypes and biases in recent Asian American fiction for adolescents. *Ethnic Forum, 14*(2), 44–58.

Harrison, P. C. (1972). *The drama of nommo*. New York: Grove.

Harry, B. (1992). *Cultural diversity, families, and the special education system: Communication and empowerment*. New York: Teachers College Press.

Haskins, J., & Butts, H. F. (1973). *The psychology of Black language*. New York: Barnes & Noble.

Heath, S. B. (1983). *Ways with words: Language, life, and work in communities and classrooms*. Cambridge, England: Cambridge University Press.

Hegi, U. (1997). *Tearing the silence: On being German in America*. New York: Simon & Schuster.

Heller, C. (1997). Selecting children's picture books with strong Black fathers and father figures. *Multicultural Review, 6*(1), 38–53.

Hill, K. (1990). The Detroit Area Pre-College Engineering Program, Inc. (DAPCEP). *Journal of Negro Education, 59*(3), 439–448.

Hilliard, Jr., A. G. (1991/1992). Why we must pluralize the curriculum. *Educational Leadership, 49*(4), 12–14.

Hoijer, H. (1991). The Sapir-Whorf hypothesis. In L. A. Samovar & R. E. Porter (Eds.), *Intercultural communication: A reader* (6th ed.) (pp. 244–251). Belmont, CA: Wadsworth.

Holliday, B. G. (1981). The imperatives of development and ecology: Lessons learned from Black children. In J. McAdoo, H. McAdoo, & W. E. Cross, Jr. (Eds.), *Fifth conference on empirical research in black psychology* (pp. 50–64). Washington, DC: National Institute of Mental Health.

Holliday, B. G. (1985). Towards a model of teacher–child transactional processes affecting Black children's academic achievement. In M. B. Spencer, G. K. Brookins, & W. R. Allen (Eds.), *Beginnings: The social and affective development of Black children* (pp. 117–130). Hillsdale, NJ: Erlbaum.

Hollins, E. R. (1996). *Culture in school learning: Revealing the deep meaning*. Mahwah, NJ: Erlbaum.

Hollins, E. R., King, J. E., & Hayman, W. C. (Eds.). (1994). *Teaching diverse populations: Formulating a knowledge base*. Albany: State University of New York Press.

Hoover, M. H. (1998). Ebonics: Myths and realities. In T. Perry & L. Delpit (Eds.), *The real Ebonics debate: Power, language, and the education of African-American children* (pp. 71–76). Boston: Beacon.

Howard, T. C. (1998). *Pedagogical practices and ideological constructions of effective teachers of African American students*. Unpublished doctoral dissertation, University of Washington, Seattle.

Howe, M. J. A. (1984). *A teacher's guide to the psychology of teaching*. New York: Blackwell.

Hoyenga, K. B., & Hoyenga, K. T. (1979). *The question of sex differences: Psychological, cultural, and biological issues*. Boston: Little, Brown.

Hudley, C. A. (1995). Assessing the impact of separate schooling for African American male adolescents. *Journal of Early Adolescence, 15*(10), 38–57.

Huffman, T. E., Sill, M. L., & Brokenleg, M. (1986). College achievement among Sioux and White South Dakota students. *Journal of American Indian Education, 25*(2) 32–38.

Hurston, Z. N. (1990). *Their eyes were watching God: A novel*. New York: Perennial Library.

Hutchinson, E. O. (1997). The fallacy of Ebonics. *Black Scholar, 27*(1), 36–37.

Hymes, D. (1985). Introduction. In C. C. Cazden, V. P. John, & D. Hymes (Eds.), *Functions of language in the classroom* (pp. xi–xvii). Prospect Heights, IL: Waveland.

Igoa, C. (1995). *The inner world of the immigrant child*. New York: St. Martin's Press.

Irvine, J. J. (1990). *Black students and school failure: Policies, practices, and prescriptions*. New York: Greenwood.

Irvine, J. J., & Foster, M. (Eds.). (1996). *Growing up African American in Catholic schools*. New York: Teachers College Press.

Irvine, J. J., & York, D. E. (1995). Learning styles and culturally diverse students: A literature review. In J. A. Banks & C. A. M. Banks (Eds.), *Handbook of research on multicultural education* (pp. 484–497). New York: Macmillan.

Jackson, J. J. (1997). On Oakland's Ebonics: Some say gibberish, some say slang, some say dis den dat, me say dem dumb, it be mother tongue. *Black Scholar, 27*(1), 18–25.

Jackson, G., & Cosca, C. (1974). The inequality of educational opportunity in the Southwest: An observational study of ethnically mixed classrooms. *American Educational Research Journal, 11*(3), 219–229.

Johnstone, B. (1993). Community and contest: Midwestern men and women creating their worlds in conversational storytelling. In D. Tannen (Ed.), *Gender and conversational interaction* (pp. 62–80). New York: Oxford University Press.

Jones, F. (1981). *A traditional model of educational excellence.* Washington, DC: Howard University Press.

Jordan, C. (1985). Translating culture: From ethnographic information to educational reform. *Anthropology & Education Quarterly, 16*(2), 105–123.

Jordan, C., Tharp, R. G., & Baird-Vogt, L. (1992). "Just open the door": Cultural compatibility and classroom rapport. In M. Saravia-Shore & S. F. Arvizu (Eds.), *Cross-cultural literacy: Ethnographies in communication in multiethnic classrooms* (pp. 3–18). New York: Garland.

Journal of Black Psychology, 23(3). (1997, August).

Kane, J. (1994). Knowing and being. *Holistic Education Review, 7*(12), 2–4.

Kanganis, C. T. (Director). (1996). *Race the sun* [Film]. Culver City, CA: TriStar Pictures.

Kiang, P. N., & Kaplan, J. (1994). Where do we stand? Views of racial conflict by Vietnamese American high school students in Black-and White context. *The Urban Review, 26*(2), 95–119.

Kim, B. L. (1978). *The Asian Americans: Changing patterns, changing needs.* Montclair, NJ: Association for Korean Christian Scholars of North America.

Kim, E. (1976). *Survey of Asian American literature: Social perspectives.* Unpublished doctoral dissertation, University of California.

King, J. E. (1994). The purpose of schooling for African American children: Including cultural knowledge. In E. R. Hollins, J. E. King, & W. C. Hayman (Eds.), *Teaching diverse populations: Formulating a knowledge base* (pp. 25–56). Albany: State University of New York Press.

King, J. E., Hollins, E. R., & Hayman, W. C. (Eds.). (1997). *Preparing teachers for cultural diversity.* New York: Teachers College Press.

King, J. E., & Wilson, T. L. (1990). Being the soul-freeing substance: A legacy of hope in Afro humanity. *Journal of Education, 172*(2), 9–27.

King, N. (1993). *Storymaking and drama: An approach to teaching language and literature at the secondary and postsecondary levels.* Portsmouth, NH: Heinemann.

Kitano, H., & Daniels, R. (1995). *Asian Americans: Emerging minorities* (2nd ed.). Englewood Cliffs, NJ: Prentice-Hall.

Klein, S. S. (Ed.). (1982). *Handbook for achieving sex equity through education.* Baltimore: Johns Hopkins University Press.

Kleinfeld, J. (1973). Effects of nonverbally communicated personal warmth on the intelligence test performance of Indian and Eskimo adolescents. *Journal of Social Psychology, 91*(1), 149–150.

Kleinfeld, J. (1974). Effects of nonverbal warmth on the learning of Eskimo and White students. *Journal of Social Psychology, 92*(1), 3–9.

Kleinfeld, J. (1975). Effective teachers of Eskimo and Indian students. *School Review, 83*(2), 301–344.

Kleinfeld, J., & Nelson, P. (1988). Adapting instruction to Native Americans' learning style: An iconoclastic view. In W. J. Lonner & V. O. Tyler, Jr. (Eds.), *Cultural and ethnic factors in learning and motivation: Implications for education* (pp. 83–101). Bellingham, WA: Western Washington University Press.

Koch, L. M., & Gross, A. (1997). Children's perceptions of Black English as a variable in interracial perception. *Journal of Black Psychology, 23*(3), 215–226.

Kochman, T. (Ed.). (1972). *Rappin' and stylin' out: Communication in urban Black America.* Urbana: University of Illinois Press.

Kochman, T. (1981). *Black and White styles in conflict.* Chicago: University of Chicago Press.

Kochman, T. (1985). Black American speech events and a language program for the classroom. In C. B. Cazden, V. P. John, & D. Hymes (Eds.), *Functions of language in the classroom* (pp. 211–261). Prospect Heights, IL: Waveland.

Kozol, J. (1991). *Savage inequalities: Children in America's schools.* Boston: Houghton Mifflin.

Krater, J., Zeni, J., & Cason, N. D. (1994). *Mirror images: Teaching writing in black and white.* Portsmouth, NH: Heinemann.

Ladson-Billings, G. (1992). Reading between the lines and beyond the pages: A culturally relevant approach to literacy teaching. *Theory Into Practice, 31*(4), 312–320.

Ladson-Billings, G. (1994). *The dreamkeepers: Successful teachers for African-American children.* San Francisco: Jossey-Bass.

Ladson-Billings, G. (1995a). But that's just good teaching! The case for culturally relevant pedagogy. *Theory Into Practice, 34*(3), 159–165.

Ladson-Billings, G. (1995b). Multicultural teacher education: Research, practice, and policy. In J. A. Banks & C. A. M. Banks (Eds.), *Handbook of research on multicultural education* (pp. 747–759). New York: Macmillan.

Ladson-Billings, G. (1995c). Toward a theory of culturally relevant pedagogy. *American Educational Research Journal, 32*(3), 465–491.

Ladson-Billings, G., & Henry, A. (1990). Blurring the borders: Voices of African liberatory pedagogy in the United States and Canada. *Journal of Education, 172*(2), 72–88.

Lakoff, R. (1975). *Language and women's place.* New York: Harper & Row.

Landrine, H., & Klonoff, E. A. (1996). The schedule of racist events: A measure of racial discrimination and a study of its negative physical and mental health consequences. *Journal of Black Psychology, 22*(3), 144–168.

Lane, S. (1993). The conceptual framework for the development of a mathematics performance assessment. *Educational Measurement: Issues and Practice, 12*(2), 16–23.

Lane, S., Silver, E. A., & Wang, N. (1995, April). An examination of the performance of culturally and linguistically diverse students on a mathematics performance assessment within the QUASAR project. Paper presented at the annual meeting of the American Educational Research Association. San Francisco.

Lazarus, M. (Producer & Director). (1979). *Killing Us Softly* [Video]. Cambridge, MA: Cambridge Documentary Films.

Lazarus, M. (Producer & Director). (1987). *Still Killing Us Softly* [Video]. Cambridge, MA: Cambridge Documentary Films.

Lazear, D. (1991). *Seven ways of knowing: Teaching for multiple intelligences.* Palatine, IL: Skylight.

Lazear, D. (1994). *Multiple intelligence approaches to assessment: Solving the assessment conundrum.* Tucson, AZ: Zephyr.

Lee, C. (1991). Big picture talkers/words walking without masters: The instructional implications of ethnic voices for an expanded literacy. *Journal of Negro Education, 60*(3), 291–304.

Lee, C. (1993). *Signifying as a scaffold to literary interpretation: The pedagogical implications of a form of African-American discourse* (NCTE Research Report No. 26). Urbana, IL: National Council of Teachers of English.

Lee, C. D., & Slaughter-Defoe, D. T. (1995). Historical and sociocultural influences on African American education. In J. A. Banks & C. A. M. Banks (Eds.), *Handbook of research on multicultural education* (pp. 348–371). New York: Macmillan.

Leung, B. P. (1998). Who are Chinese American, Japanese American, and Korean American children? In V. O. Pang & L-R. L. Cheng (Eds.), *Struggling to be heard: The unmet needs of Asian Pacific American children* (pp. 11–26). Albany: State University of New York Press.

Lilly, D. (1997, September 4). Seattle schools just got tougher. *The Seattle Times,* pp. B1–B2.

Lipka, J., & McCarty, T. L. (1994). Changing the culture of schooling: Navajo and Yup'ik cases. *Anthropology & Education Quarterly, 25*(3), 266–284.

Lipman, P. (1995). "Bringing out the best in them": The contribution of culturally relevant teachers to educational reform. *Theory Into Practice, 34*(3), 202–208.

Lipsitz, J. (1984). *Successful schools for young adolescents.* New Brunswick, NJ: Transaction Books.

Longstreet, W. (1978). *Aspects of ethnicity: Understanding differences in pluralistic classrooms.* New York: Teachers College Press.

Losey, K. M. (1997). *Listen to the silences: Mexican American interaction in the composition classroom and community.* Norwood, NJ: Ablex.

Maccoby, E. E. (1988). Gender as a social category. *Developmental Psychology, 24*(6), 755–765.

Malcolm X, & Haley, A. (1966). *The autobiography of Malcolm X.* New York: Grove.

Maltz, D. N., & Borker, R. A. (1983). A cultural approach to male–female miscommunication. In J. J. Gumperz (Ed.), *Communication, language, and social identity* (pp. 196–216). Cambridge, England: Cambridge University Press.

Mandelbaum, D. G. (Ed.). (1968). *Selected writings of Edward Sapir in language, culture and personality.* Berkeley: University of California Press.

Marcia, J. (1980). Identity in adolescence. In J. Adelson (Ed.), *Handbook of adolescent psychology* (pp. 159–187). New York: Wiley.

Margulies, S., & Wolper, D. L. (Producers). (1977). *Roots,* Parts I–VII [Video]. Burbank, CA: Warner Home Video.

Margulies, S., & Wolper, D. L. (Producers). (1978). *Roots: The next generation,* Parts I–VII [Video]. Burbank, CA: Warner Home Video.

Marlowe, J. (1997). Beyond "Ebonics": What the Oakland uproar drowned out. *The American School Board Journal, 184*(7), 30–31, 39.

Masland, S. W. (1994). Gender equity in classrooms. The teacher factor. *Equity & Excellence in Education, 27*(3), 19–27.

Mason, J. M., & Au, K. H. (1991). *Reading instruction for today.* Glenview, IL: Scott Foresman.

Mathews, J. (1988). *Escalante: The best teacher in America*. New York: Henry Holt & Company.

Matthews, C. E., & Smith, W. S. (1991). Indian-related materials in elementary science instruction. (ERIC Document, Reproduction Service No. ED 344 752)

McCarty, T. L., Wallace, S., Lynch, R. H., & Benally, A. (1991). Classroom inquiry and Navajo learning styles: A call for reassessment. *Anthropology & Education Quarterly, 22*(1), 42–59.

McDonnell, T. L., & Hill, P. T. (1993). *Newcomers in American schools: Meeting the educational needs of immigrant youth*. Santa Monica, CA: Rand.

McFadden, A. C., Marsh, G. E., Price, B. J., & Hwang, Y. (1992). A study of race and gender in the punishment of school children. *Education and Treatment of Children, 15*(2), 140–146.

McWhorter, J. H. (1997). Wasting energy on an illusion. *Black Scholar, 27*(1), 9–14.

Mehan, H., Hubbard, L., Lintz, A., & Villanueva, I. (1994). *Tracking untracking: The consequences of placing low track students in high track classes*. San Diego: University of California, San Diego, National Center for Research on Cultural Diversity and Second Language Learning.

Mehan, H., Hubbard, L., Villanueva, I., & Lintz, A. (1996). *Constructing school success: The consequences of untracking low-achieving students*. New York: Cambridge University Press.

Menendez, R. (Director). (1988). *Stand and deliver* [Film]. Burbank, CA: Warner Home Video.

Mercado, C. I. (1993). Caring as empowerment: School collaboration and community agency. *The Urban Review, 25*(1), 79–104.

Michaels, S., & Cazden, C. B. (1986). Teacher/child collaboration as oral preparation for literacy. In B. B. Schieffelin & P. Gilmore (Eds.), *The acquisition of literacy: Ethnographic perspectives* (pp. 132–154). Norwood, NJ: Ablex.

Mickelson, R. A. (1990). The attitude-achievement paradox among Black adolescents. *Sociology of Education, 63*(1), 44–61.

Mihesuah, D. A. (1996). *American Indians: Stereotypes & realities*. Atlanta: Clarity Press.

Miller, P. S. (1991). Increasing teacher efficacy with at-risk students: The sine qua non of school restructuring. *Equity & Excellence, 25*(1), 30–35.

Min, P. G. (1995). Major issues relating to Asian American experiences. In P. G. Min (Ed.), *Asian Americans: Contemporary trends and issues* (pp. 38–57). Thousand Oaks, CA: Sage.

Montagu, A., & Matson, F. (1979). *The human connection*. New York: McGraw-Hill.

More, A. J. (1989). Native Indian students and their learning styles: Research results and classroom applications. In B. J. Shade (Ed.), *Culture, style, and the educative process* (pp. 150–166). Springfield, IL: Thomas.

Morgan, H. (1990). Assessment of student's behavioral interactions during on-task activities. *Perceptual and Motor Skills, 70*(2), 563–569.

Morris, L., Sather, G., & Scull, S. (Eds.). (1978). *Extracting learning styles from social/cultural diversity: A study of five American minorities*. Washington, DC: Southwest Teacher Corps Network.

Mun Wah, L. (Producer and Director). (1994). *The color of fear* [Film]. Berkeley, CA: Stir Fry Productions.

Nakamura, R. A. (Producer). (1994). *Something strong within* [Film]. Los Angeles: Japanese American National Museum.

Nakanishi, D. (1994). *Asian American educational experience*. New York: Routledge.

Nicolopoulou, A., Scales, B., & Weintraub, J. (1994). Gender differences and symbolic imagination in the stories of four-year-olds. In A. H. Dyson & C. Genishi (Eds.), *The need for story: Cultural diversity in classroom and community* (pp. 102–123). Urbana, IL: National Council of Teachers of English.

Nieto, S. (1999). Critical multicultural education and students' perspectives. In S. May (Ed.), *Critical multiculturalism: Rethinking multicultural and antiracist education* (pp. 191–215). Philadelphia: Falmer.

Noddings. N. (1992). *The challenge to care in schools: An alternative approach to education*. New York: Teachers College Press.

Noddings, N. (1996). The cared-for. In S. Gordon, P. Brenner, & N. Noddings (Eds.), *Caregiving: Readings in knowledge, practice, ethics, and politics* (pp. 21–39). Philadelphia: University of Pennsylvania Press.

Norton, D. (1992). *Through the eyes of a child: An introduction to children's literature*. Columbus, OH: Merrill.

Oakes, J. (1985). *Keeping tracks: How schools structure inequality*. New Haven, CT: Yale University Press.

Oakes, J. (1986a, September). Keeping track, Part 1: The policy and practice of curriculum inequality. *Phi Delta Kappan, 68*, 12–17.

Oakes, J. (1986b, October). Keeping track, Part 2: Curriculum inequality and school reform. *Phi Delta Kappan, 68*, 148–153.

Oakes, J., & Guiton, G. (1995). Matchmaking: The dynamics of high school tracking decisions. *American Educational Research Journal, 32*(1), 3–33.

Olneck, M. R. (1995). Immigrants and education. In J. A. Banks & C. A. M. Banks (Eds.), *Handbook of research on multicultural education* (pp. 310–327). New York: Macmillan.

Ormrod, J. E. (1995). *Human learning* (2nd ed.). Columbus, OH: Merrill/Prentice-Hall.

Osajama, K. H. (1991). Breaking the silence: Race and the educational experiences of Asian-American college students. In M. Foster (Ed.), *Readings on equal education: Vol. 11. Qualitative investigations into schools and schooling* (pp. 115–134). New York: AMS Press.

Otnes, C., Kim, K., & Kim, Y. C. (1994). Yes, Virginia, there is a gender difference: Analyzing children's requests to Santa Claus. *Journal of Popular Culture, 28*(1), 17–29.

Page, R. (1987). Teachers' perceptions of students: A link between classrooms, school climate, and the social order. *Anthropology & Education Quarterly, 18*(2), 77–99.

Pai, Y. (1990). *Cultural foundations of education*. New York: Merrill/Macmillan.

Palardy, J. (1969). What teachers believe—What students achieve. *Elementary School Journal, 69*(7), 370–374.

Palcy, E. (Director). (1998). *Ruby Bridges* [Film]. Home Box Office.

Pang, V. O., & Sablan, V. (1995, April). *Teacher efficacy: Do teachers believe they can be effective with African American students.* Paper presented at the annual meeting of the American Educational Research Association, San Francisco.

Parent Handbook. (n.d.). Seattle, WA: African American Academy of Seattle Public Schools.

Pasteur, A. B., & Toldson, I. L. (1982). *Roots of soul: The psychology of Black expressiveness.* Garden City, NY: Anchor Press/Doubleday.

Perkins, K. R. (1996). The influence of television images on Black females' self-perceptions of physical attractiveness. *Journal of Black Psychology, 22*(4), 453–469.

Perry, T., & Delpit, L. (Eds.). (1998). *The real Ebonics debate: Power, language, and the education of African-American children.* Boston: Beacon.

Persell, C. H. (1977). *Education and inequality: A theoretical and empirical synthesis.* New York: Free Press.

Peters, J., & Barone, T. (Producers). (1997). *Rosewood* [Film]. Burbank, CA: Warner Brothers.

Pewewardy, C. D. (1991). Native American mascots and imagery: The struggle of unlearning Indian stereotypes. *Journal of Navajo Education, 9*(1), 19–23.

Pewewardy, C. D. (1994). Culturally responsive pedagogy in action: An American Indian magnet school. In E. R. Hollins, J. E. King, & W. C. Hayman (Eds.), *Teaching diverse populations: Formulating a knowledge base* (pp. 77–92). Albany: State University of New York Press.

Pewewardy, C. (1996/1997). The Pocahontas paradox: A cautionary tale for educators. *Journal of Navajo Education, 14*(1/2), 20–25.

Pewewardy, C. (1998). Fluff and feathers: Treatment of American Indians in the literature and the classroom. *Equity & Excellence in Education, 31*(1), 69–76.

Philips, S. U. (1983). *The invisible culture: Communication in classroom and community on the Warm Springs Indian Reservation.* Prospect Heights, IL: Waveland.

Philips, S. U. (1985). Participant structures and communicative competence: Warm Springs children in community and classroom. In C. B. Cazden, V. P. John, & D. Hymes (Eds.), *Functions of language in the classroom* (pp. 370–394). Prospect Heights, IL: Waveland.

Piestrup, A. M. (1973). *Black dialect interference and accommodation of reading instruction in first grade* (Monograph of the Language Behavior Research Laboratory). Berkeley: University of California.

Plummer, D. L., & Slane, S. (1996). Patterns of coping in racially stressful situations. *Journal of Black Psychology, 22*(3), 302–315.

Porter, R. E., & Samovar, L. A. (1991). Basic principles of intercultural communication. In L. A. Samovar & R. E. Porter (Eds.), *Intercultural communication: A reader* (6th ed.) (pp. 5–22). Belmont, CA: Wadsworth.

Powell, R. R., & Garcia, J. (1985). The portrayal of minorities and women in selected elementary science series. *Journal of Research in Science Teaching, 22*(6), 519–533.

Ramírez, M., III, & Castañeda, A. (1974). *Cultural democracy, bicognitive development and education.* New York: Academic Press.

Ramírez, M., & Dowd, F. S. (1997). Another look at the portrayal of Mexican-American females in realistic picture books: A content analysis, 1990–1997. *Multicultural Review, 6*(4), 20–27, 54.

Reed, F. (Producer & Director). (1995). *Skin deep* [Video]. Berkeley, CA: Iris Films.

Riley, D. W. (1995). *The complete Kwanzaa: Celebrating our cultural heritage.* New York: HarperCollins.

Rist, R. C. (1970). Student social class and teacher expectations: The self-fulfilling prophecy in ghetto education. *Harvard Educational Review, 40*(3), 411–451.

Ritts, V., Patterson, M. L., & Tubbs, M. E. (1992). Expectations, impressions, and judgments of physically attractive students: A review. *Review of Educational Research, 62*(4), 413–426.

Rocha, O. M. J., & Dowd, F. S. (1993). Are Mexican American females portrayed realistically in fiction for grades K–3? A content analysis. *Multicultural Review, 2*(4), 60–69.

Roper Organization. (1993). *America's watching: Public attitudes toward television.* New York: Network Television Association.

Rosaldo, R. (1989). *Culture & truth: The remaking of social analysis.* Boston: Beacon.

Rosenthal, R., & Jacobson, L. (1968). *Pygmalion in the classroom: Teacher expectations and pupils' intellectual development.* New York: Holt, Rinehart & Winston.

Sadker, M., & Sadker, D. (1982). *Sex equity handbook for schools.* New York: Longman.

Sadker, M., & Sadker, D. (1994). *Failing at fairness: How our schools cheat girls.* New York: Touchstone.

Sanchez, R. (1998, April 19). After Ebonics controversy, Oakland seeks viable lesson plan. *The Washington Post,* p. A10.

Sapir, E. (1968). The status of linguistics as a science. In D. G. Mandelbaum (Ed.), *Selected writings of Edward Sapir in language, culture and personality* (pp. 160–166). Berkeley: University of California Press.

Saville-Troike, M. (1989). *The ethnography of communication: An introduction* (2nd ed.). New York: Blackwell.

Schneider, B., & Lee, Y. (1990). A model of academic success: The school and home environment of East Asian students. *Anthropology & Education Quarterly, 21*(4), 358–377.

Schoem, D., Frankel, L., Zuniga, X., & Lewis, E. A. (Eds.). (1993). *Multicultural teaching in the university.* Westport, CT: Praeger.

Schram, T. (1994). Playing along the margin: Diversity and adaptation in a lower track classroom. In G. Spindler & L. Spindler (Eds.), *Pathways to cultural awareness: Cultural therapy with teachers and students* (pp. 61–91). Thousand Oaks, CA: Corwin.

Scott, E., & McCollum, H. (1993). Making it happen: Gender equitable classrooms. In S. K. Biklen & D. Pollard (Eds.), *Gender and education,* Part 1. (92nd Yearbook of the National Society for the Study of Education) (pp. 174–190). Chicago: University of Chicago Press.

Scott, K. P., & Schau, C. A. (1982). Sex equity and sex bias in instructional materials. In S. S. Klein (Ed.), *Handbook for achieving sex equity through education* (pp. 218–232). Baltimore: Johns Hopkins University Press.

Shade, B. J. (Ed.). (1989). *Culture, style, and the educative process.* Springfield, IL: Thomas.

Shade, B. J. (1994). Understanding the African American learner. In E. R. Hollins, J. E. King, & W. C. Hayman (Eds.), *Teaching diverse populations* (175–189). Albany: State University of New York Press.

Shade, B. J., Kelly, C., & Oberg, M. (1997). *Creating culturally responsive classrooms.* Washington, DC: American Psychological Association.

Shade, B. J., & New, C. A. (1993). Cultural influences on learning: Teaching implications. In J. A. Banks & C. A. M. Banks (Eds.), *Multicultural education: Issues and perspectives* (2nd ed.) (pp. 317–329). Boston: Allyn & Bacon.

Sheets, R. H. (1995a). From remedial to gifted: Effects of culturally centered pedagogy. *Theory Into Practice, 34*(3), 186–193.

Sheets, R. (1995b). *Student and teacher perceptions of disciplinary conflicts in culturally pluralistic classrooms.* Unpublished doctoral dissertation, University of Washington, Seattle.

Sheets, R. H. (1996). Urban classroom conflict: Student–teacher perception: Ethnic integrity, solidarity, and resistance. *The Urban Review, 28*(2), 165–183.

Shinn, R. (1972). *Culture and school: Socio-cultural significances.* San Francisco: Intext Educational Publishers.

Shor, I. (1992). *Empowering education: Critical teaching for social change.* Chicago: University of Chicago Press.

Shor, I., & Freire, P. (1987). *A pedagogy for liberation: Dialogues on transforming education.* South Hadley, MA: Bergin & Garvey.

Siddle-Walker, E. V. (1993). Interpersonal caring in the "good" segregated schooling of African-American children: Evidence from the case of Caswell County Training School. *The Urban Review, 25*(1), 63–77.

Silver, E. A. (1995). Rethinking "algebra for all." *Educational Leadership, 56*(6), 30–33.

Silver, E. A., & Lane, S. (1995). Can instructional reform in urban middle schools help to narrow the mathematics performance gap? Some evidence from the QUASAR Project. *Research in Middle Level Education, 18*(2), 49–70.

Silver, E. A., & Stein, M. K. (1996). The QUASAR Project: The "revolution of the possible" in mathematics instructional reform in urban middle schools. *Urban Education, 30*(4), 476–521.

Simkins-Bullock, J. A., & Wildman, B. G. (1991). An investigation into the relationship between gender and language. *Sex Roles, 24*(3/4), 149–160.

Slavin, R. E. (1987). *Cooperative learning: Student teams* (2nd ed.). Washington, DC: National Education Association.

Slavin, R. E. (1992). When and why does cooperative learning increase achievement? Theoretical and empirical perspectives. In R. Hertz-Lazarowitz & N. Miller (Eds.), *Interaction in cooperative groups* (pp. 145–173). Cambridge: Cambridge University Press.

Slavin, R. E. (1995). Cooperative learning and intergroup relations. In J. A. Banks & C. A. M. Banks (Eds.), *Handbook of research on multicultural education* (pp. 628–634). New York: Macmillan.

Sleeter, C. E., & Grant, C. A. (1991a). Mapping terrains of power: Student cultural knowledge versus classroom knowledge. In C. E. Sleeter (Ed.), *Empowerment through multicultural education* (pp. 49–67). Albany: State University of New York Press.

Sleeter, C. E., & Grant, C. A. (1991b). Race, class, gender, and disability in current textbooks. In M. W. Apple & L. K. Christian-Smith (Eds.), *The politics of textbooks* (pp. 78–110). New York: Routledge.

Smart-Grosvenor, V. (1982). We got a way with words. *Essence, 13*(6), 138.

Smith, B. O. (1971). On the anatomy of teaching. In R. T. Hyman (Ed.), *Contemporary thought on teaching* (pp. 20–27). Englewood Cliffs, NJ: Prentice-Hall.

Smith, E. (1998). What is Black English? What is Ebonics? In T. Perry & L. Delpit (Eds.), *The real Ebonics debate: Power, language, and the education of African-American children* (pp. 49–58). Boston: Beacon.

Smith, G. P. (1998). *Common sense about uncommon knowledge: The knowledge bases for diversity.* Washington, DC: American Association of Colleges for Teacher Education.

Smitherman, G. (1972). Black power is black language. In G. M. Simmons, H. D. Hutchinson, & H. E. Simmons (Eds.), *Black culture: Reading and writing Black* (pp. 85–91). New York: Holt, Rinehart & Winston.

Smitherman, G. (1977). *Talkin' and testifyin': The language of Black America.* Boston: Houghton Mifflin.

Smitherman, G. (1998a). Black English/Ebonics: What it be like? In T. Perry & L. Delpit (Eds.), *The real Ebonics debate: Power, language, and the education of African-American children* (pp. 29–37). Boston: Beacon.

Smitherman, G. (1998b). Dat teacher be hollin at us—What is Ebonics? *TESOL Quarterly, 32*(1), 139–142.

Smitherman, G. (1998c). What go round come round: King in perspective. In T. Perry & L. Delpit (Eds.), *The real Ebonics debate: Power, language, and the education of African-American children* (pp. 163–171). Boston: Beacon.

Smitherman, G., & Cunningham, S. (1997). Moving beyond resistance: Ebonics and African American youth. *Journal of Black Psychology, 23*(3), 227–232.

Songhai Empire, The (n.d.). Philadelphia, PA: Philadelphia Public Schools, Northwest Region. Mimeograph.

Sowell, T. (1976). Patterns of Black excellence. *The Public Interest, 43*, 26–58.

Spindler, G. D. (Ed.). (1987). *Education and cultural process: Anthropological approaches* (2nd ed.). Prospect Heights, IL: Waveland.

Spindler, G., & Spindler, L. (1993). The process of culture and person: Cultural therapy and culturally diverse schools. In P. Phelan & A. L. Davidson (Eds.), *Renegotiating cultural diversity in American schools* (pp. 21–51). New York: Teachers College.

Spindler, G., & Spindler, L. (Eds.). (1994). *Pathways to cultural awareness: Cultural therapy with teachers and students.* Thousand Oaks, CA: Corwin.

Spring, J. (1992). *Images of American life: A history of ideological management in schools, movies, radio, and television.* Albany: State University of New York Press.

Spring, J. (1995). *The intersection of cultures: Multicultural education in the United States.* New York: McGraw-Hill.

Springer, S. P., & Deutsch, G. (1998). *Left brain right brain: Perspectives from cognitive neuroscience* (5th ed.). New York: Freeman.

Squire, J. (1995). Language arts. In G. Cawelti (Ed.), *Handbook of research on improving student achievement* (pp. 71–95). Arlington, VA: Educational Research Service.

St. John, N. (1971). Thirty-six teachers: Their characteristics and outcomes for Black and White pupils. *American Educational Research Journal, 8*(4), 635–648.

Steele, C. M. (1997). A threat in the air: How stereotypes shape intellectual identity and performance. *American Psychologist, 52*(6), 613–629.

Steele, C. M., & Aronson, J. (1995). Stereotype threat and the intellectual test performance of African Americans. *Journal of Personality and Social Psychology, 69*(5), 797–811.

Stevens, R. J., & Slavin, R. E. (1995). The cooperative elementary school: Effects on students' achievement, attitudes, and social relations. *American Educational Research Journal, 32*(2), 321–351.

Streitmatter, J. (1994). *Toward gender equity in the classroom: Everyday teachers' beliefs and practices.* Albany: State University of New York Press.

Sullivan, A. R. (1974). Cultural competence and confidence: A quest for effective teaching in a pluralistic society. In W. A. Hunter (Ed.), *Multicultural education through competency-based teacher education* (pp. 56–71). Washington, DC: American Association of Colleges of Teacher Education.

Swanson, M. C., Mehan, H., & Hubbard, L. (1995). The AVID classroom: Academic and social support for low-achieving students. In J. Oakes & H. Quartz (Eds.), *Creating new educational communities* (94th Yearbook of the National Society for the Study of Education, Part I) (pp. 53–69). Chicago: University of Chicago Press.

Tan, A. (1989). *The joy luck club.* New York: Ivy Books.

Tannen, D. (1990). *You just don't understand: Women and men in conversation.* New York: Morrow.

Tannen, D. (1994). *Gender and discourse.* New York: Oxford University Press.

Tarlow, B. (1996). Caring: A negotiated process that varies. In S. Gordon, P. Brenner, & N. Noddings (Eds.), *Caregiving: Readings in knowledge, practice, ethics, and politics* (pp. 56–82). Philadelphia: University of Pennsylvania Press

Taylor, M. D.(1981). *Let the circle be unbroken.* New York: Dial.

Taylor, M. D. (1984). *Roll of thunder, hear my cry.* New York: Bantam.

Taylor, T. (1969). *The cay.* New York: Doubleday.

Tetreault, M. K. T. (1985). Phases of thinking about women in history: A report card on the textbook. *Women's Studies Quarterly, 13* (2/3), 35–47.

Tharp, R. G., & Gallimore, R. (1988). *Rousing minds to life: Teaching, learning, and schooling in social context.* Cambridge, England: Cambridge University Press.

Tong, B. R. (1978). Warriors and victims: Chinese American sensibility and learning styles. In L. Morris, G. Sather, & S. Scull (Eds.), *Extracting learning styles from social/cultural diversity: A study of five American minorities* (pp. 70–93). Washington, DC: U. S. Office of Education, Southwest Teacher Corps Network.

Treisman, P. U. (1985). *A study of the mathematics achievement of Black students at the University of California, Berkeley.* Unpublished doctoral dissertation, University of California, Berkeley.

Tuck, K. (1985). *Verve inducement effects: The relationship of task performance to stimulus variability and preference in working class Black and White school children.* Unpublished doctoral dissertation, Howard University, Washington, DC.

Tuck, K., & Boykin, A. W. (1989). Verve effects: The relationship of test performance to stimulus preference and variability in low-income Black and White children. In A. Harrison (Ed.), *The eleventh conference on empirical research in Black psychology* (pp. 84–95). Washington, DC: National Institute of Mental Health Publications.

Tyson-Bernstein, H., & Woodward, A. (1991). Nineteenth century politics for twenty-first century practice: The textbook reform dilemma. In P. G. Altbach, G. P. Kelly, H. G. Petrie, & L. Weis (Eds.), *Textbooks in American society: Politics, policy, and pedagogy* (pp. 91–104). Albany: State University of New York Press.

U. S. Civil Rights Commission. (1973). *Mexican American education study. Report V. Differences in teacher interaction with Mexican American and Anglo students.* Washington, DC: U. S. Civil Rights Commission.

Valuing diversity [Video]. (1987). San Francisco: Copeland-Griggs Productions.

Vernez, G., & Abrahamese, A. (1996). *How immigrants fare in U. S. education.* Santa Monica, CA: Rand.

Vygotsky, L. S. (1962). *Thought and language.* Cambridge: MIT Press.

Wade, R. C. (1993). Content analysis of social studies textbooks: A review of ten years of research. *Theory and Research in Social Education, 21*(3), 232–256.

Wade-Gayles, G. (Ed.). (1997). *Father songs: Testimonies of African-American sons and daughters.* Boston: Beacon.

Walker, A. (1985). *Color purple.* New York: Pocket Books.

Ward, C. J. (1994). Explaining gender differences in Native American high school dropout rates: A case study of Northern Cheyenne schooling patterns. *Family Perspective, 27*(4), 415–444.

Washington, V. (1982). Racial differences in teacher perceptions of first and fourth grade pupils on selected characteristics. *The Journal of Negro Education, 51*(1), 60–72.

Watson, C., & Smitherman, G. (1996). *Educating African American males: Detroit's Malcolm X Academy solution.* Chicago: Third World Press.

Webb, J., Wilson, B., Corbett, D., & Mordecai, R. (1993). Understanding caring in context: Negotiating borders and barriers. *The Urban Review, 25*(1), 25–45.

Whorf, B. L. (1952). *Collected papers on metalinguistics.* Washington, DC: Department of State, Foreign Service Institute.

Whorf, B. L. (1956). Language, mind, and reality. In J. B. Carroll (Ed.), *Language, thought, and reality: Selected writings of Benjamin Lee Whorf* (pp. 246–270). Cambridge, MA: MIT Press.

Wilkins, R. (1982). *A man's life: An autobiography.* New York: Simon & Schuster.

Williams, C. (1998, June). *African American Academy school wide project update, 1997–1998.* Mimeographed. African American Academy, Seattle Public Schools.

Williams, P. (1997). The hidden meaning of "Black English." *Black Scholar, 27*(1), 7–8.

Williams, R. L. (1997). The Ebonics controversy. *Journal of Black Psychology, 23*(3), 208–214.

Wong, M. G. (1980). Model students?: Teachers' perceptions and expectations of their Asian and White students. *Sociology of Education, 53*(4), 236–247.

Wong, M. G. (1995). The education of White, Chinese, Filipino, and Japanese students: A look at "High School and Beyond." In D. T. Nakanishi & T. Y. Nishida (Eds.), *The Asian American educational experience: A source book for teachers and students* (pp. 221–234). New York: Routledge.

Wong Fillmore, L., & Meyer, L. M. (1992). The curriculum and linguistic minorities. In P. W. Jackson (Ed.), *Handbook of research on curriculum* (pp. 626–658). New York: Macmillan.

Woodson, C. G. (1969). *Mis-education of the Negro.* Washington, DC: Associated Publishers. Original work published 1933

Zuniga, X., & Nagda, B. A. (1993). Dialogue groups: An innovative approach to multicultural learning, In D. Schoem, L. Frankel, X. Zuniga, & E. A. Lewis. (Eds.). (1993). *Multicultural teaching in the university* (pp. 233–248). Westport, CT: Praeger.

Index

Abella, R., 175, 176, 178, 179
Abrahamese, A., 17
Abrahams, R. D., 26, 92
Academic achievement
  active and affective engagement and,
    168–172
  assertions about improving, 8–20
  caring and, 49–52
  conventional reform and, 12–13, 203–
    209
  cooperative learning and, 158–166
  cultural diversity and, 14–16
  culture and, 8–12
  effects of culturally diverse curriculum on,
    130–142
  ethnic-centered classes and schools and,
    172–181
  gender and, 65–67
  grades and, 16–20, 25
  impact of attitudes and expectations on,
    46–47
  intention versus action and, 13–14
  multiple aspects of, xiii
  other dimensions of, xix
  patterns of minority groups, ix, xiii–xiv, 1.
  test scores and, 7–8, 15, 16–20, 25, 177–181
Adenika-Morrow, T. J., 137, 139–140
Advancement Via Individual Determination
  (AVID) project, 12–13, 32–33, 163–166,
  180, 205
African American Academy (Seattle, WA),
  176–177, 178
African Americans
  achievement patterns of, ix, xiii–xiv, 16–20,
    25, 177–181
  active and affective engagement of,
    168–172
  caring and, 47–52, 75
  communication style, xv, 78, 81–102
  cultural diversity and, 15
  curriculum and, 114–115, 118–119, 121–122,
    124, 125, 126, 127–135, 137–140, 155–
    158, 211

  Ebonics and, xv, 78, 81–90, 190–191
  ethnic-centered classes and schools for,
    175–181
  European-American teachers and, 12–13,
    32–33, 51–52, 163–166, 180, 205
  expectations and, 54, 56, 58, 59, 60, 61
  intentional silence in class and, 19
  Kwanzaa and, 176, 197
  learning styles, 93–95, 152, 154–172
  marginalization of, xix, 203
  post-Civil War experience of, 13
  teacher interactions with, 63–65
  as teachers, 36, 205
Afrocentric Enhancement, Self-Esteem Oppor-
  tunity Program (AESOP), 178–179
Afrocentrism, 175
Albury, A., 160–161, 166
Allen, B. A., 15, 168–171, 170
Allen, J. E., 127–128
American Association of University Women
  (AAUW), 56, 64, 116
American Indians. See Native Americans
American Indian Science and Engineering So-
  ciety (AISES), 139, 141
Anderson, R. C., 88, 89–90
Angelou, Maya, 83
Anyon, J., 1, 62, 68, 114
Apache students, 22–23
Apple, M. W., 113
Aragon, J., 28
Archer, E., 137, 140
Arciniega, T. A., 26–27
Armstrong, L. A., 9
Armstrong, T., 152
Aronson, J., 18
Asante, Molefi K., 35, 82, 91, 175
Ascher, M., 81
Ashton, P. T., 60–61
Asian/Pacific Islander Americans
  achievement patterns of, ix, xiii–xiv, 16–20,
    25
  communication style, 92, 93, 94–95, 96–97,
    99, 102–105

241

About the Author

Geneva Gay is Professor of Education and Associate of the Center for Multicultural Education at the University of Washington–Seattle. She is the recipient of the 1990 Distinguished Scholar Award, presented by the Committee on the Role and Status of Minorities in Educational Research and Development of the American Educational Research Association, and the 1994 Multicultural Educator Award, the first to be presented by the National Association of Multicultural Education. She is nationally and internationally known for her scholarship in multicultural education, particularly as it relates to curriculum design, staff development, classroom instruction, and culture and learning. Her writings include 115 articles and book chapters, co-editorship of *Expressively Black: The Cultural Basis of Ethnic Identity* (Praeger, 1987), and author of *At the Essence of Learning: Multicultural Education* (Kappa Delta Pi, 1994). Her professional service includes membership on several national editorial review and advisory boards, such as the *National Alliance of Black School Educators Journal, The Educational Forum, The Social Studies*, and the Advisory Council of the Black Family Studies Program at Philander Smith College in Little Rock, Arkansas. International consultations on multicultural education have taken her to Canada, Brazil, Taiwan, Finland, Japan, England, Scotland, and Australia.